The Public Value of the Social Sciences

The Public Value of the Social Sciences

An Interpretative Essay

John D. Brewer

B L O O M S B U R Y

LONDON · NEW DELHI · NEW YORK · SYDNEY

Comments on this book

This is a very important work. While many have attempted to champion favoured definitions of social science, very few have done so with the level of historical circumspection and critical understanding that is on display in this book. Very few, moreover, have ventured to provide such a wide-ranging survey and informed analysis of the current condition of social science in public life and how it might be fashioned to meet the demands of our day. There is much food for thought and much ground is cleared for further debate. I particularly welcome and value the emphasis that is placed upon the importance of recovering a tradition of social inquiry that serves as a means to nurture moral sentiment and human-social understanding; and all the more so insofar as this is also advanced as a vital component of the attempt to better understand and ameliorate the many urgent social problems we face. Here, the argument that social science should be normatively geared is also set into practice in the style of writing and argumentation. The argument in the book is designed to involve the reader in a series of critical reflections on their teaching and research practice; and further, the manner of their moral and political engagement with social problems in public life.

Iain Wilkinson, sociologist, University of Kent

It is a pleasure reading [this] manuscript, which I thoroughly enjoyed. It is a bracing read, provocative as intended and both inviting and welcoming engagement at many different levels. I thought it was magnificent in presenting such a compelling argument in what is otherwise a thoroughly muddied field. The text is provocative and I was provoked as you intended. However, I see no reason to soften or qualify your arguments. On the contrary, they should retain the vigour with which they are currently expressed. This is a really good read that carried me along. The text was both inspirational and liberating, and offers new ways to think about and approaches to issues that are critical.

Hastings Donnan, social anthropologist, Queen's University of Belfast

I particularly enjoyed the critical dissection of the UK impact agenda and the survey of the health of the social sciences. It's a pity that in the former regard it hasn't appeared earlier in the current REF cycle. It is a spirited defence/mission statement for public value social science – and I was to some extent reminded of Bernard Crick's In Defence of Politics, *which was by no means as defensive as the title implies – he ends (in the mid-1960s) with a rallying cry, as do you. The book certainly made me think – a lot. I found myself saying 'hear hear'. It also irritated me – but then again, that's a measure of its success in getting under my skin.*

Rick Wilford, political scientist, Queen's University of Belfast

I think this is a really big issue. Chapter 3 almost had me leaping up and cheering. The bit about the loss of manners was particularly pointed. It is wonderful. You are really on the money. I couldn't agree more.

David Livingstone, human geographer, Queen's University of Belfast

I agree especially [with] the importance of increasing the appreciation of the public value of social science and the need for a more open intellectual approach to understanding the challenges that will emerge in this century (your 'wicked questions'). Your concern about the impact of 'impact' comes across vividly in the passionate way you have written.

John Beath, economist, St Andrew's University

I very much enjoyed reading your book. I have to nail my colours to the mast as someone who has never regarded law as a social science strictly speaking. I am not sure that the otherness of law comes through strongly enough here. When I read what you say about what has happened in universities during our careers and what is on the near horizon, I find myself in total agreement with your analysis. It has been a fascinating read.

Norma Dawson, private law, Queen's University of Belfast

Could I thank you for giving me the opportunity to look over your essay? I can say with complete honesty I found it both fascinating and at the same time profoundly depressing, in many ways confirming all my worst fears as to the perilous state in which the social sciences now find themselves. While I think your diagnosis of the problem facing the social science(s) is elegant and

I fully endorse your analysis and interpretation, where we differ is that I can see no happy ending. The quasi-marketization of UK higher education has spawned an HE culture and a generation of social scientists, including social psychologists, that would have no capacity or appetite to embrace the new world of public social science that you envisage. Their world is myopic, short term and risk-averse, driven by the next audit, and sadly no opportunity is thereby afforded to lift heads up out of the gutter to sniff any prospect of change, never mind grand revolution. I sincerely wish that I could share your optimism that a phoenix will rise from these ashes, but unless you can conjure up a Harry Potter pretty soon, I think it more likely all you will see is a continuation of the production line of expert procedural technicians, trying their best to do what they think they've been told to do.

John Kremer, social psychologist, Queen's University of Belfast

For my granddaughter,
Matilda Somerville Brewer,
born 17 August 2011.

Bloomsbury Academic

An imprint of Bloomsbury Publishing Plc

50 Bedford Square	175 Fifth Avenue
London	New York
WC1B 3DP	NY 10010
UK	USA

www.bloomsbury.com

First published 2013

British Library Cataloguing-in-Publication Data
A catalogue record for this book is available from the British Library.

ISBN: HB: 978-1-7809-3522-5
PB: 978-1-7809-3174-6
ePub: 978-1-7809-3177-7
ePDF: 978-1-7809-3178-4

Library of Congress Cataloging-in-Publication Data
A catalog record for this book is available from the Library of Congress.

Typeset by Deanta Global Publishing Services, Chennai, India
Printed and bound in Great Britain

Contents

About the Author

John D. Brewer takes up a position as Professor of Post Conflict Studies in the Institute for the Study of Conflict Transformation and Social Justice at Queen's University Belfast, from Spring 2013. Prior to this he was Sixth Century Professor at the University of Aberdeen. He has held visiting appointments at Yale University (1989), St John's College Oxford (1992), Corpus Christi College Cambridge (2002) and the Research School of Social Sciences at the Australian National University (2003). He has been a Leverhulme Research Fellow (2007–08). He is a Fellow of the Royal Society of Arts (1998), an Academician in the Academy of Social Sciences (2003), a Member of the Royal Irish Academy (2004), then only the third sociologist to be elected in the Academy's history, and a Fellow of the Royal Society of Edinburgh (2008). He is one of only a handful of people worldwide who are members of the Royal Irish Academy and the Royal Society of Edinburgh. In 2012, he was awarded an Honorary Degree from the University of Brunel for services to social science. He has been President of the British Sociological Association (2009–12), a member of the Governing Council of the Irish Research Council for Humanities and Social Science (2008–12) and served on ESRC boards and on the national committees of the BSA and the Royal Irish Academy. In 2012, he was appointed by the Irish government to the Council of the new Irish Research Council, which integrates humanities, social science, engineering and the natural sciences, and to the Council of the Academy of Social Sciences.

He is author or co-author of 17 books, most recently *Ex-Combatants, Religion and Peace in Northern Ireland: The Role of Religion in Transitional Justice* (Palgrave 2013), *Religion, Civil Society and Peace in Northern Ireland* (Oxford University Press, 2011) and *Peace Processes: A Sociological Approach* (Polity Press, 2010). His latest research is on the sociology of peace processes, and he is Principal Investigator on a £1.26 million grant from the Leverhulme Trust for a 5-year study of compromise among victims of communal conflict, focusing on several case studies, including Northern Ireland, South Africa and Sri Lanka. He has earned over £6.4 million in grants. He publishes in the following areas: peace processes and post-violence adjustments, religion and peacebuilding, religion and conflict, qualitative research methodology, especially ethnography, Adam Ferguson and the Scottish Enlightenment, crime and policing and interpretative sociological theory.

As examples of public engagement, he regularly teaches peace and reconciliation workshops in Sri Lanka and for Mediation Network in Northern Ireland, and was active in the Northern Irish peace process as facilitator for the Faith in a Brighter Future Group of leading ecumenical churchmen and women in their dialogue with governments and paramilitary groups. He has also been involved as a policy advisor on policing reform in South Africa and Northern Ireland and is a member of the United Nations' Roster of Global Experts for his expertise on peace processes and religious peacebuilding. He regularly speaks to civil society and grassroots groups, including in 2011, Journey Towards Healing (Belfast) and the Gulen Institute's Dialog of Civilizations (Houston, Texas).

John Brewer is in his fifth decade as a self-consciously committed sociologist, having started as an 'A'-level student in sociology in 1968. He has always been persuaded by the views of Charles Wright Mills on the sociological imagination, in which the discipline tries to make a difference to the lives of ordinary men and women. Mills originally referred to this approach as characterizing 'social studies' generally, which was to form the original title of his book, and it is used here as the motif for the social sciences as a whole.

Preface and Acknowledgements

The economist Joan Robinson once said that when you cannot find an answer there is something wrong with the question. I have taken this as sound advice and deliberately framed my chapter titles – as well as most of their subsections – as questions purposely to show there are answers, including to the most profound of these about the public value of social science. And what is my answer? There are two dimensions to the public value of social science: it not only generates information about society, it is a medium for society's reproduction. Put another way, it is the way in which society finds out about itself and in so doing generates the idea of society itself. The social sciences have public value, therefore, because they nurture a moral sentiment in which we produce and reproduce the social nature of society itself, enabling us to develop a sympathetic imagination towards each other as social beings and to recognize we have a shared responsibility for the future of humankind through understanding, explaining, analysing and ameliorating the fundamental social problems stored up for us. Social science, thus, becomes a public good for its own sake for cultivating this moral sentiment and sympathetic imagination through its subject matter, teaching, research and civic engagements. There is no incompatibility between the status of social science as science and its public value as a moral sentiment in disclosing through *science* that society is a social entity premised upon our nature as social beings.

The case for the public value for social science is not being heard in the public sphere. This has to do in part with the arts and humanities background of higher education journalists and government politicians, and the public attention given to vociferous humanities scholars in claiming as part of their defence of the principle of public universities that the humanities are the only civilizing tendencies left in higher education (Martha Nussbaum), or are more central to what the idea of a university means (Stefan Collini), but social scientists have also failed to articulate their case. The latter is as much due to hostility towards the rhetoric of value as diffidence. I suffer from neither.

I am aware, however, that many people could have written this defence of the social sciences and restated their public value for the twenty-first century, most of them better than me, and I am conscious that the topics I touch on superficially here are better known to many others. I fear my inadequacy may be further reinforced among professional social scientists because I have deliberately written this book in a popular style and with a minimum of citations and discussion of actual social science research in order to make it accessible to a wide audience.

However, to avoid any suggestion that I am treating as shallow topics that have been subject to enormous debate by academics, I resort to the extensive use of footnotes and the occasional boxed vignette to capture some of this intensity (which can be ignored by those without interest in the arcane debate). It is necessary to labour this point a moment. The footnotes and vignettes serve a special purpose. I consider them very important to my argument, for they mostly highlight significant debates among professional social scientists, offer relevant illustrations of my argument or reinforce my point with examples. They have not been included in the text, however, because I do not wish to disrupt the narrative or overburden the general reader. I have left readers the choice of taking time out to pursue in further depth an issue in a way on the printed page that can only be achieved my means of footnotes and vignettes. In this manner, I have tried to balance the different needs of general readers and those of my colleagues.

I am grateful to Emily Drewe from Bloomsbury Academic for the invitation to take this overview and to Caroline Wintersgill, who replaced Emily as my editor, for looking after the project. I suspect I was commissioned because I occupied the post of President of the British Sociological Association (BSA) between 2009 and 2012, and had set my tenure to encourage a constructive engagement with the idea of impact and to demonstrate by a range of public events and initiatives the public relevance of sociology. I am grateful to the Association for the honour and privilege to act as President and to the number of colleagues and friends in the BSA who supported me, including earlier when I was Chair of the National Executive Committee (2004–06), especially

Judith Mudd, Gayle Letherby, Rob Mears, John Scott, Tim Strangleman, Susan Halford, David Inglis, Tom Hall, Geoff Payne, Iain Wilkinson, Linda McKie and the late Liam Murphy and Ray Pahl.

I am aware that the invitation also lay in part in the sort of work I have done as a sociologist throughout my career – publicly engaged, empirically oriented yet attuned to conceptual clarification, and popularly written; and that a background in research on topics like social division, political change, policing and police reform, crime, sectarianism, religion and peace and reconciliation was sufficiently cross disciplinary to enable me to write as a social scientist, as well as one experienced in doing socially relevant research. I, thus, owe a lot to the friends and colleagues I have talked with down the years, sharing many helpful discussions and receiving much good advice, such as David Livingstone, Bernie Hayes, Francis Teeney, Steve Bruce, Richard Breen, Chris Jenks, Duncan Rice, David Inglis, Liz Stanley, Myra Hird, David McCrone, Jack Spence, the late Fatima Meer, Peter Derman, Greg Kelly, Hastings Donnan, John Spencer, Sally Shortall, Rick Wilford, John Kremer and Shirley Lal Wijesinghe. They represent a multidisciplinary bunch, covering all the major social sciences, as well as demonstrating my affection for the University of Kwa-Zulu-Natal, Queen's University Belfast and the University of Aberdeen, places of work I am proud to be associated with.

I would also like to acknowledge my colleagues on the Leverhulme Trust-funded 'Compromise after Conflict' project (http://www.abdn.ac.uk/compromise-conflict), with whom I work on a daily basis, for the congeniality of my working life: Bernie Hayes, Francis Teeney, Katrin Dudgeon, Natascha Mueller-Hirth, Corinne Caumartin, Shirley Lal Wijesinghe, Rosemary McGarry and Jennifer McNern, including the linked PhDs – Dave Magee, Laura Fowler Graham, Sandra Rios, Clare Magill, Rachel Anderson, Aimee Smith and Duncan Scott – whose enthusiasm and drive inspires me about the future of the social sciences.

I am very grateful for a number of friends and colleagues across the social sciences that have read this volume in draft form and I apologize where I have not taken their sound advice: John Beath (economics), Dave Byrne (social policy), Norma Dawson (law), Hastings Donnan (social anthropology), John Kremer (social psychology), David Livingstone (human geography), Rick Wilford (politics) and Iain Wilkinson (sociology).

Finally, I want to express my love and gratitude to my family, Caitríona, Fiachra, Bronwen, Gwyn, Lori and, of course, Matilda; and also to my brother Colin. There is something in this volume of all these mentioned, although I am entirely responsible for what this is. But thank you everyone.

Kings College, Aberdeen

13 July 2012

Introduction

Why write this book?

This book is about the public value of the social sciences in the twenty-first century. I anticipate a groan from some readers already who will not be immediately convinced of the point of discussing public value. The adjective 'public', after all, is overused. It is stuck before so many nouns that it is almost tiresome. Michael Burawoy's Presidential Address to the American Sociological Association in 2004 (printed as Burawoy 2005) did not invent public sociology but he certainly gave us the term, and in the process made the adjective part of the zeitgeist. Most social science disciplines now come in a 'public' version. Web blogs abound devoted to the idea of the public – and, of course, creating publics in the very process. We are urged to differentiate 'publics', and to recognize that not all will be progressive (Calhoun 2007), to reinvent the idea of the public university (Holmwood 2011a), to become public spirited, to engage with, and be responsive to, the public and so on. The Open University's Centre for Citizenship, Identities and Governance in the United Kingdom (UK) has a research project called 'creating publics', with a lecture series and a web blog, designed to interrogate what public engagement means and how it might be enhanced (see http://www8.open.ac.uk/ccig/programmes/publics). There are countless other examples that I could mention: there are nearly six trillion references to 'public' on Google.

Its popularity resonates with the return of another closely related adjective, 'civil'. The 'public sphere' and 'civil society' are often run together as terms, and there are good reasons for this. 'Civil society' (see Edwards 2004) and 'the civil sphere' (see Alexander 2006) are arenas where we encounter publics, do the public engagement, garner and display our public spiritedness and mediate between governments and civil society. Edwards (2004: vi) asked at the turn of the new millennium if civil society was the 'big idea' whose time had come. Not only does this seriously overlook the antiquity of the term, but it is also, I suggest, the adjective 'public' that is the mantra of late modern society. This is because it is part of its own subject matter, with the term 'public' successfully penetrating people's contemporary consciousness and discourse, and thus also that of social science.

Regardless of any cynicism provoked by the adjective, it is necessary to understand why 'public' has become popular as a term for our time. It is code for a series of normative questions that have emerged in late modernity about the nature of power. These questions are raised locally, nationally and globally by governments, citizens, civil society groups and social scientists, as power competes and fragments across its various sources as a result of what Foucault and others call the domestication or dispersal of power. Use of the adjective 'public' not only implies fundamental questions about accountability, but also poses additional queries about to whom should we as social scientists primarily feel accountable. It also moderates questions about accountability with others about responsibility, shifting focus away from our answerability towards our responsibility, by asking to whom should social scientists primarily feel obligated. It not only defines sets of issues in which we as social scientists should be interested, but asks whose perspectives on these issues we should consider the most important. If not anymore a question of which side social science is on, as Howard Becker (1967) put it in the heady days of the 1960s, since in late modernity there are no stark zero-sum answers, the adjective 'public' nonetheless conjures up deeply normative questions about the purpose and point of social science. My use of the term 'public value' is, therefore, meaningful because I intend to address these normative purposes and restate for the twenty-first century the public value of social science, showing how, in Orlie's (1997) evocative phrase, we can in *our practice as social scientists* live ethically and act politically.

'Value', however, is another term dismissed by cynics. I was once asked about the value of discussing value. I thought it a daft question, but it made me realize that the obvious answer could not be taken for granted. While I will be distinguishing types of value – for just as there are different publics, so there are different notions of value – it is first important to highlight, as it were, the value of public value.

The social sciences are under attack. They are assailed from without and within. Social scientists have always been introspective, but to this is now added genuine insecurity. The British government minister with responsibility for science and the universities, David Willetts confirmed, during a speech at the British Academy on 1 March 2011, that the humanities and social sciences are at the heart of contemporary enquiry. He has said something similar many times. During a speech in November 2011, for example, at the Economic and Social Research Council's (ESRC) Festival of Social Science, which launched its video *Celebrating Social Science*, he was very emphatic, using terms resonant of the ESRC 2011–15 Delivery Plan.

> Quite simply, the social sciences are essential to understanding human behaviour, the wellbeing of citizens and promoting sustainable growth. The UK has an internationally acclaimed social science research community, championed by ESRC. Social science research generates vital knowledge that informs policy, helping us navigate our way through the world as individuals and as a society.

The problem is that few social scientists believe him for his government continues to pare their budgets. Self-protection within the social sciences now reinforces long-established professional separation as public expenditure constraints define the contemporary experience. The social sciences seem to exist not so much in disciplinary silos as in bunkers; feelings of threat envelop us.

This moment, therefore, is precisely the right time to restate the purpose and value of social science. The twenty-first century is a time when the social sciences are needed even more than they were in the eighteenth and nineteenth centuries to make sense of rapid and profound social change and to proffer analysis, if not also solutions. Society will need to make sense of itself in the whirlwind of crises the twentieth century has stored up for humankind in the twenty-first. However, practising social science ethically and politically, as the 'wicked problems' we face in the twenty-first century suggest we must, requires a different kind of social science.[1] If the future needs social scientists, I argue that it must be a new kind of public social science, more post-disciplinary

---

[1] The term 'wicked problem' is explained further in later chapters and is not intended to infer a moral judgement about their character but the complexity and danger associated with them. The term is not mine; I overheard it from a member of the audience at a meeting to discuss impact. If I knew who said it I would acknowledge them.

than interdisciplinary, with a new sense of its public value and new attitudes towards some old orthodoxies, like value neutrality and moral relativism. The challenges we face in the future are not only from government policies towards the social sciences and the public university as a place of learning, but also our own practices as social scientists.

The critical stance I take towards my own subject area does not seem to be shared by the humanities scholars who are championing their field, and look at the humanities uncritically as the sole resting place of either ancient scholarship (Collini 2012) or moral virtue (Nussbaum 2010). My view is that social science needs to be engaged with critically. But I differ from them also in my emphasis on the necessity of post-disciplinary collaboration between social science, the humanities and natural and medical sciences. There is nothing quite as grubby in the face of a common threat as arguing for 'ourselves alone'.[2] Bunkers are bad places from which to lead forward charges; post-disciplinarity equips universities for the twenty-first century rather than the fifteenth.[3]

Why an interpretative essay?

My argument is developed in the manner of an interpretative essay, a format I encountered a great deal as a young student when authors wrote with more hesitancy but which seems to have gone out of fashion as certainty and assertiveness get used to stamp a strong authorial voice on the argument; a time when authors pursued a tentative style rather than a dogmatic one, crafting a prolegomenon towards an argument rather than claiming a polished statement.[4] This describes my ambition here.

---

[2]   This is a recurring phrase in the text and I use it generically to refer to disciplinary closure, occasionally, as here, in the context of the disciplinarity of the separate subject areas that constitute the 'three cultures' in British intellectual life (Kagan 2009), but mostly to tendencies within the separate social science disciplines to privilege themselves above the rest. I am not using it as a pun on the name Sinn Féin, which is sometimes mistranslated from the Irish as 'ourselves alone'. Sinn Féin more properly translates as 'ourselves' or 'we ourselves'.

[3]   Of course, universities go further back than this but my own institution, Aberdeen University was founded in 1495 so just qualifies the fifteenth century as a relevant comparison for my stylistic rather than historical purposes here.

[4]   What I have in mind is Fox's 'Prolegomenon to the Study of British Kinship' (1965) and Blau's prolegomenon towards a theory of bureaucracy (1956). I have used the term before in an early attempt to develop a sociological approach to peace processes (Brewer 2003).

By an interpretative essay, I also mean a genre that involves new interpretations of evidence rather than new facts, in which personal opinion and perspective are permitted, but which deliberately seeks to confront orthodoxy and to critique taken-for-granted interpretations. It is very much a personal argument, but it is intended to throw out a challenge to contemporary ways of thinking about an issue. It, thus, speaks from a personal standpoint to a wider audience in the hope it raises ideas they had not to this point anticipated or expected. I see my audience as comprising practitioners in the social sciences, politicians, policy makers in higher education and members of the public. This is a powerful alliteration that requires me to write in a popular style. It is written with the nervousness of knowing the arguments are likely to be unpopular, but also with a confidence that derives from believing the challenge to be necessary. This genre of writing, after all, is concerned more to provoke debate than derive agreement and is oriented to change rather than consensus.

The public value of the social sciences is currently misconceived both by the majority of practitioners in the separate social sciences and the government managers of social science education and research in the United Kingdom.[5] I seek to challenge social scientists as much as education managers; those eager to throw up the barricades to protect the social sciences against government attacks, as much as the policy makers and planners who are potentially driving them into the ground; a challenge to government policies on the universities generally and to the very nature of social science itself. I hope also to rally the public, whom I want to convince about the value of social sciences enough that they see them as relevant to the twenty-first century and therefore worth defending.

A succinct summary of my argument is worthwhile. I apologize in advance for the repetition since this précis outlines ideas, terms and examples elaborated throughout the later text, but I think it is important that a short digest is given for those readers who first appreciate an overview and abridgement.

---

[5] By government managers, I mean the politicians who decide education policy, in the universities and beyond, and the managers in the various bodies that operationalize and implement it, such as the Economic and Social Research Council, the Higher Education Funding Councils and the institutions of higher and further education themselves, whose autonomy has been dramatically eroded for reasons that form a central tenet of my argument about the need to restate the public value of the social sciences for the twenty-first century.

What is the public value of the social sciences?

Public value is integral to the very nature of the social sciences, since they emerged as separate disciplines out of moral philosophy in the eighteenth century precisely in order to better diagnose and improve the social condition. Engagement with social and human progress, improvement and betterment marks social science as a public good. Two threats exist to social science, however. The first is the global university crisis and its local form in Britain, epitomized by the audit culture and marketization in higher education (this crisis is captured in three edited collections, Bailey and Freedman 2011; Holmwood 2011b; Molesworth et al. 2010). Yet this threat is simultaneously an opportunity to empower the social sciences in a new form of 'public social science'. Public social science has both a research and teaching agenda, and involves a commitment to promote the public good through civic engagement.

The second threat is the impact agenda, which is linked to the first but has developed dynamics of its own in Britain. Paradoxically, the new public social science permits engagement with the impact agenda since the process of impact is easy to demonstrate for the social sciences. However, impact is a deeply flawed approach to assess the public value of social science research. There are diverse views on its meaning, it is very difficult to measure, even within the policy evaluation tradition for which the idea of impact slips easily off the pen, and the hostility generated by the impact agenda, associated as it negatively is with the audit culture, has turned the debate gangrenous and ruled out the possibility of reasoned argument. This volume argues that the debate needs to move on from the public impact of social science to its public value. Impact is about effects, value about worth; effects are instrumental and shifting, worth is inbuilt and unchanging. Public value is a vocabulary around which it is easier to develop a common conversation in order to conduct reasoned debate. The idea of public value, however, needs to be deconstructed in order to outline its various types and the different ways in which the public value of the social sciences can be articulated.

However, at this point it is all too predictable to anticipate three complaints: that the argument is UK-centric; that I am gullible, even naïve, about the impact agenda; and that I am following a government agenda. Before the summary argument proceeds further, therefore, it is essential to clear some ground.

The processes affecting UK higher education policy are international. The contemporary conjuncture for higher education is marked by worldwide assaults on the idea of the public university, arising from neoliberal attacks on 'Big Government', global economic privations and public expenditure cuts, the marketization of higher education, the growth of the audit culture, the emphasis on accountability in public funding and increased regulation of higher education. Many of these processes are contradictory: the withdrawal of government funding for the social sciences and humanities by ending the block grant and replacing it by fees, which amounts to the wholesale privatization of public education, occurs simultaneously with increased government regulation of universities. However, while this conjuncture is international and the opportunities and threats it offers social science global, the British university system has been subject to marketization further and faster than anywhere else. My argument will place emphasis on the United Kingdom in order to critique its impact agenda and British social sciences' ambivalent response to it. It is British higher education policy after all that has forced the social sciences into restating their value and purpose (and raised the interest of publishers in their defence). This also gives my argument a tighter focus, since broad international coverage of social science research globally risks an over-ambitious book.

We are at a moment of near total degradation of the public university in the United Kingdom and social scientists are rightly critical of the public attack on social sciences, the ending of public provision for social science university education and the policy emphasis on their impact and value. By writing on the public value of social science, I might, therefore, be portrayed as reproducing the logic of this degradation and contributing to their ruin. However, I seek to respond to the disservice being done to British social science when social scientists react to the crisis facing them by refusing to engage with the impact agenda. In my view, we have no choice. Rather than 'doing the government's job for them', or 'prostituting social science to the powerful', allegations that have attached themselves to me for nudging the BSA into a constructive engagement with the impact debate, I will argue that critical engagement facilitates the renewal of the social sciences. Ours is an occasion of empowerment for the social sciences as much as defeat, a moment for stating the case for 'public social science'.[6]

It is for this reason also that I refute any suggestion that I am responding to the British government's crude neoliberal economism by writing about value in a way that tries to please everybody. I suspect I will please no one. More to the point, while the government's neoliberal agenda has, indeed, occasioned my reflections on public value, my primary purpose is to initiate debate among social scientists about their craft as we enter the twenty-first century and have to deal with 'wicked problems' that have never been encountered before in such complexity and severity. Marketization may have provoked interest in redefining our public value, but it is the essential worth of social science, which is encapsulated by its normative public value, that is the real driver of change, for this notion of our value requires us to be relevant to diagnosing, analysing, understanding and ameliorating the conditions of culture, the market and the state in the twenty-first century.

Inaugurating the 'new public social science' is the kernel of this interpretative essay. A brief explanation of the idea is, thus, necessary. First, it implies a critique of the limits of social science as traditionally conceived. Secondly, it involves a declaration of principle that posits a new form of social science appropriate for the dramatically changed landscape of higher education in the aftermath of the global university crisis – a social science for the twenty-first century.

What might be called 'old' or 'traditional' social science involved governments suspicious of, and often critical of, social science research, rarely using it to inform policy despite the mantra of 'evidence-led policy', and often disagreeing with its findings or ignoring critical ones. On the part of social science, there was a position of mostly principled distance from and critique of government under the ethos of academic freedom, intellectual autonomy and research independence. The social sciences practised disciplinary closure and mostly competed with one another from separate silos. Public universities were *sui generis* as largely unregulated ivory towers, with the principles of

---

[6] Christensen and Eyring (2011) make a similar point with respect to universities as institutions generally in the United States, where they claim that they are ripe for destruction but also for innovation from within, facing threats and danger as well as evincing reasons for hope.

academic freedom and autonomy used to support professional-driven, single-disciplinary social science. On the part of government, this gave us 'negative impact', social science research that governments disliked and ignored because it showed policy to be wrong and ill-founded. On the part of social science, disciplinary closure and academic autonomy were often disguises for disconnected and disengaged research, removed from community concerns, and people's 'private troubles' and public issues, as Charles Wright Mills once put it, and written in a style that the public could not comprehend. Traditional social science often wrote only for the like-minded and was impenetrable to the public and policy makers alike. Policy-oriented social science was done aplenty but it was marginalized and ridiculed within mainstream social science, and, deeply ironical, mostly ignored by policy makers and government. 'Disguised impact' is, thus, real, comprising that social science research that has public benefits but of which policy makers, governments and the media are wholly ignorant. Disguised impact fills the black hole that often exists between a research input and its eventual outcome.

The current conjuncture threatens to reinforce traditional social science. Seemingly opposite pressures actually pull in the same direction to solidify traditional notions of social science. The marketization of social scientific knowledge, via ideas of 'impact', 'use', 'knowledge transfer' and 'benefit', combines with the privatization of public university education through the withdrawal of public funding for humanities and social science, and enhanced state regulation of universities through the audit culture, to reinforce mutual suspicion and contempt between government and social science, making government approaches to social science ideological. This is the horn of a dilemma on which the development of social science is caught. Social science research risks being rendered by the government and proponents of the audit culture as impactful only when carried out on behalf of narrow government policy objectives, like the Big Society, while social science researchers who try to engage with impact are negatively stereotyped by social science critics of the impact agenda for conducting narrow, 'professional' policy research and of 'prostituting social science to the powerful'.

However, the present conjuncture can be turned to the advantage of social science and current exigencies used as a form of empowerment. My argument is intended to make the case for the new public social science that can emerge from the current university crisis. What is the new public social science? Devising strategies for improving governments' receptivity to social science is part of the new social science as much as improving social science's attitude towards political and public engagement and the pursuit of publicly relevant research – mostly done in participatory forms in conjunction with communities, non-governmental organizations (NGOs), civil society and the people directly involved in or affected by it. Public social science has porous borders and requires enhanced collaboration between the social science disciplines; it transcends national borders to engage with global society; and it moves from traditional disciplinary agendas, many rooted in narrow twentieth-century notions of professionalism within the separate social science disciplines, to engage with public issues affecting the future of humankind. This affects the teaching agenda of the new social sciences as much as their research concerns.

Social science has necessarily always been transgressive and its critical edge is what makes it distinctive. The new public social science retains its identity as a form of critique by continuing it transgressiveness. There are at least three borders it transgresses – disciplinary, national and political – and it transcends at least one divide – that between teaching and research. It is post- or interdisciplinary and global. Disciplines like sociology, politics, economics, social psychology, anthropology, international relations, social policy, human geography, demography, law and criminology offer perspectives better in combination than separately. Post-disciplinarity is finding expression in hived-off new subject areas, like gender and sexuality studies, cultural studies, auto/biography and narrative studies, peace studies, transitional justice studies, development studies, security studies and memory studies among others. However, I suggest its home is better found in the idea of public social science itself.

But it is the political boundaries that make public social science most challenging. Because it is the responsibility of us all to deal with the complex issues facing humankind in the twenty-first century, the new public social science has to engage with those considered by us up to now as 'strangers' – natural scientists, governments, international agencies like the European Union, United Nations and international NGOs. If we take climate change as an instance, there has to be useful engagement between sociologists, environmentalists, transport policy makers, oceanographers and the like.

Governments are the strangest of all our 'dragons',[7] but the new social science needs to engage with them as much as civil society and organic community groups.

There is an imperative here that also affects social science teaching. Alongside the core areas of traditional social science disciplines, the new public social science also needs to teach courses that deal with some of the public issues that affect the future of humankind. Teaching courses on sustainability, oceans, well-being and happiness, East-West, North-South, humans and other animals, climate, organized violence and peace, for example, make social science inherently post-disciplinary and help transcend the social/natural science divide. International NGOs and civil society groups can be brought into the classroom so that, in our teaching, students see what it means to think globally and act locally. Public social science is a practice for the classroom and the real world, and one that tries to narrow the gulf between the two.

In all these ways, public social science returns to its eighteenth-century roots as a diagnosis of the social condition, with a moral vision committed to social and human improvement and betterment. I cannot emphasize this point more strongly so as to avoid any suggestion I am claiming originality. There are a few other formulations than my own that are struggling with making social science relevant to the twenty-first century, but I wish to stress that mine returns us to the eighteenth century, and to the eighteenth-century Scottish moralists in particular; to an era when the separate social sciences emerged out of moral philosophy precisely in order to engage with the various dimensions of culture, the market and the state; to a time when my view of public value was taken for granted by the way in which social science was designed to diagnose and improve the human condition.[8] This sense of public value was lost – with some notable individual exceptions – as the social sciences subsequently professionalized and became more esoteric and technical in their knowledge production, forcing them to be inward looking rather than publicly engaged, and to separate from each other and become specialized rather than combine

---

[7] Intended as a phrase to invoke the practice of medieval map makers who always referred to areas of the globe unknown to them as 'here be dragons'. I return to this metaphor in Chapter 5.

[8] For readers who wish to trace the historical development of moral philosophy into the separate social sciences in eighteenth-century Scotland and afterwards, I suggest they consult with the work of Gladys Bryson (1932a, 1945) or Brewer (1989). To deal with it here would be overly disruptive to my narrative about public value.

and be generic. My argument is that we should rekindle the sense of public value that specialization and professionalization destroyed. In reclaiming this form of social worth, I am arguing that the new public social science in and of itself is a public good.

This is not an argument in support of the narrow impact agenda that is currently dominating social science and government education managers. I advance four claims with respect to impact: (a) the new form of public social science is well equipped and readily capable of demonstrating the impact of social science research; (b) impact, however, is a deeply flawed way of approaching the public value of social science since the term is difficult to define and measure, as even the policy evaluation tradition demonstrates; (c) it is necessary to shift the terms of the debate away from the public impact of social science to its public value; and (d) value can be deconstructed into several types which show the diverse ways in which the social sciences have value.

Public social science requires broadening our understanding of the idea of value. It is proposed that shifting the terms of the debate from the public impact of social science to the public value of social science brings four advantages: it better constitutes a vocabulary that permits common conversations to develop; it involves rhetoric that is consensual not divisive, thus helping to move social scientists on from the unfortunate tone into which the impact debate has sunk; it transcends the localized form of the debate about impact, which is perceived to be peculiarly British, to link with an international discourse about public value; and it offers the best prospect of restating for the twenty-first century the principles on which social science can justify itself against the neoliberal push towards using economic impact as their sole measure of effectiveness.

It is possible to develop a definition of public value that speaks to the inherent principle and purpose of social science as a public good. This involves deconstruction of the term 'value'. There are at least three different meanings to the term: value as usefulness and utility; value as quality and worth; value as judgement and evaluation. The first we might rename *use value*, the second *price value*, the third *normative value*.[9] They prompt further deconstruction. Use value can be direct or indirect, price value intrinsic or added (giving us

---

[9] I explain in Chapter 4, where I develop these ideas, why I do not use the popular term of exchange value instead of price value.

the phrase 'value added') and normative value private or public. Direct use value describes the level of usefulness of an item unmediated by other things, indirect is the utility accorded when used in combination with other things. Use value does not necessarily diminish when it is indirect. A single chair has direct use value but its indirect use value can be enhanced when set in relation to other chairs and a table. Intrinsic price value is the worth of the item inherent unto itself, such as the cost of the raw materials and labour power to make a single chair or set of chairs and table. Added price value describes the worth of things when put to use indirectly, such as the price value attributed to a meal in a restaurant that utilizes chairs and tables. Private normative value refers to the quality attributed to an item by an individual in terms of the status to them derived from possessing it, public normative value to the quality attributed to it more widely, such as its social status and cultural significance. Personal sentiment can attach immense normative value to an item which is of little meaning and status to other individuals or collectively, and vice versa.

Elements of use, price and normative value are run together in current debates, where 'impact' is often narrowly reduced to use-value and where arguments about the defining purposes of subjects is often related exclusively to their public normative value. By developing an appropriate sense of the purpose of the social sciences, it is possible to establish a definition of their value that broadens it from economic usefulness.

This conceptual vocabulary means that we have to assess the value of the social sciences across different dimensions of value, and that the assessment of their worth varies accordingly. For example, this conceptual deconstruction allows us to argue that the value of the social sciences is not to be found solely in direct use value (say, economic usefulness), as if this can be assessed in isolation from indirect use value (say, their economic usefulness when assessed in relation to other things, such as the economic usefulness of social science graduates across their working lives, or the indirect use value of social science research in combination with other scientific research, in the form of medical-social science research, biological and social sciences research, climate change science and the sociology of climate change and so on).

We can further argue that the price value of the social sciences (their cost to the public exchequer set against what they realize by their direct use value) is a very poor measure of value. If the focus is on price value, we should properly calculate both the indirect use value of the social sciences and their 'value added' price value – the price value of the social sciences when measured by what they add to the use, price and normative value of other things. The price value of the social sciences, for example, should be set in the context of what they add to the price value derived from, say, student exchanges, intellectual tourism and social and cultural events, or the impact of social science research on transport policy, housing, the welfare state, 'race' relations, better hospital care for the dying, crime rates and so on, and what added price value accrues from having people educated in the social sciences (in terms of, say, socially informed citizenry, workforces, communities and the like). The social sciences as a rule do not have direct links with industry and the market, and knowledge transfer in the social sciences does not tend to reflect in spin-off companies and the like. But social science research on intercultural and interethnic relations, ageing and population demographics, sport, heritage and so on can be stressed as part of their added price value.

This multidimensional view of value also means that the normative value of the social sciences is an important dimension equal to their use and price value. This is not just meant in the narrow sense of what they add to the quality of life and status of individuals educated in the social sciences or to the lives of people affected by social science research, important as these are as a measure of private normative value; it is that the value of the social sciences can be assessed by their contribution to the social values they help garner and disseminate in culture, the market and the state deriving from people's awareness of themselves as forming a society, whether local, national or global.[10] The public normative value of the social sciences, therefore, gives the social sciences two qualities against which their status should be evaluated: they not only generate information about society, they are a medium for society's reproduction. They are the way in which society can find out about itself and in so doing generate the idea of society itself. If it is thought that this sort of value is incalculable, it is no more so than the proper enumeration of the use and price value of the social sciences. However, the language of 'public value', as distinct from 'public impact', is challenging precisely because it is not

---

[10] I explain in the next chapter why I refer to culture, the market and the state as synonymous with 'society' in its inclusive sense and why I emphasize local, national and global spaces.

reducible to monetary calculation in the same way price and use value are, which is why establishing the public value of social science is so important for rescuing the debate from the marketeers who reduce everything to use and price value.

The argument in this interpretative essay is, thus, simple and clear cut: making people aware of themselves as comprising a society helps in the development and dissemination of key social values that render society possible – cultural values like trust, empathy, altruism, tolerance, compromise, social solidarity and sense of belonging – and assists in society's ongoing betterment and improvement. The social sciences help us understand the conditions which both promote and undermine these values and identify the sorts of public policies, behaviours and relationships that are needed in culture, the market and the state to ameliorate their absence and restore and repair them. It is for these reasons that social science is a public good and has inherent worth.

The public normative value of the social sciences lies, therefore, in their direct engagement with the DNA of society – individuals, groups, social relations, civil society, culture, law, legal governance, the market and the state. They are modes for understanding the mechanisms through which we live socially and as such are essential for making social life possible. The medical analogy is worth emphasizing, especially since an organic analogy was so important to the public understanding of the social sciences at their inception. DNA is not only important to helping us understand biological life, knowing how DNA works helps improve the *quality* of biological life. Social sciences dissect the DNA of society and the information this discloses helps them improve the quality of social life. As such, the social sciences exist within a moral and ethical framework, and simultaneously help to consolidate it as the framework within which everyone exists as social beings.

The public value of social science research is enhanced by the way the social sciences compress time and space and thus make society aware both of the global dimensions to local issues and the catalogue of dangerous issues stacking up for humankind in the future. Use and price values are located in the immediate here-and-now of current time and place; public normative value is attentive to the humanitarian future. The vocabulary involved in debating the public value of the social sciences can make reference to social science engagement with the 'big issues' of future industrial, scientific and economic change – sustainability, labour migration, climate change, peace processes, the link between demographic shifts and welfare demands to name a few. If the traditional standards by which we judged the purpose of social sciences research have been replaced by economic utility, then the new public value narrative should not ignore this but stress that scientific, economic, political, industrial, climatic and social changes in the future will be mediated by the capacity of the social sciences to enable culture, the market and the state to make sense of them.

Users of this value narrative need to recognize that the notion of public value into which it fits is multidimensional. 'Economic benefits' have to form part of the value narrative and use and price value are part of the debate about the public value of the social sciences. This means articulating that the social and cultural relevance of social science research on quality of life issues, well-being, climate change or intercultural understandings, for example, has economic utility in addition to its other benefits. My argument, however, is not restricted to economic utility and broadens the debate. Current notions of impact value are seriously distorted by their narrowness.

The notion of value explicit in the volume demonstrates, however, the extent of the challenge facing the social sciences, not only in the sense of undergoing change in order to make themselves relevant to the difficult issues facing the future of humankind, but also to their own modes of practice. We need more than interdisciplinarity if we are to deal with the impending crises affecting the future of humankind; we need to be post-disciplinary: not just linking across the disciplinary boundaries within social science but to the humanities and the natural sciences, looking to connect with civil society and government, being theoretically astute, evidenced based and policy engaged. We need to be able to let the problem define the disciplinary perspectives needed, not the other way round. The new public social science will challenge our orthodox commitments to value freedom and moral relativism, two principles of the old social science. The new public social science is value-committed, undertaking ethical-based research and teaching, done for the purpose of promoting the public good broadly conceived, in which values matter and notions like 'good', 'sustainability', 'social justice', 'equality of opportunity', 'fairness', 'wrong-doing', 'evil', 'human betterment' and the like are objective rather than relative categories. The new public social science sees the end of value neutrality and moral relativism. But normative social science has to remain still as science, and living with tensions between civic engagement and detachment and normative and scientific practice mark some of the challenges of public social science in the twenty-first century. This signals my argument as highly controversial and provocative; qualities eminently suitable to the genre of an interpretative essay.

What is the organization of this essay?

I have given this digest of the argument at this early point because it will be a long time before we discuss public value again (in Chapter 4). I wish to present the essay in a way that I think will be more attractive to popular readers. I do not wish to start with a declaration and substantiation of the public value of the social sciences and then work slowly backwards to show how this is premised on my definition of the generic nature of social science. Establishing the public value of social science, after all, is not the culmination of the essay; my endpoint is identifying the new form of public social science that emerges from the inherent worth of social science. I wish to proceed in a more logical fashion by moving forwards not backwards, building each additional layer of the argument on carefully laid foundations. In Chapter 1, I define social science, and in Chapter 2, I outline its scale and assess its quality and strength in the United Kingdom. In Chapter 3, I establish the nature of the threat it faces and to which my account, in Chapter 4, of its public value is a defence. In Chapter 5, I outline the new public social science that follows on from this sense of public value. In the Conclusion, I discuss the broader implications of this view for making social science relevant to the twenty-first century. My discourse on public value, in other words, is merely the medium through which a wider discussion about the nature and content of social science in the future is possible.

1

What is Social Science?

Introduction

I see the social sciences, for all their obvious differences in content, approach and methodology, as united in two senses. First, they have a shared subject matter (which I call the social nature of culture, the market and the state). This permits huge variety in the way they each approach and tackle this subject matter and what they focus on. Secondly, they have a common public value that derives from this subject matter. Two things follow for the way I construct my argument. While disciplines have historically contingent boundaries and are obviously shaped by the conversations that take place across them, the social sciences have an essential, generic nature; and their public value is a common denominator. Focusing on their public value serves to demonstrate this essential unity. My later description of the normative public value of social science, as I call it, is, therefore, premised on a view of their common character. This chapter is devoted to defining this generic quality.

This is a difficult argument, given that specialization and professionalization in the twentieth century have destroyed any sense of generic unity among the separate social sciences and turned them against one another. Many economists, for example, think they are the only social science that is scientific, and those prejudicial to economics think it too dismal a failure to be considered a social science.[1] However, in this chapter, I venture to outline what I consider to be the generic nature of social science.

---

[1] In a personal communication with the author David Byrne was blunt: 'Basically I think you have a real problem in trying to assert the public value of the social sciences on behalf of the social sciences as a whole because their whole methodological and problematic bases are often incompatible. For example, while Steuer whom you quote more than once asserts that economics is the only real social science, I would say contemporary mathematical neo-classical economics is utterly unscientific since it is based on a deductive development from manifestly false premises and has no empirical foundation whatsoever' (dated 21 April 2012). These views are expanded in his book *Applying Social Science* (Byrne 2011).

It is necessary to explain that I develop this working definition of generic social science as I go along, building up to a definition incrementally, arriving fully only at the end of the chapter. I am not working backwards in this chapter, unpicking a definition stated categorically at the beginning, since I think the general reader unfamiliar with the idea of social science appreciates going forwards as each block is built on bit by bit. I will conclude by dealing with the issue of disciplinarity and disciplinary closure, by which I mean the tendency for the separate social sciences to erect fences between one another, marking off each other as different and distinct. Disciplinary closure is about emphasizing dissimilarities and it is necessary that we dismantle these fences before we can build the new public social science that is premised on my generic definition of social science.

Two problems in particular arise from disciplinarity for a generic definition of social science. First, the very meaning of the word 'social' has become subject to disciplinary closure, where it is now closely identified with the subject matter and domain of sociology to the point that it complicates our sense of what generic social science is. We, therefore, need to rescue the concept of society from sociology. Secondly, so difficult is it to define social science that people resort to listing the separate subjects within the field. There is no sense of the generic features of this branch of scientific study; it is what its separate subjects do. This sort of definition is particularly inadequate if we are to advance the idea of a new public social science that has a special and unique public value. Therefore, we must build up to such a definition by first deconstructing what is 'social' and 'science' about social science.

What is 'social' about social science?

Some august bodies connected to the social sciences shy away of trying to define them or resort to rather tepid common denominators. The United Kingdom's Academy of Social Sciences, for example, takes it so for granted what the social sciences are that it does not define them on its website (http://www.acss.org.uk/). Neither does the US Social Science Research Council on its website (http://www.ssrc.org/).[2] The worst cases of this oversight are the

---

[2]   Consulted 25 October 2011.

International Social Science Council, whose 2010 *World Social Science Report* (UNESCO 2010: 3) considers that it constitutes merely the professional associations affiliated to it, and the Commission on the Social Sciences, an *ad hoc* body set up by the Academy of Social Sciences at the new millennium to report on the state of social science in Britain, which described social science as a misnomer given the divergences between the separate disciplines (2003: 6), although it went on to define it as 'disciplined curiosity about societies in which we live' (2003: 32).

Those tempted to define social science agree around the notion that it is the scientific study of society, although this is variously worded. In its pioneering Foundation Module in Social Sciences, the Open University in the United Kingdom, for example, defined social science as the study of society, justifying a module on general social science on the grounds that society provoked such a broad range of questions that no one discipline could possibly answer them all (Porter 1981: 3). Perhaps the definition used by the ESRC is the most appropriate.

> Social science is, in its broadest sense, the study of society and the manner in which people behave and influence the world around us. Some social scientists argue that no single definition can cover such a broad range of academic disciplines. Instead, they simply define the social sciences by listing the subjects they include. The main social science disciplines include: anthropology, communication, criminology, cultural studies, economics, human geography, linguistics, public law, political science, psychology, sociology, development studies.[3]

Such a response is the common one: social science is what social scientists do in their separate disciplines. This will not suffice here. If what is 'social' about the social sciences is that their field of enquiry is society, we need to know first what society is.

The ESRC's change of name from the Social Science Research Council in 1983, under a Conservative government hostile to social science, reflects the storm about the term 'science' when applied to society, but the term 'society' itself is controversial. It is particularly important to disabuse readers of the view that society does not exist, that only individuals are real. This is what philosophers call a 'category mistake' (which Gilbert Ryle, the Oxford

---

[3]   ESRC website (www.esrc.ac.uk/about-esrc/what -we-do/what-is.aspx), consulted 10 October 2011.

philosopher used to illustrate by contrasting Oxford University's Colleges with Oxford University as a collectivity; in seeing the former, we see the latter: what differs is simply that nature of the category). Society *is* real and without it individuals could not exist, let alone function; people are, to borrow the title of W. G. Runciman's introduction to social science (1999), 'a very social animal'.

Society consists of individuals, groups and institutions. Individuals are not its basic unit; and groups and institutions are as tangible as people. Therefore, society is more than the aggregation of all the interactions of the people who comprise it. This was recognized even in early social psychology. James Mickel Williams, for example, wrote that the 'social mind', as he called it, exercised a dominant influence over individuals' minds (1920: 442), a view prevalent in American social psychology, in people such as Cooley, and in early British psychology, notably William McDougall – who went on to work and live in the United States – as well as social theorists like Hobhouse.[4] An example can illustrate this point. The social significance of multimillions of people honouring the Armistice silence at 11 o'clock on the 11th day of the 11th month each year is a property of a collectivity different in kind from the motivations of each person on the day. Each person has their own motive for participating, but their joint actions have a collective significance that transcends each individual. The event draws on ideas about the nation and culture, and points to shared beliefs across national and cultural boundaries, it evokes such things as national narratives of honour and sacrifice, its connects generations across time and space, the long-since dead with present and future generations, and it involves collective rituals as much as individual emotional responses, collective behaviour as well as personal action. That is to say, people are not islands unto themselves, living in isolated and separate worlds inhabited only by themselves as single individuals. Individuals live, work and behave within groups; people cannot exist without each other in groups.

This is not to say that social science only studies groups, as suggested by the Mass Observation organization in 1937 when it wrote 'collective habits

---

[4] McDougall wrote a text in 1908 entitled *An Introduction to Social Psychology* in the same year as the American E. A. Ross published his text with the title *Social Psychology*. I owe to John Kremer the observation that the differences between the two mark the beginnings of the later schism within social psychology between those who look towards the natural sciences for an understanding of human social behaviour and those who see the social sciences as their natural home. From within psychology it is only really the latter that fall within the bailiwick of my essay.

and social behaviour are our field of enquiry, and individuals are only of interest in so far as they are typical of groups' (quoted in Stanley 2001: 92). Nor does social science claim, even worse, that there is a 'group mind'.[5] People always retain some novel and unique features compared to their fellow group members in terms of social and demographic characteristics or particular beliefs and practices, so social science studies *people in groups*, but it is the case that the groups' shared beliefs and practices shape what individual members believe, say and do, so social science focuses as well on *groups in people*. It is like the difference between an individual tree and the forest of which the tree is a small part. Extending this analogy, social science is constantly in the fruitful tension of exploring the individual tree, the wood which it comprises and the relationship between the two. That is to say, society is composed of individuals who live and work in groups, having relationships with other people and other groups to which everyone attaches meaning. There would be no culture, commerce or communication without groups. Individuals are made for group living; human nature *is* social.

It is worth quoting another Aberdonian on this. Robert MacIver joined the University of Aberdeen in 1907 as lecturer in politics, but in 1911 taught courses in sociology before moving to the University of Toronto as associate professor in political economy in 1915, and thence to Columbia University in New York where he held a combined chair in economics and sociology. He ended his days as Chancellor of the New School of Social Research in the city (for further details of MacIver's career, see Brewer 2007a). He was, thus, accomplished enough to write a short text in 1921 entitled *The Elements of Social Science* (MacIver 1921), which was the first academic textbook to recognize this field of enquiry under that name in Britain (readers who wish to pursue the history of the term 'social science' in Britain should see **Vignette 1**), going through at least seven editions (my copy is dated 1944). It was published a whole generation before the volumes of the *Encyclopaedia of Social Science* first appeared between 1930 and 1935. He begins his opening paragraph as follows (1921: 1). 'Wherever there is life there is society. For life can arise and

---

[5]   It was popular once to claim there was such a thing when, in early sociology and psychology, group behaviour was explained in terms of features of individuals (James Mickel Williams, an early social psychologist, referred to this as the 'social mind', 1920: 442). But the expansion in our idea of the social allows us to see such arguments as pre-social science. Today, with recognition of such phenomena as crowd behaviour and collective behaviour, we are more alert to the impact of the group on individual participants' minds.

Vignette 1 The origins of the term
social science in Britain

By 1887, Beatrice Webb was deploying the term commonly and it was sufficiently established for her to write about its methodology (see 1926: 356–7), but its origins go much further back. I would like to emphasize three related but distinct precursors: Victorian social ameliorism; Christian social ethics; and the emergence of professional sociology. Victorian Britain was replete with references to 'social science' and it had a strong institutional presence. The British Association, later to become the British Association for the Advancement of Science (BAAS), had a Statistics section from 1833, only 2 years after formation of the Association itself, which became the Economic Science and Statistics section in 1856. The National Association for the Promotion of Social Science (NAPSS), sometimes shortened to the Association of Social Science, was created in 1857 and held annual conferences, published a regular series of its transactions and the *Journal of Social Science* until 1884 (see Abrams 1968; Goldman 2002; Huch 1985). The NAPSS was an amalgam of several local statistical societies and reform groups concerned to understand and ameliorate social problems. Under the sway of Victorian altruism and religious social activism, the NAPSS appealed to the British Establishment – its Council included 31 Peers, 48 MPs, 19 Doctors of Law and QCs, 14 Fellows of the Royal Society, as well as numerous Baronets, Knights, medical professionals and churchmen (Abrams 1968: 45) – as well as the growing middle classes in the cities worried at the effects of urbanization and industrialization. It had sections dealing with law, education, crime, public health and 'social economy'. It linked with the British Medical Association, the Law Amendment Society and the BAAS, drawing on faith in religion, science and social progress in an exercise of remarkable disciplinary openness. The *Journal of Social Science* reflected, among other things, concerns over sanitation, air pollution ('noxious vapour') and acid rain ('coal acidity' in rain), nursing care and hospital design; and, unusually for a time when women had to have their papers read by men, the NAPSS encouraged the participation of women and the working class. The Association's demise in the mid-1880s is explained by the failure of ameliorism in the face of a more aggressive working class and trades union movement (Huch 1985: 281 n 13). Its notion of social science was very much restricted to problem-oriented, technical knowledge to assist improvement, and was atheoretical. There was no sense in which these social ills were connected to the kind of social structure generated by nineteenth-century industrialization; or at least, the NAPSS became redundant when this sort of analysis was pursued by social reformers more closely interested in the condition of the working class, like Booth, Rowntree and the Webbs (Abrams 1968: 52). Christian ethics was also social ameliorist but had a much more elaborate sense of society as an interlocking set of institutions, primarily as a result of the application of the organic analogy to society. Elsewhere, I have addressed the influence of Christian groups on British sociology (see Brewer 2007b) and the same impulses to Christian sociology gave direction to social science. On the one hand, there was an essentially conservative view of society that was ambivalent towards modernism, in which religion, scientifically understood, could supply its moral canopy, and, conversely, a Christian socialist ethos concerned to make sense of social progress. Most of Catholic and 'high' Anglican sociology was shaped by the former, the latter by the sociology of Maurice Reckitt and his journal of Christian sociology *Christendom*. The Catholic Social Guild, involved in seminary training and work with the laity, produced *A Primer of Social Science* in 1913. Written by the Right Rev Monsignor Henry Parkinson, it went through several editions. Parkinson was a Jesuit, Rector of Oscott College in Birmingham, and the book was designed for members of the Guild who wished 'for a simple yet comprehensive manual of social science . . . under the light of Catholic principle' (1920[1913]: v). Despite his Catholic ethos, social science was defined reasonably well, as 'the systematic study of the social organism. By the social organism is understood the structure of Society (comprising individuals, families, groups, the Church and State) together with the mutual action of its various elements' (1920[1913]: 9). The book – my 1920 edition runs to 285 pages – has chapters on all the above but was primarily concerned with economic relations and 'social failures' (seen as personal and social; among the latter were included poverty and unemployment). The book was heavily focused on the conditions of the working class, taking up encyclicals by Pope Leo XIII, and featured a great deal of Catholic social teaching. Parkinson made the point, however, that social science is more than social ameliorism: 'it has for its special object the existing inequalities of the different classes, the deficiencies of society and their removal' (1920[1913]: 11). No single subject could give adequate expression to 'these myriad relations and forces [so] social science must presuppose the sciences of religion and morals but also that of politics, jurisprudence and economics' (1920[1913]: 11). Sociology was oddly missing from this list. That discipline's contribution to the etymology of social science, however, starts with MacIver in 1921. MacIver's *The Elements of Social Science* is more secular and modern than Parkinson's. It was designed partly for a readership in the Workers Educational Association in Britain, showing both continuity with the ameliorist tradition and the emerging interest in class, but also for MacIver's university students in Toronto as a textbook.

continue only in the society of like beings. Life is always obviously social. It is born and nurtured in society, it finds its degree of fulfilment, its character, its limitation, in society. Society is more than our environment: it is our nature. It is within us as well as around us'.

That we now take this for granted as our original state of nature, when it was once thought not to be the case, is the result of the expansion of social science knowledge about ourselves. We might say that social science has become part of common sense knowledge and has become routinized – that is, social science is now a routine part of our taken-for-granted knowledge. The way we understand ourselves as human beings living in society is the product of what social science has enabled us to see about ourselves and the way we live in groups. As Giddens puts it (1996: 76), the major achievement of social science, which the natural sciences cannot emulate, is the realization that social science constitutes the very social world it studies by the absorption of social science into the sense people make of society. That is to say, social science has enabled us to see ourselves in a new light. We will return to this point, but in passing we can note as evidence of routinization the enculturation of social science terms into popular and media discourse, notably concepts like 'moral panic', inflation, social capital, McDonaldization,[6] social class, infant nurturing, the division of labour, the law of diminishing returns, risk, socialization, introversion-extroversion, globalization and role, among many others.

The groups to which people belong can be large and amorphous collectivities with blurred boundaries, like social classes, genders, neighbourhoods, ethnic groups and nationalities, and more clearly marked and identifiable collections, like churches, factories, business organizations, political parties, families, schools and the like. The term 'institution' covers all these groupings and is, thus, open to confusion, in a way that the term 'individual' is not, because the nature of the loyalties represented by these various groups and their boundaries differs. Some institutions are very prescriptive in what they lay down for people to follow, such as legal rituals in courts of law, others permit choice, such as the institution of marriage. People also have different sorts of closeness to these institutions and relate to them in different ways,

---

[6] George Ritzer, the inventor of the term, reflects on its wider use in the United Kingdom compared with the United States, which he takes as evidence of the greater capacity for social scientists to be public intellectuals in Britain (2006: 212).

and the groups change over time and with it our relationship to them. People change churches, vote for different parties and move in and out of different employment, so institutions reflect patterns of continuity and change. These patterns reflect the behaviours of many individuals, so while single individuals may change their behaviour little in the course of their lifetime, or a lot, patterns of continuity and change within institutions reflect those of the many more people who constitute the whole group. In this way, institutions take on behaviours and structures separate from the individuals who comprise them.

These institutional structures can in turn affect people. These effects vary with the nature of the institution. Some institutions have very direct effects that are immediately apparent. The decisions business firms make about production affect people who work there. Changes in party manifesto can influence people's decision about the casting of their vote. The more opaque and amorphous the boundaries that mark the institution, however, the more indirect these impacts seem, especially where they occur only slowly over time. These impacts on individual behaviour can be so indirect that attributing their cause to broader institutional change can be contested. For example, the extent to which changes in family structure (such as the rise of single-parent and multiple step-family structures) have impacted on children's educational performance, or their participation in crime, is not clear and is a matter of debate between social scientists. Other forms of institutional change are clearer in their effect on individual behaviour as a result of long-established social science analysis, such as the growth of consumer culture on young people's behaviour, the effects of long-term unemployment on the individual's health and well-being or the consequences of social class for children's language skills and verbal repertoire.

In saying that social science studies institutions and individuals, we are therefore also saying that it studies *social relationships*. To quote again MacIver's programmatic outline of social science at the beginning of the twentieth century: 'Society in the very widest sense include[s] every kind and degree of relationship entered into by social creatures. Society means the whole system of social relationships' (1921: 8). These social relations can be those between people themselves (such as the way family members relate to one another across the generations, or do members of a trade union with managers or businesses with workers) and the relations the groups to which they belong have as groups (such as the behaviour of trade unions, businesses, political parties, social classes and the like), as well as the relations these groups and institutions have to one another (such as the link between female gender and church attendance or the links between business firms and political parties).

These relations are two-way. Social science studies people's behaviour in groups, the way in which institutions are in part constituted by people acting together within them, as well as studying the impact institutional structures have on people's behaviour, the way in which institutions constrain and shape people's behaviour. In this way, social science studies the relationships both people and institutions have to the collectivity called 'society' and the way in which society is simultaneously both the outcome of people's relationships and the context within which they relate. Society is seen as a myriad of complex interrelations, going off in all directions, at the same time both cause and effect of ordinary people's behaviour. Society, thus, has a dual character. It is both external and internal to people, something that exists beyond people to shape what they do, while being the creation of people who act in socially acceptable and agreed ways. It is the framework for human behaviour, the apparatus of rules, regulations, norms and values that shape people's interrelationships, but constructed by humans themselves. Peter Berger (1963) once put this aptly: people exist in society and society in people. For simplicity's sake, we might call the one societal reproduction, the other societal production: society is reproduced (replicated over time and space) by what people produce (behaviour, social relationships), which then shape people's future production and, by further regression, society's continued reproduction, and so on.

Some broad characterizations of social science might be suggested by this working definition thus far. Particular social sciences have placed emphasis on the question of how it is that society exists in people (societal reproduction). Cultural studies, social psychology, education, language and communication studies and social anthropology have in their different ways all contributed significantly to our understanding of the process of child socialization, language acquisition and the multiple ways culture is learnt. This left the other social sciences to primarily focus on the question of people's behaviour in society (societal production). And the professionalization of the social sciences into disciplinary blocks resulted in attention to political, economic, sociological and legal behaviour, by individuals and institutions, among many other things.

However, the whole point about the dual character of society is that the two sides are intertwined to the point that it is too crude to demarcate the particular social sciences by separating them according to one or other side of a Janus face. All social sciences concern themselves with both societal reproduction and production. Economics is as much interested in how people internalize economic norms and behave in markets as sociology is in the process of cultural learning and change. Economics does not only deal mathematically with quantity but also with subjective perceptions of quality of life and value, with the impact of external factors *on* markets as well as traders' emotional states *in* markets. Economic markets could not operate unless people make sense of the meaning of key economic processes like investment and risk, and make evaluations of them. Social psychology addresses childhood socialization (society in people) but also issues around identity and how identity formation shapes people's behaviour in settings of inter-group interaction (people in society). This is to say, in studying the social relationships individuals and institutions have in society, social science necessarily studies the social relationships individuals and institutions have with each other *and* towards society itself.

Putting this in a slightly more complicated way, the subject matter of social science is the *social* nature of society, its continual reproduction through people's production. This is not to claim, of course, that social science necessarily has to focus on societal production and reproduction at the same time. By this I mean that social science is demarcated by its interest in addressing the ways in which individuals and institutions internalize society and behave within it, but the two sides of the Janus face can be studied together or separately.

Three features of society need to be stressed at this point. First, social science is not restricted just to what people in society say about themselves in the process of societal production and reproduction. This enables us to demarcate professional social science from common sense. Secondly, society is spatial and temporal but knows no spatial or temporal bounds, and thus neither should social science. This requires us to take account of the globalization of society. Thirdly, our notion of society has to be broad and inclusive in order to avoid privileging any particular social science take on it. This means that we have to rescue the idea of society from sociology. Let me deal with each briefly in turn.

The subject matter of social science is defined by its *own* criteria of significance not common sense. Sociologists in particular have struggled to comprehend this, even fearing that sociology might be replaced in the media and popular culture by the common sense routinization of sociological knowledge (for example, Savage and Burrows 2007: 894). Social science would be mere reportage if members' own accounts settled the task of understanding social life. Social science puts these accounts to test; they are our starting point but they are rarely our end. There are several reasons why people's accounts should be treated as problematic. They may not be aware of the reasons why they hold these beliefs or behave in the way they do, or their reasons may be partisan and partial or too deeply emotional to be articulated readily. These beliefs are often embedded in common sense (and the common sense translation of social science knowledge back into common sense) and common sense needs to be assessed for its correspondence to the evidence. People's accounts also vary (both between people and perhaps in the same person over space and time) and the variations need to be placed in the context that explains them. Furthermore, people are often unaware of both the implicit biological and emotional knowledge and the broad social structural forces impinging on their lives, and people's narratives, thus, underplay the structural factors in culture, the market and the state, locally, nationally and globally, that fully explain their views, behaviours and beliefs. People are deeply affected by global economic markets, for example, of which they have no clear knowledge, nor any understanding of the causes of their plight, which can only be brought to light by highly technical social science knowledge. They are also often oblivious to the unintended consequences of their actions and those of others (which makes the unforeseen and unanticipated nature of social, political and economic action a central interest of social science).

People's accounts are also affected by the operation of power, inequality and prestige; it may well be that people's definition of their situation becomes real in its consequences, as the sociologist W. I. Thomas argued in 1929, but some have the power to impose their definition on others, and under-standing whose views count the most and why is a key task of social science. People are also unaware of regularities, patterns and standardized practices across time and space, which the social scientist is able to observe. Conceptual advances in understanding made by social science on the basis of observed regularities – the law of diminishing returns in economics, the impact of anomie on suicide within sociology, the impact of embourgeoisement on working class voting patterns or the glass ceiling in women's empowerment in work – are only conscious to people as personal experiences, which underscores their wider effects in culture, the market and the state globally. For these reasons and more, social science does not stop at the understanding of society that members themselves have.

Secondly, it is one of the successes of social science knowledge and its routinization that we can confidently assert, and the lay person in the street fully appreciate, that society is spatial but not constrained by space, and is both in time and out of time. 'Society' always has some spatial and temporal referent, some physical location in time; this is inevitably so if it consists of people and institutions, since these naturally imply place and time. Even in its analytic sense of 'society' in the abstract, it is always evidence from some place or other at one time or another that goes into our understanding of what society means, whether or not the analysis makes this clear. And the lay person's appropriation of social science knowledge about society tends to place it – locate it – in time and physical space somewhere. We know, however, that the globalization of society has proceeded apace so that our idea of society needs to go beyond our immediate experience of society in our locality and neighbourhood, even our national society, to now incorporate global society over time. In this sense, society transcends space and time. The behaviour and social relationships of people and institutions that social science studies, therefore, need to be extended to include their local, national and global dimensions across time. Indeed, the social sciences have been very successful in charting the growth and expansion of global interconnections, whether in economic and financial links, political and geopolitical strategic relations, military connectedness, cultural and diasporic links, cultural homogenization, global civil society, the development of international humanitarian law to regulate the conduct of war and the like. There is no social science discipline that is unaffected by globalization and no aspect of society that is not in some way impacted by it.

This reinforces the public importance of social science. If we are to properly understand the contemporary world and the issues it presents us and future generations, whether we mean by this our local neighbourhood, nation or global society, then social science is essential. Society needs social science to make sense of itself, to show how society works and how the complexity of the public issues society faces now and in the future are intertwined with globalization and operate in local, national and global spaces. This is more clearly understood for some public issues than others, such as the worldwide banking crisis or industrial restructuring, because global economic connectedness is an everyday experience for the worker whose job is under threat or the small business and ordinary family suffering under the credit crunch. But it applies generally. The army of helpers on wet Saturday mornings standing on the high street distributing leaflets for some charity or other, or the small band of dedicated Christian or Islamic extremists bellowing hellfire or martyrdom down loudspeakers as shoppers pass by, are all members of civil society groups in a neighbourhood who, while thinking globally, act locally on humanitarian, civil and human rights issues, motivated in their philanthropy by evidence of global suffering, or in their fundamentalism by reaction to international geopolitical strategy or to cultural homogenization that has provoked fierce religious reaction. It is social science analysis that helps us understand the plight of the starving child in Africa and the problem of AIDS in Rwanda, or the outbreak of the Arab Spring or the summer riots in England in 2011 (on the latter, for example, see Morrell et al. 2011).

Social science provides a double insight, however. Social science helps us understand both the global, national and local nature of these issues *and* why people react to them in the way they do in whatever spaces they find themselves. That is to say, we owe to social science both the awareness we have of the complex nature of public issues in the contemporary world and the way in which the rhetoric of globalization is mobilized by politicians and the public alike to make sense of them.

Thirdly, it matters greatly for the insightfulness of social science that society is understood broadly to empower *all* social sciences. Philippe Fontaine (2006: 193) made the telling observation that all social science disciplines have a tendency, arising from disciplinary specialization, to see the working of the whole society through one of its segments – economists the economy, political scientists the polity, anthropology culture and so on. But sociologists are especially vulnerable to this temptation because sociology is supposedly the most general or synthesizing of the social sciences. Disciplinary closure has seen 'society' become narrowly claimed by sociology as its domain, when what we need is an overarching conception of society which holds the social sciences together.

For all my eulogizing of Robert MacIver's pioneering introduction to social science in 1921 that made it the study of society in its broadest sense, he thought sociology proffered a privileged perspective on society. 'There is a group of sciences which study particular aspects of social life', he wrote, but 'none of these studies society as a whole. They thus leave room for, in fact they invite, a more comprehensive science. This is the science now named sociology' (1921: 12).[7]

Sociology is not unique in aggrandizing itself. Geography and anthropology see themselves as synthesizing social sciences based around the centrality, respectively, of space and culture. The comparative study of social institutions within anthropology, for example, furnishes economic anthropology, political anthropology, religion and social relations (of kin, family and neighbour), among others, which are connected by its emphasis on culture. James Mickel Williams's textbook on social psychology, written in 1917 but published after World War I, saw 'human motives' as the base to all phenomena in social science and it was, thus, he wrote, the task of social psychology to co-ordinate the work of all social scientists (1920: vii). He proceeded to illustrate this point with reference to political science, jurisprudence, economics, history and sociology. All social science, he wrote, is premised on 'fundamental psychological assumptions' (1920: xiii) and every discipline in this field needed the aid of social psychologists for interpretation (1920: xiv). This is a truism but it impacts on sociology above other social sciences. It is for this reason that most of the early professional sociologists – people like Durkheim in France and MacIver in Britain – singled out psychology and eagerly wrote programmatic statements on the boundaries between them, in which psychology was the secondary discipline.

---

[7] It is for this reason that MacIver's introductory text in sociology was entitled *Society*. First published in 1937 (1950 in the United Kingdom), it went through 11 reprints, the last in 1967, when it was co-written with Charles Page (see MacIver and Page 1967). In another of the early sociology textbooks in Britain, Morris Ginsberg's *Sociology* (Ginsberg 1934), sociology was again seen as the most general and synthesizing of the social sciences. I owe to John Scott the observation that this was a trait of early British sociology generally, in people like Branford, Geddes and Hobhouse, who saw in sociology a bridge between the ethical interests of social philosophy and empirical social science. This was not, however, MacIver's motivation. This may be linked to the fact that, by the time *The Elements of Social Science* was published, he had spent six years in Canada, where he was pioneering sociology in a different national context.

Sociology emerged as a word in the mid-nineteenth century to describe the scientific study of society but was only becoming currency when MacIver wrote his assessment decades later. While Auguste Comte, who gave us the term, saw the discipline as the Queen of the Sciences, with sociology universalized as the final stage of knowledge, most of the classical practitioners of sociology who are appropriated by the discipline for shaping sociology as the scientific study of society, such as Mark, Weber and Durkheim, were working across disciplines (the exception being psychology), and, as a result, have been taken as representatives in economics, education, politics, social anthropology, public law and history. This is perhaps epitomized by Weber's monumental contribution to social science going under the title *Economy and Society*. There is in the early discipline of sociology, therefore, an inherent interdisciplinarity – psychology excepted – that fits uneasily with its later practices of disciplinary closure.

Two books written by sociologists in the period when the discipline was just entering its moment of rapid expansion in Britain and which went under titles that invoked social science, Julius Gould's *Penguin Survey of the Social Sciences* (Gould 1965) and W. G. Runciman's *Social Science and Political Theory* (Runciman 1965), not only considered sociology and social science as interchangeable terms, sociology's triumphalism shone through as the premier social science. 'We are all sociologists now', Gould declared in his opening paragraph (1965: 9), while Runciman commenced his first chapter by stating: 'If sociology is defined as the systematic study of collective human behavior, then such separate disciplines as economics, or demography, or criminology, or politics should be regarded as co-ordinate but distinctive branches of sociology (or social science)' (1965: 1). There is little diffidence about disciplinary closure here.

Whatever ambivalence there may be among some sociologists 50 years on about disciplinarity,[8] which John Urry captures in his portrayal of sociology

---

[8] For example, Holmwood (2010) refers to sociology as interdisciplinary but construes this as problematic, threatening its intellectual coherence and disciplinary core. His argument reflects my earlier point about the ambiguity in the relationship between sociology and other social sciences. Sociology (like anthropology and geography to some extent) makes claims to a synoptic view of 'society', while economics, criminology, politics and the rest make claims to specialized competence in relation to particular social phenomena. My argument is that this claim reflects sociology's practices of disciplinary closure and that this synoptic, synthesizing perspective can be found in the generic definition of social science proffered here, whose subject matter is the social nature of culture, the market and the state, locally, nationally and globally. Whether contemporary social science disciplines lay claim to it is another matter given their tendencies to disciplinary closure.

as parasitic on other disciplines (1981) and Liz Stanley in the notion that the discipline has always been hybridic (2005), it is necessary to avoid privileging sociology for its attention to society. A definition of social science that valorizes the notion of society, therefore, needs to make it absolutely clear that society is a multidisciplinary entity that contains within it intellectual arenas and institutional spaces that facilitate insight from the full range of social sciences. Society broadly conceived includes intellectual arenas like culture, civil society, economy and markets, government and the state, and law and legal governance, all of which can be further subdivided into smaller interconnected arenas; and all of these come within the broad rubric of 'society'. In this respect, one can agree with Runciman (1965: 176) that, for example, Bendix and Lipset's famous argument (1957) that political science studies the effects of the state on society and sociology the effect of society on the state, is a misconception for the state and society so closely involve each other. Society, in other words, is not reducible to culture, is much broader than markets and the state, being inclusive of them, as well as of law, civil society and the array of individual and institutional behaviours that occur within these spheres.

These intellectual arenas not only represent cognate fields of enquiry about society, they have embedded within them various sets of ideas, concepts and theories, as well as methods of research by which to pursue these ideas, which go towards constituting a vocabulary for talking about society, understanding it and representing it to people who wish to know how society works. These arenas furnish vocabularies and practices by which social scientists do their research, giving ways of talking about society which are mediated by the public in the sense they make of social science knowledge.

These arenas are further codified by the range of institutional spaces within which these vocabularies and practices operate. These institutional spaces include places where the sets of ideas are taught, like schools, colleges and universities, places where the ideas are developed, extended and progressed through research, like universities, institutes and research centres, and specialist institutions that promote and sponsor the insights garnered within these arenas, such as learned societies, professional associations, publishers, journals, editors and editorial boards and, in a few cases where professional accreditation is necessary, like psychology and law, professional bodies capable of determining rights to practise in the arena.

We might consider these intellectual arenas, vocabularies and institutional spaces as defining the separate social sciences. The separation of society into cognate arenas, which is reinforced by the intellectual practices and institutional spaces that mark the individual social sciences as discrete, should not disguise, however, that society is the unifying subject matter of them all. This is concealed when considering society the special domain of sociology. So ingrained is this disciplinary closure that it is difficult now to use the term 'society' in its inclusive sense (especially given that it is a sociologist using it here). To represent society in its inclusive sense, meaning culture, civil society, economy and the market, law, governance and the state, I will run together three terms that summarize the arenas that comprise it – 'culture, the market and the state' is my longhand for 'society'.[9] This gives us, I think, the overarching conception of society that ties the social sciences together.

Culture, market and the state are discrete domains in society but they clearly penetrate each other to an extent that they act as a synonym for society. The 2011 Eurozone currency crisis illustrates how closely connected are markets and states, with Greek political interests skirmishing with global market considerations; and the suggestion from religious bodies in the meleé that bankers should be levied a 'Robin Hood tax' highlights the intrusion of cultural beliefs about fairness and moral obligations. While social scientists and philosophers have always noted the moral limits of markets, articulated most recently by Satz (2010) and Sandel (2012), some economists are themselves recognizing that governments can be against markets (for example, see Bayer and Drache 1996).[10] The Euro crisis, for all its financial dimensions, is now

---

[9] I am grateful to Hastings Donnan for the observation that anthropology utilizes 'culture' as its unifying theme and thus does not regard culture as an isolatable domain alongside the market and the state. For anthropologists it is not one of society's segments, a variable alongside others, but is the central factor through which all else is mediated and articulated. This view is not problematic to my argument. Social anthropologists use 'culture' in the way I do 'society' to signify the encompassing domain through which the study of social relations and social institutions is best approached. I prefer my terminology because the subject area I am discussing after all is called 'social science' not 'cultural science', which has an entirely different connotation. Hence, when I use the term 'culture' I am not referring to it as the central prism for understanding social institutions and social relations but in a more restrictive manner as thoughts, perceptions, values and symbols. That is to say, to learned behaviour and beliefs. This falls short of making culture the organizing principle for human society as a whole.

[10] Ever since we recognized the 'two Adam Smiths' – the author of arguments about moral sentiments and the progenitor of the division of labour and the wealth of nations – debate has raged over whether markets are amoral or not. Free markets were once thought of as just that, devoid of agency. Yet moral neutrality is impossible in one sense because markets are composed of individuals and institutions with values. This is where we get ideas from about corporate social responsibility. The more important issue is whose values? But if in terms of motivations we can see markets as moral,

also about the clash between market principles and local cultural practices in Greece and Spain, and highlights the conflict between politics in the nation state and global economic markets.

If I can recap the argument so far, what is 'social' about social science, is that it studies how society in its inclusive sense works, reproduces itself and operates across time and space in local, national and global contexts. Putting this in a verbose way, social science studies individuals and institutions as they interrelate within culture, the market and the state, thereby making culture, the market and the state arenas that are reproduced by the behaviour, relations and interrelations of people and institutions but which simultaneously constrain and shape what they do. This process of societal reproduction, which creates culture, the market and the state as constraining frameworks, operates on three levels – local, national and global – ensuring that culture, the market and the state exist both in time and space and across time and space. The 'social' gives social science a very wide remit when understood in this way.

We can catch a glimpse of the scale and breadth of the 'social' by considering the phenomenon of farming, as one aspect of society, from a social science perspective. The topic implicates economics and business through the relevance of markets, production, supply and demand and the growth of agribusiness; it implicates human geography through land use and changing land use, or population relocations with the arrival of the ex-urban middle class as commuters and second-home owners; law through inheritance of land, as well as legal regulations of farming and animal welfare; cultural studies through the symbolic meaning of land and the countryside; sociology through notions of community and social and family relations in rural areas, or the gendered experiences of farming and rural isolation; environmental studies through land and wildlife protection, or the negative impact of agrichemicals;

---

it is less certain that in terms of their financial consequences markets act morally. Markets have always been subject to legal regulation and constrained by politics and government; this was what gave meaning to Keynesian economics as a response to the Great Depression in the 1930s. The current debate about a Robin Hood tax, a term ironically first used by an Italian Treasury minister in 2008 but now taken up by many charities and civil society groups, including the Church, is about the moral responsibilities of markets for some of the financial consequences of aggregate market outcomes. The intrusion of culture, as distinct from politics, into the operation of markets will be fascinating to see unfold. The Anglican and Catholic churches support the idea of a Robin Hood tax, which suggests that the culture war between science and religion will take on another dimension in the confrontation between religion and economics, itself an ancient battle over such things as usury, but now given a modern twist. When crossing the Atlantic to Britain, the 'occupy Wall Street' movement occupied cathedral grounds – St Paul's, Sheffield, Exeter, Glasgow – throwing up as much a challenge to the Anglican Church as to bankers.

psychology through such issues as rural isolation, well-being and loneliness, or the high incidence of farming-related suicides; criminology through rural crime, or the problem of the rural underclass, out-bought for houses and jobs by the ex-urban incomers; politics would address the rural vote, the politics of class relations in the countryside or the politicization of the so-called 'country way of life' through such things as the foxhunting ban; social policy would consider transport policy or policies of elder care in rural areas. And social anthropology's significant contribution is to remind us that farming practices are encultured, taking different forms in various cultural spaces, and that classification systems that are self-evident in the West – wild/domestic, cultivated/uncultivated, nature/culture – are not always understood in the same way in other agricultural modes of production; and so on.

These examples do not come even close to exhausting the sorts of issues an interdisciplinary social science addresses about farming. The fact that readers may object to my construal of them in disciplinary terms, since population change in rural areas, for example, is not the sole preserve of human geography, nor rural loneliness and suicides of psychology, only proves my argument about the essential unity between the social sciences deriving from an inclusive notion of society. And these issues have local, national and global dimensions, since concern over the 'food miles' farm produce travels or animal welfare concerns for exported beasts, for example, shows farming to be global, national and local all at once, existing across space and time. Agribusiness, international food markets, futures trading in world markets on cereals, for example, reflect locally on decisions an individual farmer makes about what crops to grow or beasts to keep on a single farm, but this global-local nexus, which Roland Robertson captures wonderfully with his term 'glocalization' (1995),[11] radiates out from the domain of economics when it has consequences for land use or ownership in the area, or environmental protection, rural unemployment or housing, rural crime, farm suicides or whatever, drawing in other social sciences.

It is a truism accepted I think by practitioners and the public alike now that society in this inclusive sense is a myriad of complex interrelations mediating culture, markets and the state, spreading across time and space. What needs

---

[11] This term began in the discipline of economics in Japan but was popularized in Western social science by Roland Robertson to mean a combination of globalization and localization.

to catch up with this commonplace is the realization that social science also has to be decompartmentalized.[12] Social life knows no hermetic separation, neither should social science, for the 'social' is a thread that unites the infinite variety of processes, activities and relationships studied by them.

What is 'science' about social science?

There are some disciplines that transcend the natural and social science divide and have elements of both – physical and social/cultural anthropology, cognitive psychology and social psychology, or physical geography and human/cultural geography – and while the 'social science' end is mostly marked by a qualifier, occasionally it is not and cultural and physical anthropologists, for example, exist side by side under the one label.[13] The exchanges between them can be acrimonious, and sometimes they exist almost as separate intellectual arenas, as they do notably in anthropology and psychology, but there is at least in principle the possibility of the social science component building on the natural science one. In much the same way, in sexuality studies, social science interest in transgender has drawn on developments in biological science (see Hird 2004), the sociology of climate change on environmental science (see Urry 2011), and the human brain has become an object of sociological interest (Bone 2010). I will be dealing here with the social sciences and, where there is an internal divide, with the 'cultural', 'human' and 'social' end of those disciplines. I want to address the kind of science it is they do, for if 'society' is a contested notion within social science, the idea of 'science' is even more so.

We can dismiss outright those critics of social science who deny the appellation science on grounds there is no such thing as society to have a scientific study of, for reasons established in the previous section. A much more serious criticism is that the very nature of society precludes science. It

---

[12] C. Wright Mills (1959) also railed against the compartmentalization of the social sciences and his book on the sociological imagination was, despite its title, a platform for their unification. Ironically, disciplinary closure proceeded apace in the 1960s, when professionalization accompanied the expansion of the social sciences.

[13] A similar disjuncture exists, of course, in law between private and public law, only the latter of which can be seriously considered a social science, although this is more a division between the orientation towards either humanities (private law) or social science (public law). I owe to Norma Dawson the observation that some private lawyers strictly speaking consider law *sui generis*, a subject area unto itself.

has long been wondered how a science of society is possible when social life is not subject to the same predictable, universal laws as the natural world, making replication of findings almost impossible, when causal variables are hard to isolate in experimental settings, or causality is rendered pointless with the uniqueness of particular historical sequences of behaviour and contexts, when researchers are themselves part of the social world they are studying and their presence a variable in it, and when our subject matter is people who have their own interpretations and senses of how the social world works (and of social science itself). Social scientists make claims that are capable of being interpreted by the subject matter they purport to explain.

Paradoxically, the very success of social science in routinizing its knowledge within common sense adds to its difficulties in claiming status as a science, for not only are 'social meanings', what Max Weber called 'understandings' or *Verstehen*, part of our subject matter, people's common sense rendering of professional social science knowledge gets incorporated into our subject matter as an infinite regression. What I have in mind here, for example, is the way in which taxi drivers, hair stylists and neighbours in shopping queues or over garden fences talk about the topics that interest social scientists and develop their own answers to the questions we ask about economic risk and markets, or why crime is rising (or not), schools are failing (or not) or unemployment increasing (or not), which are in part based on their own common sense knowledge but also the popularization of social science knowledge into common sense by the way in which the media, politicians, journalists and other mediators of social science in popular culture interpret and make sense of social science knowledge.[14] In my discipline, this is called 'lay sociology' and lay sociological thinking is practised fulsomely by ordinary people as part of their everyday life and work. This lay sociology then gets studied by sociologists and incorporated into further social science knowledge (such as decision-making by police officers based on their lay sociology about crime; see Bennett 1979). This makes our subject matter appear slippery with few of the 'objective' qualities of the natural world.

It was, thus, boldly asserted in 1970 by a practising social scientist that the social sciences 'are not, and cannot hope to become, sciences at all'

---

[14] It is worth recalling that some sociologists see this as a source of anxiety (for example, Savage and Burrows 2007: 894), others as the discipline's major achievement (for example, Giddens 1996: 76).

(Ryan 1970: 125), a view Ryan has held to since (see Ryan 1981). The date is deeply significant. This was the heyday of scientific social science, almost 20 years on from when Madge (1953), in explaining the 'tools of social science' in a book of the same title, had self-assuredly exclaimed the possibility of experimentation in social science and use of the hypothetico-deductive method.[15] However, Ryan's judgement was not iconoclastic, for it was made precisely at the time when attacks on positivist notions of science were gaining sufficient ground for many in the social sciences not to care, let alone aspire, to be scientific.[16] Derek Phillips (1973) judged his book title at this time very well, *Abandoning Method.* The near half-century since then has seen the 'science war' unabated, refreshed even, with ever more troops.[17]

Responses to the conflict have been several. I identify three ideal types, all of which undertake worthwhile studies of culture, the market and the state and make significant contributions to social science, but which put down different claims to scientific status. I call these *science-loyalism, science-rejectionism* and *science-affirmation.* Science-loyalists unashamedly see themselves as scientists (sometimes deleting 'social' from the couplet) and address those areas of culture, market and the state which do more readily lend themselves to scientific methods. In Steuer's otherwise highly critical depiction of the scientific claims of the social sciences (2002), he still recognized that some social science research differed from natural science only by degree: there was just not very much of it outside economics. Science loyalists look for evidence that can be quantified and replicated. For example, Skinner's behaviourist approach in psychology, psephology (voting and election studies) in political science, econometrics in economics, population statistics and trends in demography, the 'political arithmetic' tradition in social policy or 'analytical sociology', as the Nuffield College Oxford sociologists like to characterize their quantitative approach, remain experimental, mathematical, statistical and deductive, and often involve theoretically led computer modelling.

---

[15] This is a theory of explanation that requires the development of general laws, from which various empirical statements are deductively drawn, which are then tested through research, leading to further refinement of the general statements and further testing.

[16] Positivism is a methodological tradition that seeks to emulate the practices and approach of the natural sciences. On positivism and its critics in social science see Giddens (1974, 1996: 65–77).

[17] Livingstone (2012) has shown how the science wars in human and cultural geography are enlivened by interpenetration from the culture wars, including such notions as the cultural meaning of science, which often has geographic and place variations, and the aged battle lines between science and religion.

Science-loyalists do not dominate a whole social science discipline, perhaps with the exception of demography and social statistics (omitted from Steuer's critical analysis), although they would like to and urge on their uncommitted peers the virtue of their theoretical ideas and quantitative research methods. But some were very popular for a long while – notably behaviourism in psychology (which has now also expanded into behaviourist economics) – and significant sub-areas of social science disciplines are commanded by them. Econometrics and quantitative sociology, for example, receive preferential allocation of research resources and postgraduate studentships from the ESRC in order to boost their skills base, and concern over undergraduate and postgraduate teaching of statistics and quantitative methods is voiced by science-loyalists in most social science disciplines.

Science-rejectionism comes in at least two sub-types. First are those science-rejectionists who deconstruct the scientific method to render it merely a series of social practices and thus without honour. This itself comes in two colours. The 1960s'–70s' hue was persuaded by Thomas Kuhn (1962) that 'normal' science was an ideological practice and thus should not be held up as a role model for the social sciences. The 1980s'–90s' version was shaped by European postmodernism and alleged that all research practices are social constructs, social as well as natural sciences, thereby removing any distinction between professional and lay knowledge. If in 1965 we were all sociologists then, by 1985 we were all mythmakers, just like the Azande in our witchcraft. Science-rejectionists of this first type remain committed to the study of culture, the market and the state but rarely self-identify as social *scientists*, preferring other identifiers. If not a disciplinary term, the prefix 'social' can be put before a whole number of options – philosopher, theorist, historian – but 'social' is always there as an important identity marker.

The second type of science-rejectionist does not wish to impugn the scientific method, much less the practices of social science. They look to the humanistic and literary traditions within social science, accepting – celebrating – that their subject matter and approach is different in kind not just complexity from natural science. The role models here are the humanities, with their literary, cultural and philosophical emphases (hence, for example, Robert Nisbet's 1976 book *Sociology as an Art Form*), or the *Verstehende* tradition, with the search for meaning, understanding and empathy replacing cause and effect relationships. The emergence of social constructionism in psychology in the 1990s (on which see Burr 1995), has proved seismic in a discipline that is noted for its commitment to rigorous scientific method,[18] as earlier did the linguistic and conversation analysis-turn in social science, which Gellner famously dismissed as 'the Californian way to subjectivity' (1975), although he was no practitioner of empirical research himself. The 'cultural turn' in sociology from the 1990s caused some sociologists to express anxiety for the future of sociological methods (see Rojek and Turner 2000), as did British sociology's expertise in qualitative and ethnographic methods among at least two well-known analytical quantitative sociologists (Goldthorpe 2000; Erikson 2005). The London School of Economics (LSE) economist Max Steuer (2002) only partly facetiously suggested all social scientists be trained as economists because everything else was 'pretend social science', bearing no resemblance to science in any form (2002: 55).[19] And who can forget the demographer, David Glass, famous for being the only sociologist in modern times elected to the Royal Society, for his put-down of the community studies tradition as 'the poor sociologist's substitute for the novel' (quoted in Bell and Newby 1971: 13)?

However, new literary and culture-oriented subject areas like cultural studies, postmodern studies, celebrity studies and media studies have replaced sociology as the butt of the science-loyalists' rebuke against pretend

[18] Social psychology, along with political psychology, has long wrestled with what type of science it aspires to be and many would agree with Brinkmann (2011) that it is a moral science. I owe to John Kremer the observation that it was in the 1970s that a very healthy and vibrant critical version of social psychology emerged in European social psychology, with the likes of Henri Tajfel, Michael Billig and Serge Moscovici. Social psychology positioned itself perilously between psychology and the social sciences, recognizing the contribution of many different approaches, operating at different levels of analysis, from the micro to the macro. The hard science end of psychology, though, adheres to the natural sciences. Social psychology was rocked as a discipline in 2010–11 by discovery that one of its leading practitioners, Diederick Stapel, from Tilburg University, fabricated some of his data. Many of his publications have been withdrawn. In 2011, he voluntarily returned his 1997 PhD to the University of Amsterdam. Stapel was considered one of Europe's leading cognitive social psychologists and in response to this fraud the discipline has sought to restore replication and falsification as the cornerstone of its commitment to the scientific method. Sir Cyril Burt's fraudulence in his quantitative psychological research on IQ in twins illustrates, of course, that fabrication is not restricted to social psychology or non-numerate disciplines. There is an impression that fabrication of data is becoming more common and is linked to the marketization of higher education and the concomitant stress on performance indicators, although it remains to be proved whether the publish-or-perish ethos of marketized higher education has led to more fraud or better ways of detecting it.

[19] We should be reminded, I think, that economics is not everywhere held as the model for scientific practice. Ormerod (1994: 67) in particular considers it 'virulently esoteric chat' and its 'bad science', in the form of macroeconomics, responsible for bringing capitalism to the brink of global depression (Ormerod 2010).

or non-science (and ridicule in sections of popular culture), although, with the exception of postmodernism, there is nothing in principle that prevents a quantitative approach being applied in these fields or the collection of numerical data rather than extracts of natural language, as content analysis in media studies illustrates. Science-rejectionists of this second type are comfortable about the appellation 'social scientist' but look on the second part of the couplet as a convenience, devoid of meaning to them, or put the term 'science' in quotation marks. Where it matters to them the word social is used again as a prefix to a number of more preferable options; their commitment to the label social, however, remains keen.

The third response I call science-affirming. It upholds the *idea of science* (a phrase I will define shortly), believes in the possibility of a scientific study of culture, the market and the state, and adopts an attitude towards research practice and data that is thought of as scientific, but science means something different than in the natural sciences. While natural science models of social science research are rejected, scientific practice is still valued. This affirming view was the one adopted by the 1996 Gulbenkian Commission on the future of the social sciences (Gulbenkian Commission 1996). It was this affirmation, after all, that permitted Malinowski, the founder of modern social anthropology, to describe it in 1922 as a discipline based on 'scientific ethnography' (a view that came under attack as part of the science wars inside social anthropology in the 1980s). The science-affirmers, however, can be found working in all the social sciences, even in the same areas and, where this is feasible, on the same topics as those who are science-loyalists or advocates of the literary, humanistic and *Verstehende* traditions, but are distinguished from the former by their honest realization that they are science-like in their practice, and from the latter by their affirmation of science as an aspiration and intent. Both terms in the couplet 'social scientist' have meaning here and are equally important.[20]

It is worth elaborating on the meaning of science to the science-affirmers and how they can sustain their avowal in the light of the objections raised against 'the idea of a social science' – a phrase that gave the title to Peter

---

[20] One of the strong advocates of the Gulbenkian Commission's approach to science is Byrne (2011), who appropriated the Commission's definition of science, which portrays it as any systematic secular knowledge that is empirically grounded (Byrne 2011: 2). This idea of science is quite loose and inclusive and contrasts only slightly with my own definition below.

Winch's defence more than 50 years ago (Winch 1958) – since this, I proffer, is the ideal type that corresponds closest to most people's practice. To suggest that social science is a kind of social physics, as Comte claimed of sociology in the nineteenth century, or that we adopt more of the scientific practices of physics, as Taagepera (2008) argues, requires that our subject matter be treated as if it was inanimate matter in motion affected only by external stimuli. This would deny social science the perspicacity of understanding what is distinctive about its subject matter.

To appreciate the force of this point, it is necessary to be reminded of our earlier discussion that the subject matter of social science is the *social* nature of society. Society has a dual character: people are in society and society in people. People, groups and institutions act within culture, the market and the state across time and space, in part producing them and produced by them, so that local, national and global society is both the outcome of individual, group and institutional behaviour and the framework that shapes this behaviour. Thus, some social science investigation addresses what culture, the market and the state mean to people, groups and institutions, how they understand, make sense of and reproduce culture, markets and the state across time and space (societal reproduction), while others investigate what people, groups and institutions believe, how they act and interrelate in culture, the market and the state (societal production). A social physics would be incapable of capturing what marks the social sciences as special in their insightfulness because it is blind to the reproduction side of society's Janus face.

If not social physics though, there are characteristic traits of investigation and practice that define the aspiration to be scientific among the science-affirmers. These can be listed as follows:

- the commitment to developing evidence-based observations, descriptions and explanations (where 'evidence' is understood to include empirical data as well as theoretical ideas and models);
- the commitment to professional and ethical practice, including accuracy, honesty and integrity, in all stages of the investigation;
- the commitment to objectivity (since even subjectivity can be studied objectively); and
- the separation of value and evidence.

These are self-explanatory and need no special justification. They are worded carefully to avoid any suggestion of privileging empiricism or 'practical knowledge', since I wish to make clear that major theoretical contributions are part of social science (and it is worth remembering, for example, the profound theoretical ideas about culture established through ethnographies in early British social anthropology).

However, a brief comment is necessary on the latter because of the hoary old debates about value, ideology and the 'open society' that have characterized much of the philosophy of the social sciences over the last century. I will be dealing with moral values and the idea of value neutrality in the last chapter, but it is important here to explain that what I mean by this is not that social scientists be value free in the sense of having no values – which would be absurd – but that their values are separated from the evidence they collect, so that evidence is not distorted for the sake of the values they hold. I believe this interpretation is entirely consistent with Weber's meaning of value neutrality, as I will argue later. Note, I am not saying that values should be separated from the investigation completely, since it is widely accepted, in the natural and social sciences, that researchers are often drawn to their topics precisely for value reasons. It is the separation of values from evidence that is the key to scientific practice and objectivity.

In its generic sense, science involves the observation, description and identification of phenomena by empirical and theoretical investigation to enable phenomena to be explained. It does not implicate any one kind of evidence, nor any one research method or practice to obtain it. The natural sciences are associated with particular sorts of phenomena, evidence and practices, *most* of which *most* social sciences cannot follow. But the *idea of science* – the generic commitment to observation, description and identification of phenomena by empirical and theoretical investigation in order to explain – remains very strong in science-affirmers. Their commitments to the idea of science do not privilege any one kind of evidence or any one research method or practice for collecting it, unlike the science-loyalists whose preference for numerate data via quantitative methods is a fetish.

Gone, however, are the commitments that privilege the natural sciences' practice of science, which the science-loyalists in social science seek to emulate, such as causation, deduction, the development of universal law-like generalizations and (it follows on naturally) prediction. It is the absence of these sorts of practices that provoke the regular complaint that the social sciences are not scientific enough;[21] but this is just one mode for practising the idea of science.

More openness and tolerance about what science means might end the science wars. The meaning of the term 'science', however, tends to be narrowed into specific sets of methods and practices that implement it, not the generic idea of science. Science-affirmers believe strongly in the *idea of science* and in practising it; what they practise in terms of methods just happens to vary from natural scientists and, on the whole, from science-loyalists in the social sciences. It is for this reason I have avoided use of the terms 'hard' and 'soft' sciences to describe the difference between the science-loyalists in social science (along with natural science) and the science-affirmers, although this is a very popular characterization, since 'soft' is a pejorative term and it conceals that the generic idea of science unites them all.

So what is social science?

We have arrived finally at our conclusion, where the previous arguments can be brought together into a general definition of social science.

> *Social science is the observation, description and identification of the social nature of society by empirical and theoretical investigation, in order to explain what culture, the market and the state mean to people, groups and institutions, how they understand, make sense and reproduce culture, markets and the state across time and space; and what people, groups and institutions believe, how they act and interrelate in culture, the market and the state, in local, national and global settings.*

Put more succinctly, social science is the scientific study of the processes of societal production and reproduction in culture, the market and the state across time and space.

---

[21] For example, it is a recurring complaint from science-loyalists within social science down the generations that the social sciences are not predictive enough and need to be made more so. In the 1950s, see Madge (1953: 290), in the 1990s Horowitz (1995) and more recently Taagepera (2008).

Generic definitions such as this, however, confront the problem of disciplinary closure which separates the social sciences into distinct intellectual fields and arenas. There is nothing sacrosanct about the current configurations of social sciences (see Abbott 2001 for a discussion of how configurations can and have changed). Disciplines are not naturally differentiated, nor for once and all time, since new issues can emerge and internal practices of specialization change. Bridges are built between some of them, and drawbridges pulled up behind others. However, tendencies towards disciplinarity are strong; strong enough to make many social scientists reluctant to define generic social science and to want instead to list the disciplines that comprise it. Disciplinarity needs to be addressed, therefore, if a new public social science is to be articulated with a special public value.

Disciplinarity and disciplinary closure in the social sciences

It is deeply paradoxical that, at a time when the big issues facing the future of humankind are multifaceted and require post-disciplinarity, the social science disciplines remain separated into their own silos. Even more so that disciplinary closure is encouraged by some aspects of higher education policy itself. While the effects of policy are contradictory in this respect, some areas encourage disciplinarity by evaluating and assessing subjects individually in teaching and research terms, funding their research separately, allocating PhD student quotas according to disciplines and, until recently, also undergraduate student places. The audit culture that has been imposed on British higher education institutions (HEIs) over recent years, which we will explore further in Chapter 3, reinforces disciplinarity as a defence; subjects look to their survival and continuity because the audit culture increases their sense of being under threat. They exist, perhaps, not so much in silos as bunkers.

British academic culture, moreover, forces a huge divide between the humanities, natural science and the social sciences, which according to Kagan (2009) constitute themselves as three separate cultures. But even where the cultural barriers are breaking down – as they are under higher education policies that promote interdisciplinarity and which fund some cross-culture research initiatives – this highlights the contradictions in policy, for it is happening only slowly and at the edges. Proponents of interdisciplinarity universally complain that they encounter an academic system that has not yet found ways of dealing with cross-disciplinary activity, much less funding, measuring and assessing it (the Commission on the Social Sciences, 2003, was strongly in favour of interdisciplinarity as a future strategy for the social sciences in Britain and make this point strongly).

However, while higher education policy is counterproductive in reinforcing disciplinarity, the bunker mentality of most disciplines is primarily the result of practices by the subjects themselves. It is practitioners who practise disciplinarity. This is why the response to the emergence of multidisciplinary administrative units in HEIs, has mostly been one of complaint and fear at the threat of subject fragmentation. Single subject schools are looked on with nostalgic fondness by most academics, a remembrance of times past and things lost (as much for the democratic ethos that came with their single disciplinary identity).

This strong sense of disciplinarity among practitioners occurs simultaneous with the rise of joint degrees in HEIs, the emergence of interdisciplinary degrees, such as women's studies, peace studies, security studies and the like, and, under the modular structure, the capacity for students to make a cafeteria style selection of courses that fit inaptly under a single subject name. This reflects both that some students' preferences are not disciplinary based and, since it is HEI staff teaching them, not all practitioners work in silos.

The push towards interdisciplinarity, however, meets strong forces of resistance. The subject of women's studies, for example, has more or less moved out of the undergraduate market in Britain, in large part because of the inability to persuade departments to free-up staff time to teach courses under pressure from discipline-based teaching and research assessment exercises. Development studies, a rich amalgam of economics, sociology and politics, with some anthropology alongside, has gone much the same way. Peace studies is very small in the United Kingdom compared with the United States.[22] And while new subject areas are burgeoning as research

---

[22] It is interesting to speculate that the strong survival of women studies as an undergraduate programme in the United States, for example, and the expanding presence of peace studies in the undergraduate curriculum there, is because the United States has escaped so much of the audit culture that characterizes British higher education policy, although the prevalence of peace studies is also linked to the place of civics in US education. There is greater institutional conservatism in British HEIs and the 'A' level curricula reinforces this.

interests – transitional justice studies, security studies, memory studies, auto/biography and narrative studies, sexuality studies, cultural studies – on the whole they are not establishing themselves as undergraduate degree subjects because of the ethos of disciplinarity. Even long-established and very popular interdisciplinary subjects with their own degrees, like criminology and media studies, find themselves located in more established disciplinary 'homes', such as law, sociology, social policy, English and communications, and have not emerged as units in their own right for research quality assessment purposes.[23] And practitioners in these established disciplines often express anxiety at the threat the newcomers pose to their own student quotas, staff numbers and research opportunities. Only where there is no competition for prime undergraduate income (and now fees), such as at the taught postgraduate level, do these interdisciplinary subjects thrive as degree topics.

The rise of interdisciplinary administrative units, therefore, has not impugned disciplinarity to any great extent because disciplinary closure is reproduced effortlessly in government higher education policy and disciplinary practices within each of the subjects. Disciplinarity is the norm. There are also historical reasons for this.

Disciplinarity is inherent to the professionalization of the separate disciplines as they emerged out of natural and moral philosophy in the seventeenth and eighteenth centuries. The very success of their progress and development since then has been premised on their separation into specialized subject areas, with boundaries protected by disciplinary practices that reinforced this separation. Professionalization perforce obligated separation. Their common roots are, thus, overlooked. This is nowhere better demonstrated that in the 'histories of thought'-type courses that once proliferated in the separate subjects. While the history of ideas was very popular in economics, sociology, anthropology, politics and, to a lesser extent, psychology, 'classical theory' courses are falling out of fashion in the curriculum. Yet it was always a disciplinary history that was taught, rarely an interdisciplinary one. This is despite the enduring popularity of journals catering for this interest among researchers, a few of which are interdisciplinary, such as the *Journal for the History of the Human Sciences*. Common heritage and shared lineage is underplayed to exaggerate

---

[23] Media studies, for example, finds itself in a panel with communication, cultural studies and library and information management (panel 36 in the 2014 REF).

disciplinary differences (Abbott 2001, refers to this as the 'chaos of disciplines'). The separate social sciences have a tendency to envision their histories in disciplinary terms because, to adopt Freud's term from another context, they suffer from the narcissism of small differences.

Conclusion

The power and influence of the social sciences have been undermined by their Balkanization. This is why it is so important to show their essential unity. The narcissism of small differences pulls the social sciences apart in order to exaggerate their individual distinctiveness. This has the effect of minimizing the sense among practitioners that there is a generic social science. I have argued that social science is a unified intellectual field. It is given coherence both by its subject matter, the *social* nature of society across time and place, and by its scientific practices, the objective observation and explanation of this subject matter. That society is an inclusive entity and can be expanded into arenas like culture, the market and the state reinforces the essential unity afforded by this subject matter; and that social science practices differ in their degrees of conformity to the idea of science, matters less than the common commitment to empirical and theoretical observation and explanation. To draw on Peter Winch's title again (1958), the *idea* of a social science is a very good one. And British practitioners are very good at it.

2

What is the Scale and Standing of British Social Science?

Introduction

My purpose in this chapter is very limited but also very ambitious. First, I want to give a sense of the scale of the social sciences in Britain in order to measure them against the country's provision for the sciences and humanities as well as the infrastructure for social science in other countries. This is not a modest undertaking. A lot of this information is surprisingly difficult to ascertain. Secondly, I will argue that British social science is world-class in its quality. This is not a modest claim. They are not equally good, nor everywhere good, but for a very small nation with relatively few practitioners, British social science punches well above its weight and, in terms of expenditure per head, exceeds the United States in quality. This requires stating the *social science* grounds on which I profess this claim.[1]

Consideration of the scale and standing of British social science gives a necessary background to assessing their public impact. I conclude the chapter by noting the contested terrain over the meaning of impact. This is a precursor to Chapter 3 which uses a discussion of impact, the audit culture and the potential degradation of social science in Britain to launch my argument that this present conjuncture is an opportunity for the promotion of social science.

---

[1] As we shall see shortly, one of the ironies of the current conjuncture facing British universities is that the imposition by the state of an audit culture in universities, and the introduction of several and varied performance indicators intended to regulate them, is a double-edged sword, for it allows the social sciences in Britain to show, by the state's own performance measures, that they are world class. It sits uneasily with many critics of the audit culture, however, that these performance measures should be used to argue for the quality of the social sciences in Britain, since it legitimates them; the sword is perhaps triple-edged. I do not subscribe to this view. It is wryly humorous to me to see the government hoisted on its own petard. I do, however, stress the pernicious side to this audit culture in the next chapter.

What is the scale of the social sciences in Britain?

Britain lags behind comparators in the Organization for Economic Cooperation and Development (OECD), dropping in 2010 to 15th place in the proportion of people going to university. At 1.2 per cent of Britain's gross domestic product (GDP) in 2010, it spends less on higher education than the average of OECD members at 1.5 per cent, and much less than Australia, Japan and the United States. The United States, for example, spends 2.7 per cent of GDP on its universities. Public investment in higher education in the United Kingdom is even less, at 0.6 per cent, one of the lowest in the OECD (see Oswald 2011). Expenditure on total research and development, something larger than on universities, was 1.76 per cent of GDP in the United Kingdom in 2005, comparing unfavourably with the United States at 2.62 per cent, Germany 2.48 per cent, 3.32 per cent in Japan and Israel at 4.49 per cent. The United Kingdom did much better than the BRIC countries of Brazil, Russia, India and China, areas of the world rapidly expanding in population and industrial prowess, but in 2010 came 15th in a list of 58 countries (see UNESCO 2010: 370–1), with most European nations higher than Britain.[2]

With respect to funding specifically for the social sciences, as the 'third culture' (Kagan 2009) in British intellectual life, historical funding traditions benefitted the longer-established cultures, but the scale and critical mass of social science in Britain is overturning these historic patterns. The Higher Education Statistics Agency (HESA) produces annual figures that mark this shift (see http://www.hesa.ac.uk).[3] For 2009–10, which provide the most up to date statistics available, 'total expenditure' (which includes all staff costs, operating costs and depreciation) across broad subject categories, showed that Administration, Business and Social Studies, the nearest approximation to social science,[4] got 21.9 per cent of the budget on higher education, less than Medicine, Dentistry and Health at 24.5 per cent, which is the highest, but exceeding the 14.1 per cent for Biology, Mathematics and Physical Sciences,

---

[2] Published in 2010, UNESCO's world report on social science (UNESCO 2010), sometimes utilizes old data for the United Kingdom, but this is the only comparative data available. It is always important, therefore, to specify the date of the British data.

[3] Consulted 27–31 October 2011.

[4] This covers catering and hospitality management, business and management studies, geography, media studies and 'social studies', the latter of which is an amalgam of economics, politics, sociology, social policy, social work, anthropology, human and cultural geography and 'other social studies'.

13 per cent for Engineering and Technology and 8.2 per cent for Humanities, Languages and Archaeology. Education, many parts of which are appropriately named social science, had an additional 8.1 per cent.

In terms of academic staff numbers across the whole higher education sector, Administration, Business and Social Studies has 18.2 per cent of academic staff (full and part time), 37.3 per cent of the full-time staff being female, which is higher than the sector as a whole and an increase from 31 per cent in 2002 (Commission on the Social Sciences 2003: 64). In terms of all higher education staff (which includes academic-related staff), the social science category is the second largest, behind Medicine, Dentistry and Health, and more than double that in Humanities, Languages and Archaeology. If we take HESA's broad category of Administration, Business and Social Studies as a rough approximation of social science (which, of course, excludes law and social psychology), in 2009–10, there were 44,160 social scientists employed in British HEIs.[5] However, with the category boundaries being so opaque, these sorts of calculation can only be approximations. Based on submissions to the 2001 research assessment exercise (RAE) returns, for example, the Commission on the Social Sciences in 2003 estimated the figure as 25,000 (2003: 123), which HESA figures suggest is an underenumeration.

A report by the Higher Education Funding Council for England (HEFCE) (2002) into changes in staff levels between 1995 and 2000 noted an average 6.5 per cent increase in staff levels across the sector as a whole, but 'social, political and economic studies' nearly doubled at 10.9 per cent, law increased by 12.1 per cent and business and administrative studies 13 per cent. It noted the difficulties in staff retention for law and economics, where opportunities outside HE were more lucrative than for other social sciences, and that economics in particular appointed mostly non-British staff, although this is explained as much by better quantitative training overseas than alternative employment opportunities for British-trained staff (also see Commission on the Social Sciences 2003: 61–5); the deficiencies in quantitative training in economics have largely been

---

[5] Comparing staff numbers cross-nationally is impossible because countries which include education, business and management and law within the definition of social science will have large numbers, and crude headcounts are further distorted by different employment practices whenever large numbers of casual and part-time staff are employed. The comparative statistics available in the *World Social Science Report 2010* (UNESCO 2010: 372–7) for 'researcher' head counts and full-time equivalents in 'higher education' exclude the United Kingdom and run together social science and humanities staff and thus offer no reliable comparison.

resolved since then, through selective postgraduate studentships and improved training by the ESRC.

Student numbers also give a measure of the scale of social science in Britain. Not only do the social sciences employ a lot of staff, but they also teach a high number of students. In 2009–10, the number of all students (full- and part-time, undergraduate and postgraduate) in science was just over one million, those in social studies 213,755, law 94,375, business and administration 353,910, historical and philosophical studies 96,295, languages 138,090 and education 226,385. Total enrolment statistics like this reflect also in the number of new entrants in the social sciences, the number of social science degrees awarded and other surrogates for social science demand, the repetition of which would be tedious. It is relevant, however, to give a glimpse of demand across the separate subjects that comprise HESA's 'social studies' category, along with other social sciences. This is reflected in Table 2.1, which covers all students, for all years, full- and part-time, undergraduate and postgraduate for 2009–10.

There has clearly been phenomenal growth in demand for some social sciences and steadier growth for others, but growth there has been for them all. This level of expansion in demand over the last decade is comparable across other HESA subject categories, and higher than some. That for 'social studies' as a whole was 59.5 per cent, comparing favourably with 55.7 per cent for business and administration, 52.9 per cent for languages, 52.6 per cent for medicine, dentistry and health, 30.9 per cent for the physical sciences and 26.8 per cent

Table 2.1 Student numbers in social science 2009–10

Subject	Total	% increase since 1990–2000
Economics	34,895	45.8
Politics	35,850	112.1
Sociology	34,755	49.4
Social Policy	16,215	110.0
Social Work	62,700	127.5
Anthropology	4,835	24.6
Human Geography	11,076	28.6
Other social studies	12,830	163.9
Psychology	82,510	747.1
Business and Administration	353,910	55.7
Law	94,375	63.1

Source: Worked from figures provided by Higher Education Statistics Agency at http://www.hesa.ac.uk/ content/view/1897/706/.

for engineering and technology. Historical and philosophical studies (which in 1999–2000 was called 'humanities', although the two are not entirely equivalent), witnessed growth in demand slightly higher at 60.2 per cent.

This scale needs, however, to be set in an international context. The International Social Science Council's latest figures for student numbers in 'social science, business and law' cover 2006 and are, thus, quite old, but they do give a measure of the proportion this subject area comprises of the total student enrolments for various countries at that time. The United Kingdom's was 27 per cent, equal to the United States, but the lowest in the whole of North America and Western Europe, save Ireland, Canada, Sweden and Finland (UNESCO 2010: 378–80). Not surprisingly given their recent social and political changes, countries in Central and Eastern Europe had a very large proportion of students studying in social science, business and law, as did Latin American and BRIC countries and South Africa, mostly exceeding that in the United Kingdom, United States and Canada by substantial proportions. This illustrates how 'society' as a subject matter offers a significant stimulus to social science, and those societies undergoing economic development and democratic transition are often among the keenest to ensure that they have the infrastructure in social science teaching to nurture this interest. Gross numbers studying social science are often lower in developing countries, of course, because of the limited size of total enrolments and the lag in building the infrastructure for higher education teaching. It is for this reason that Elizabeth King, from the Human Development Network at the World Bank, considers poor quality and inadequate higher education provision one of the developing world's biggest bottlenecks.[6]

Social science teaching is also vigorous and enthusiastic in the school sector in Britain. In addition to courses in the main social science disciplines, citizenship is taught at Key Stage 4 (the two years of GCSE study) and this contains a strong social science component, as does Modern Studies in Scotland. The Commission on the Social Sciences (2003: 5) estimated at any one time there were 4.5 million 11–19-year-olds studying social science subjects in schools. Nearly half a million GCSE papers are sat annually with a substantial social science focus and 163,000 at 'A' level. Interestingly, they calculated that a substantially higher proportion of students with social science GCSEs go on

---

[6] Quoted in the *Times Higher Education,* 10 November 2011, p. 17.

to take social science at university than is the case for history, mathematics and geography (2003: 79), and they noted that the number of school children exposed to social science teaching over the 20 years up to 2003 was 15 million (2003: 79): it must now exceed 20 million. All this is for subjects that are not compulsory. Add to this the two million social science graduates from HEIs over the last 30 years (estimated by the Commission on the Social Sciences 2003: 108) and social science underpins a great deal of the public education people have received in Britain.

What is the standing of British social science?

If the scale of British social science places it ambiguously in relation to its international comparators, in terms of quality it is unambiguously among the best in the world.[7] There are good reasons in British society that make it so. As the scientific study of society, social science gets its intellectual stimulus from its social location. Social science is different from natural science and the humanities therefore in being shaped – but not overdetermined – in its research and teaching agenda by the society in which it takes place. I am not implying there is a 'British national social science', although some have claimed thus (see Giddens 1996) – this is a more reasonable assertion for some social sciences than others, notably the British tradition of social anthropology (on which see Macdonald 2001)[8] – or that there were no outside influences on British practitioners. The professionalization of the separate social sciences in the 1950s and the 1960s in particular led to heavy inputs from US-based social scientists and theorists, and the mobile nature of early career appointments witnessed many of the great names from later generations study on fellowships in the United States to establish themselves; as many North Americans did likewise this side of the Atlantic. And the influence of European social theory on social science in Britain is profound today. Contemporary patterns of migration see many young talented social scientists leave peripheral regions to move to the

---

[7] This explains why Britain is so attractive to international students. In 2009–10, HESA statistics show there to be 123,940 undergraduates from outside the European Union (EU), representing 10.5 per cent, and 156,820 postgraduates, 12.7 per cent. The number of international students has doubled in the decade since 2000–01. The largest group from outside the EU comes from China, followed by India.

[8] Thus, Donald MacRea, a sociologist from the LSE, writing on 'The British Tradition in Social Anthropology' in 1961, when such a thing still existed before the disciplinary fragmentation of the 1980s, said 'the phrase social anthropology itself is very British' (1961: 30).

cultural core of the West, which the United Kingdom benefits from (but to a lesser extent than Western societies with more 'open' immigration laws). The *World Social Science Report 2010* suggests that social scientists are more mobile than they have ever been (UNESCO 2010: 143), further restricting any claims about national social science traditions. It would be foolish to contend this.

My argument is more mundane. British social change posed intellectual challenges to social scientists based here (some of whom, after all, were not British by birth), which in part they helped analyse and understand through exploiting the global market in ideas. These intellectual challenges helped cement their view that the scientific study of society was worthwhile, irrespective of the national provenance of their ideas or people's ethnicity. British society made social science seem feasible in Britain.

British society from an early stage and for a very long time threw up issues that promoted social science engagement with it. Britain's economic progress and early industrialization, first in Scotland in the eighteenth century, then England in the nineteenth, encouraged the origins of economics; and the growth in imperial trade in particular witnessed the expansion of macroeconomics and econometrics, as well as business, accountancy and finance as sub-branches of economics. As Turner (2006a: 176) notes, so closely intertwined is the idea of the free market with the free society, whether established in the seventeenth century with Locke, the eighteenth with Smith or the nineteenth with Ricardo, that economic developments in Britain also shaped intellectual ideas about liberalism, which went on to influence social science disciplines like political science and sociology. It was nineteenth-century social change that gave urgency to sociology's interest in the negative consequences of commercialization and industrialization for social relationships, and thus sociology's dominating concerns in the nineteenth and twentieth centuries with social inequality, class, poverty, distributive injustice, the social division of labour, alienation and the threat to the social bond deriving from an unfettered market.[9]

---

[9]   The contrast between the economic division of labour (the increasing specialization of work) and the social division of labour (the increasing specialization of society into classes) is worth emphasizing, for the former is rightly associated with the enhancement of productivity and trade, while the latter with inequality and social dislocation. The contrast sums up the different approach to the division of labour in economics and sociology well, and is exemplified by the varied usages of two Scots in the eighteenth century, Adam Smith and Adam Ferguson, both accredited with inventing the term but the former with an economic focus, the latter a sociological one (on which see Brewer 1986, 1989). Comparisons of the respective intellectual coherence of economics and sociology as disciplines interests sociologists for their envy of the coherence of economics (see Abbott 2001; Holmwood 2010).

Britain's early democratization and its emergence as the modern world's first parliamentary system fostered the development of political science, political theory and political sociology, as well as election studies; as did Britain's early urbanization for town planning, demography, human geography, social statistics and sociology. The development of a particular *kind* of politics in Britain, the emergence of paternalistic patrician politicians, one-nation Toryism and eventually the welfare state, shaped social science interest in this as a political expression of liberalism, as well as in the policy dimensions of social welfarism and its social consequences in British culture, the market and the state. Education, schooling, women's rights, gender and 'domestic' labour, health and medical care, poverty, slum clearance, transport policy, new town planning, citizenship rights and community rehousing are just a few of the intellectual concerns that fed into the separate social science disciplines as a result of the stimulus provided by British society and its social changes. And, of course, the link between IQ testing, the 11+ examination and policies of school selection gave psychology an additional input on top of whatever wider social concerns motivated its intellectual interest in childhood development, language acquisition and the link between poverty and infant nurturing.

One final example is worth citing to reinforce the point that British social science excelled because of what British society gave it as an initial intellectual stimulus. While there has been more British social anthropology in the post-colonial period (circa 1960) than during it, it is noteworthy that social anthropology in Britain grew apace arising from its connections to the country's colonial expansion and the need for colonial administration. This affected its area specialisms, particularly places where Britain's colonial expansion fuelled the greatest need (such as African studies and Asian studies), as well as disciplinary content (notably anthropological understanding of indigenous kinship systems, cultures and cultural beliefs in order to make sense of how its colonial territories worked). It shaped also its methodological preferences, since ethnography is premised on developing familiarization with foreign cultures. The extension of the 'exotic' anthropological tradition to the analysis of family and community life in a rapidly changing Britain, in the form of both rural and urban community studies, distances British social anthropology from the jibe of being the handmaiden of imperialism,[10] and helped lead to the development of community studies as one of the most significant forms of post-war social science, reducing further the intellectual barriers between geography, social anthropology and sociology. Many major figures in each of these disciplines started out first in one of the others. Such was this elision, that Radcliffe-Brown, one of the foremost progenitors of the British tradition in social anthropology, felt his discipline to be a form of 'comparative sociology'.

Paradoxically, this elision between human geography, social anthropology and sociology has been cemented with Britain's subsequent decolonization, for it accordingly stimulated British social science interest in 'race' relations, cross cultural contacts, immigration and housing, policies of cultural assimilation and multiculturalism and the like. Decolonization reinforced social change in Britain and, with it, shaped the subject matter of British social science. Not only did these concerns feed into the full range of social science disciplines, but they also helped give birth to new intellectual arenas, like cultural studies, black studies and post-colonial studies.

These intellectual issues also spurred methodological developments in the social sciences, ranging from sample surveys and IQ tests to qualitative interviewing and the community studies approach. According to Savage (2010), it was the combination of methodological advances and topic content that marked British social science as special in its formative years. He argued that developments in the technical apparatus of social science since World War II, particularly mass observation, interviewing and the social survey, encouraged both a scientific attitude towards data collection in practitioners, away from humanities and literary approaches, and enhanced their willingness to exploit the opportunities for social science research provided by technocratic and governmental demands for social science evidence to address problems around post-war social change. Based on analysis of seven major projects conducted between the 1940s and the 1970s, Savage emphasizes the blending that occurred

---

[10] The allegation that social anthropology was complicit in colonial exploitation is rightly dismissed by Macdonald (2001), who shows that the discipline's work was often at variance with the needs of colonial administrators, that practitioners were often left-leaning in their politics, and were more likely than not to support national independence in the societies they studied. Social anthropology was about protecting and defending the authenticity of the non-Western cultures they studied (Giddens 1996: 114). Nonetheless, it did initially benefit from the link with Empire for it had higher social status as a discipline than sociology or geography as a result of it being seen as a career – and a career for gentlemen (MacRea 1961: 36). As I make clear in the text however, the discipline has long transcended its origins.

between the methods for doing social science and the conceptual apparatus for making sense of the results, as the language of social groups, social relationships and social reproduction emerged from the technical apparatus for doing social science. All this helped generate a new kind of academic social science (which he contrasts with the amateurish 'gentlemanly' social science of the immediate pre- and post-war period).

Social science publishing accelerated in Britain in this period, as British-based publishing houses expanded their book and journal coverage of social science and, to feed the worldwide market interest in social science, themselves became global companies (to the point now where it is impossible to think of them anymore as British publishing houses). Some publish almost exclusively in social science, such as Polity Press and Sage, the latter also being a very substantial journal publisher in the social sciences (645 on the last count, with 245 journals connected to learned societies). There are also publications from learned societies in the social sciences, the Academy of Social Sciences itself, the ESRC and the various social science think tanks, policy research institutes and the like. Most of these are discipline- or thematic-based journals, but generic social science journals flourish, like the Academy of Social Sciences' *Contemporary Social Science* and Elsevier's *Social Science Research*. Proliferation, of course, is a measure of quantity; quality is something to which I return shortly.

The expanding market for social science knowledge in Britain is both cause and effect of the international profile of British social science, as companies globalized and the market increasingly became an English-speaking one, due to the dominating influence of the US market and the pressure overseas institutions are under to give their research greater international impact,[11] which French-speaking social science resented but could never rival, although the International Social Science Council is in Paris. The hegemony of English varies with social science disciplines. Economics is invariably English but the vernacular is more common in sociology, which is strong in France and

---

[11] Anglicization, which affects countries as different as Sri Lanka and Finland, results in overseas universities introducing monitoring procedures to ensure staff publish in international – which means English-medium – journals, which often requires that work is translated into English by private companies and in some cases by the English department in the university. The Polytechnic University of Milan, for example, announced in 2012 that from 2014, most of its courses will be conducted in English.

Germany. Social science subjects embedded in national contexts are more likely to use national languages and have their own journals. The rise of social science in the BRIC countries threatens the dominance of English as the language of social science publishing, but this anxiety only confirms that at the present time, British social science benefits from the market for social science publishing being Anglo-Saxon. The Thomson Social Science Citation Index records that 94.5 per cent of the articles published between 1998 and 2007 were in English (cited in UNESCO 2010: 151). And British social science helped to create this Anglo-Saxon domination. Scopus Social Science, one of several global citation indexes, covers close to 4,000 journals in the field, 13.4 per cent of which are in the United Kingdom; the United States has 30.2 per cent. Canada comes next at 5.6 per cent and China with 5.1 per cent (UNESCO 2010: 365).[12]

It is necessary here to point out, of course, that British social scientists do not benefit from an open-door policy from journal editors. In some cases, it is the reverse. In social science disciplines where US-based journals are dominant, UK academics can be forced to write to a US agenda. The government has sympathized with researchers in business and management, for example, who have complained of the dominance of US publications in their field, whose prestige makes them feel obliged to work on topics likely to be regarded favourably by their editorial boards, such as quantitative analysis of North American industry trends, rather than British or European problems (see http://www.bis.gov.uk/news/speeches/david-willetts-gareth-roberts-science-policy-lecture-2011). British social science benefits immeasurably, in other words, where there are international quality journals based on its home territory, as especially does economics, sociology, human geography and political science, reinforcing the reputation of British social scientists and the quality of research on British and European issues. The number of overseas researchers working on aspects of British economic, political and social life and publishing in British-based journals adds both to the international quality of these journals and to the hegemony of the English language.

---

[12] Strikingly comparable figures for the period 1981–2000 are supplied by the Commission on the Social Sciences (2003: 56), showing Britain to be second behind the United States in the volume of cited works.

The 2011 University World Rankings for the social sciences, published by the *Times Higher Education* in conjunction with Thomson Reuters, also shows the dominance of the English-speaking world in social science, with only five places in the top 50-ranked social science universities coming from non-English-speaking countries (see *Times Higher Education* 2011: 36). Of course, these rankings are controversial and are driven by the methodologies on which they are based, but as the *World Social Science Report 2010* noted (UNESCO 2010: 235) they have become popular and are, therefore, required to be taken seriously. Given the bias in citation indexes in favour of articles and the obvious book writing culture in some social science disciplines – the International Social Science Council cites evidence that suggests between 40 and 60 per cent of social science literature is in book form (UNESCO 2010: 251) – world rankings under-represent the contribution of social science to a university's performance. But the rankings of the *Times Higher Education* are superior because they use peer review data alongside bibliometrics and offer rankings for social science alone without the distorting publishing and citation patterns in the sciences and medicine.[13]

There is one further part of the historical context to British social science that explains its international excellence. British universities, as special spaces for the practice of social science, are among the best in the world and their structure and management facilitated the intellectual effervescence of British social science in the nineteenth and twentieth centuries. The 2011 World Rankings by the *Times Higher Education* show that Britain has 32 universities in the top 200, more than any other country except the United States; about a third of Britain's HEIs grace the list of the world's best institutions (and the top 200 represent the world's topmost 1 per cent of universities). The then Editor of the *Times Higher Education*, Ann Mroz, pointed out that this is three times as many as Germany, four times as many as Australia and six times more than Japan. When GDP is taken into account (see Oswald 2011), thereby linking performance with population size and wealth, the United States drops from first spot to fourteenth and the United Kingdom is third. What this means, first,

---

[13] Concerned about the British – and English-speaking – dominance in world rankings, the European Commission is currently testing a ranking formula called U-Multirank, developed by academics in Germany and The Netherlands, designed not to produce a league table but to allow students, policy makers, employers and universities to choose their own criteria to compare HEIs.

is that in terms of quality per pound invested in universities, Britain is ahead of the United States, and, secondly, while the United States dominates the list of the best HEIs, it has a long tail of poorly performing institutions, while the United Kingdom is good widely across the board. The United Kingdom has a critical mass of very good universities. This reflects in the 2011 social science rankings, where the United Kingdom has 9 HEIs listed in the top 50 universities for social science, 4 in the top 20, more than any other country save the United States. Only one other European country is listed, The Netherlands, with one HEI ranked. In short, British universities are special.

There are several reasons for this excellence. The right to practise as a social scientist in a British university was once constrained only by merit and the open, porous borders within British society and universities permitted waves of foreign intellectuals to escape persecution abroad to enrich British social science. British universities are free of religious and political domination by special interest groups, churches, private businesses and transnational corporations, and long-established principles of academic freedom, research autonomy and tenure once made them free of government control and regulation. The universities worked within financial tramlines set by government but otherwise were left free to run themselves. The separate social science disciplines and related professions were in charge of setting their own intellectual agendas, and key intellectual decisions were made by practitioners themselves.

The expansion of social science provision in British universities in the 1960s, with the emergence of new Robbins universities, and later in the 1990s with the ending of the binary divide between universities and polytechnics, was further encouragement to social science research, for it increased the critical mass of social science research, raised its international profile and allowed it to benefit from maximum occupational mobility. The world rankings for universities that are under 50 years old reveals the United Kingdom to have 5 in the top 20 and to have the largest number of any nation in the top 100 (with 20), reflecting, I think, the quality of the new Robbins universities established in Britain in the 1960s and the emergence of some strong post-1992 universities. Free public university education, which was reinforced for a long while by a system of maintenance grants for students from poorer economic backgrounds, also helped towards the utilization of human capital for the benefit of social science recruitment and the reproduction of the next generation of practitioners.

What is more, successive British governments promoted social science research through their recognition of the need for national data sets to facilitate policy and planning, giving us comprehensive cohort studies with longitudinal data on a whole range of issues, as well as national surveys, producing significant data on crime, educational performance, social mobility, economic trends, birth studies and the rest (something that further assisted technical and methodological development in the social sciences). A lot of the responsibility for collecting and analysing this data went to social scientists in the universities, but it also facilitated the emergence of specialist independent social science research units, such as the Policy Studies Institute (http://www. psi.org.uk/), the National Institute of Economic and Social Research (http:// www.niesr.ac.uk/) and the National Centre for Social Research (http://www. natcen.ac.uk), some of whom had long histories (on which see **Vignette 2**). There was also encouragement to the appointment of social scientists in the civil service, providing recruitment for waves of social science specialists. This threatens the place of universities in reproducing social science, to the anxiety of some university-based social scientists, but the expansion of social science in the think tanks and semi-independent research institutes is positive for the creation and consumption of social science knowledge, so long as it retains its quality, we are not sniffy about its problem-solving and policy orientation, and, in particular, the think tanks resist the temptation to be partisan (this cannot be taken for granted given some are aligned to political parties).[14]

Britain has, therefore, offered an unusually productive space for social science to develop and grow internationally. But scale is a measure of quantity; quality is quite different. There are two ways of approaching the quality of British social science, which we might call the 'great figure syndrome' and the 'critical mass argument'. The former inherently prejudices us towards the view that British social science is in decline; the other that it is uncommonly good across the board.

---

[14] Byrne (2011: 188–9) has given a negative critique of the contribution of think tanks to applied social science research, raising concerns about their narrowness of target and focus, designed as most are to engage with government within a London-centricism, which tends to make them blind to circumstances outside the South East.

Vignette 2 Independent social research centres

It is very difficult for non-commercial social research agencies to be genuinely independent and financial exigencies have forced many to develop working relationships with universities. Most have a clear policy focus to assist in generating grant and consultancy income. The *National Centre for Social Research*, for example, which began in 1969 under the initiative of the late Sir Roger Jowell and Gerald Hoinville, became in 2008 a research centre associated with the LSE, although it retains its operational independence. It describes itself thus. 'We are experts in qualitative and quantitative methods and apply rigorous and robust research methodologies to greater understand complex social policy issues. We combine our technical expertise with an indepth understanding of the policy areas we work in to ensure the highest quality results'. As one example of its many commissioned researches, in 2011 it published a Report for the Cabinet Office on the summer riots that year in England (see Morrell et al. 2011), although the Home Secretary later said she 'wholly disagreed with many of the conclusions'. The *Policy Studies Institute* had a long history of independence but in 2009 it became a wholly owned subsidiary of the University of Westminster. The Policy Studies Institute takes a politically neutral stance on issues of public policy and has no connections with any political party, commercial interest or pressure group, with its income coming from funds for individual research projects received from a variety of competitive sources. It employs a large number of staff, organized in two multidisciplinary groups: environment, and work and social policy. The Institute collaborates with colleagues in the University of Westminster but also with many other semi-independent research institutes, such as the National Centre for Social Research, the National Institute for Economic and Social Research, the Institute of Employment Research, the Institute for Public Policy Research, as well as research centres more directly linked to universities. The Policy Studies Institute began in 1931 as Political and Economic Planning, set up as an independent think tank in response to the economic depression, and can claim credit for drawing up the blueprint for what became the National Health Service and the Race Relations Act. The Policy Studies Institute was formed in 1978 through the merger of Political and Economic Planning and the Centre for Studies in Social Policy, which had been established in 1972. In January 1998, the Policy Studies Institute became a wholly owned subsidiary company of the University of Westminster, fully merging with the University in April 2009. The Institute retains its name and continues to undertake policy-relevant research. It sees its mission 'to inform public policy and practice through the provision, dissemination and promotion of high quality research. Its vision is to be highly regarded and influential in social, economic and environmental research'. In contrast the *National Institute of Economic and Social Research* has retained its independence. It is Britain's longest established independent economic research institute with over 60 years' experience of 'applying academic excellence to the needs of business and policy makers'. The Institute is independent of all party political interests. It receives no core funding from government and is not affiliated to any single university, although it undertakes projects in collaboration with leading academic institutions. The Institute's work falls into three distinct fields: economic modelling and macro analysis; education, training and employment; the international economy. Current programmes include work on productivity, pensions and the ageing population, trade and investment, European financial integration, labour markets and economic statistics. The Institute is part of the EUROFRAME network, an initiative for improved forecasting and macroeconomic analysis in the European Union set up in 1998 by nine independent European research institutes. It describes its mission statement as 'to promote, through quantitative and qualitative research, a deeper understanding of the interaction of economic and social forces that affect people's lives, and the ways in which policies can improve them'.

Where have all the giants gone?

Critics of Britain's audit culture attribute to it the blame for the disappearance of intellectual giants, for there is no personal motivation or incentive to ever become one; quite the opposite. Critics allege that the audit culture rewards those who beaver away in ever-diminishing silos, surrounded by those of their peers who can be relied on not to challenge them but to congratulate and thereby reinforce them in a continuous cycle of mutual gratification. Attractive as this is as an idea, the explanation is more complex. There is something about the very question that predisposes a negative answer. The great figure syndrome privileges the illustrious names from each discipline since the eighteenth century – many of whom qualify as British only by right of residing here, and some of whom migrated abroad after nurturing their reputations in Britain – and by positioning the classic texts within each social science discipline written by British authors. The list of such great figures and texts would be very long indeed – too long to mention here. Paradoxically, however, the great figure syndrome is highly affected both by scale, since the smaller the field the easier it to dominate, and by time, for as scale has expanded down the years the harder it is to rise above the rest. Greatness, in short, is a comparative evaluation related to the size of the field and is time dependent. It is for this reason that the great figures of British social science are thought to exist primarily in its past, when the field was easier to dominate, or reside today primarily in small subfields, where advancement is conditioned by the scale of competition. This goes some way to explaining the lament in nearly every social science discipline that there are few – none – to rival the big names of yesteryear. On this measure, British social science is in decline.

This complaint, however, is as much oriented to quantity as quality, for it was genuinely easier to be an intellectual giant when fields were new, undeveloped and relatively sparsely populated. This also puts into higher relief the true intellectual stardom of those contemporary figures – again, too invidious to mention – with reputations that transcend small subfields. The irony, of course, is that the lack of distance we have from these great figures because of the relative newness of the social sciences, coupled with the close attention the social sciences have paid to their intellectual history as part of disciplinary specialization, reinforces the great figure syndrome precisely at a time when their scale inhibits such goliaths emerging, or doing so to the sort of universal acclaim and recognition that greeted them in the past. This condemns social scientists today to forever feel that their peers lack the quality of their ancestors.[15]

It is for this reason that critical mass arguments offer an alternative way to assess the standing of British social science. The great figure syndrome significantly under-enumerates the quality-in-depth within British social science that lies beneath the great figures of the past and which characterizes the quality of the HE system as a whole rather than a few elite individuals. Strength in depth is the defining characteristic of British social science; and the mass is not standing on the shoulders of these giants, it is commanding height enough as it stands.

We have already seen, as a measure of this, the position of British universities in the 2011 world rankings for social science. Let us consider more. The research assessment exercise (RAE) is the bane of most academics' lives as

---

[15] It is my impression that reputations are not best measured by citations during someone's lifetime, but in retrospect, for citations – even for the most popular figures – mostly die off with them, leaving them to be rediscovered some decades later as part of intellectual history. The great figure syndrome, in other words, is inherently predisposed to favour the long since dead.

one of the key components of the audit culture in British higher education. It is, in the view of the Commission on the Social Sciences (2003: 9), a relentless treadmill, but they nonetheless saw the RAE as useful for highlighting the health and quality of social science research in Britain (2003: 52–6). There is a sense in which the RAE has distorted publishing patterns, accelerating the move into print, valorized the high impact journals and publishing houses, and discouraged the quiet contemplation of ideas ahead of publishing them. It has, however, had some positive effects (elaborated in Brewer 2011a: 9–12), one of which is to show the international research excellence of social science subjects objectively rather than relying on High Table gossip or the prejudices of university managements dominated by the old professions. In the 2008 exercise, 4* research was described as 'world leading in terms of originality, significance and rigour' and 3* as 'internationally excellent' in the same terms. The proportion of 3*/4* research across the social science units of assessment is revelatory, as shown in Table 2.2.

This strikes home that assessments of this level of international distinction never fell below 43 per cent of the evaluated outputs and in some cases was considerably higher. The average over the social sciences as a whole was 52 per cent. That is to say, taken as a group, one in two pieces of work produced by social scientists in Britain submitted for assessment was deemed internationally excellent. This is critical mass, and I wish to labour the point.

Table 2.2 2008 RAE scores

Social science unit of assessment	% 3*/4*
Geography	56
Economics/Econometrics	77
Business and Management	53
Law	49
Politics and International Relations	44
Social Work and Social Policy	53
Sociology	48
Anthropology	57
Development Studies	49
Psychology	45
Education	43
Average for sector as a whole	52

Source: Annex D, National Comparative Data, *RAE 2008: The Outcome*,
    December 2008, available at http://www.rae.ac.uk/results/
    outstore/raeoutcomeannexes/pdf.

The ESRC has been keen to establish value for money in the social science research it funds, and while this is usually something social scientists rail against, a useful by-product has been the benchmarking exercises it has conducted to assess British social science against international standards of quality. These began in 2005 and have been conducted for social anthropology, politics and international studies, economics, sociology and psychology; in 2012, human geography was set underway (see http://esrc.ac.uk/ funding-and-guidance/tools-and-resources/impact-evaluation/UK-human-geography.aspx?dm/).The assessments have been conducted by panels of subject specialists from overseas. Their reports are public documents available on the ESRC's website (see http://www.esrc.ac.uk/funding-and-guidance/ tools-and-resources/impact-evaluation/international-benchmarking.aspx).[16] Some extracts are worth quoting. The social anthropology panel stated: 'clearly the UK has been one of the intellectual heartlands of Anthropology; the quality of current work remains very high . . . The panel noted a lengthy list of areas of particular strength, topics in which UK Social Anthropology was indeed an intellectual leader.' The politics panel found 'considerable evidence of research quality across almost all the principal sub-disciplines . . . there is truly outstanding research in the UK profession'. The economics report stated 'the research achievements of United Kingdom scholars are exceptional by world standards; the UK economics profession is more prominent than any other country's except for the United States . . . It has attained world leadership in microeconometrics'. The comparison with the United States featured also in the sociology panel: 'it compares extremely well in a wider international frame as, perhaps, being second only to the US.' It went on: 'we attest UK sociology to be at the international forefront with its intellectual performance and research output.' 'The panel's headline finding', stated the psychology report, 'is that, overall, the quality is very high, bettered only by psychology research from the USA. In a substantial number of areas, UK psychology research is unsurpassed anywhere in the world'.

Lest it be thought that research quality is a narrow test of the standing of British social science, it is worth emphasizing that social science teaching is regarded as being excellent in quality (Commission on the Social Sciences 2003: 61). The incentives to fix any problems identified through teaching

---

[16] ESRC website accessed 31 October 2011.

evaluations, whether those done institutionally by the Quality Assurance Agency (QAA) or through universities' internal evaluation procedures, are very high, much higher than the loss of quality research funding (QR) through poor quality research, since the bulk of income is for teaching (formerly the block grant, and now fees). To support this judgement about teaching quality, it is worth employing statistical evidence from the national student satisfaction surveys conducted by the Higher Education Funding Council for England as part of its teaching quality assurance procedures.[17] The academy's attitude towards them is ambivalent, even hostile (see Furedi 2012), and given their unreliability, people complain most about the way results are utilized by public relations managers and find their way into league tables. These rankings are limited as a measure of quality inasmuch as the learning experience is greater than the level of 'overall satisfaction' expressed in it, and when disaggregated to the level of individual institutions, these surveys are hugely distorted by very low response rates. But the numbers of respondents for each discipline nationally are very reliable; and since every university participates, they are the only national measure available of teaching quality (the Quality Assurance Agency's subject reviews across UK HEIs have been abandoned long since and the original reviews are now very out of date; sociology's, for example, dates from 1995, mass communication from 1997, psychology and politics from 2000, and economics from 2001). The National Student Survey, therefore, while not perfect, supplies the only data we have (the results are remarkably consistent over time, which is another measure of the survey's reliability).

The 2010 results are summarized in Table 2.3. This shows that in every case, at least eight out of ten social science students in the major subject categories expressed overall satisfaction with the quality of the teaching they received. In all cases but one this was above the average for all the Higher Education Funding Council for England (HEFCE) subject categories. With respect to the social sciences, the number of respondents was 57,115, a large enough sample for the results to be reliable. It is a profound irony that the government is dismantling public universities, in which students clearly have satisfaction,

---

[17] HEFCE website, consulted 31 October 2011. These surveys are national and not restricted to England. In 2010–11, the survey cost £2.1 million to administer (*Times Higher Education*, 8 March, 2012, p. 5).

Table 2.3 National student survey 2010

Subject category	Number of respondents	% Overall satisfaction
Business and administration	22940	80
Education	3865	81
Geographical studies	4230	88
Law	8805	85
Social studies	17275	81
All subjects	177400	81

Source: Higher Education Funding Council for England (http://www.hefce.ac.uk/pubs/hefce/2011/ 11_11/11_11.pdf).

when the level of satisfaction expressed in government barely reaches three out of every ten respondents.[18]

If I can conclude this assessment of the standing of British social science in a pithy manner, there is a critical mass of international quality teaching and research done within British social science. If the world reputation of British universities makes them a crown of the nation, the social sciences are one of its brightest jewels. However, there is great anxiety among social scientists that government higher education policies are vandalizing them. There is a deep paradox within this fear.

What is the general impact of the social sciences?

The impact debate in higher education is one of the key components of the current conjuncture affecting the demise of the public university. Most systems of higher education involve some feature of public accountability and audit – the evaluation of grant applications in the United States and The Netherlands involves an assessment of the impact of the research, for example, and Australia has a form of research assessment exercise (see Donovan 2011) – but Britain exemplifies its fullest expression. While the impact debate in Britain needs to be placed within the wider audit culture that shapes British universities, and will be discussed as part of that analysis in the next chapter, it is worth beginning with a reminder that the social sciences are high impact subjects. Impact comes

---

[18] The 2012 Edelman Trust Barometer, for example, revealed that only 29 per cent of respondents trusted the government and 12 per cent thought they were handling 'important tasks' well. See http://www.edelman.co.uk/2012/01/levels-of-trust-hit-new-lows-among-uk-public-survey-finds/.

from their subject matter – the social nature of culture, the market and state, across time and place – and the social sciences have the least to be worried about in displaying that their research has influence in society.[19]

Impact is also, for this reason, embedded in the history and development of British social science. The social sciences emerged in Britain out of natural and moral philosophy in the seventeenth and eighteenth centuries as a diagnosis of the social condition ('social' is used here in its inclusive sense). This was initially employed in the seventeenth century among political theorists like Locke and Hobbes to deal with issues of political disorder, religious warfare and the proper balance between government and individual powers and rights; then in eighteenth-century Scotland to make sense of the economic features of commercialism and economic growth, by Adam Smith among others, and the effects of commercialization and proto-industrialization on society, such as Adam Ferguson's analysis of urbanization, alienation and the social division of labour, Millar's work on social class, Lord Kames on race and comparative mythology, Lord Monboddo on language or Dugald Stewart on comparative history and early anthropology. John Millar was a professor of civil law, and this equipped him to write on the history of English government, the origins of social class and status distinctions, and gender differences, among many other things.

These have many predecessors and intellectual history searches for early precursors as part of its *raison d'être* – for example, the Greeks in politics, Ibn Khaldun in sociology, the mercantilists in economics – but, to use the history of economic thought as the exemplar, what differentiates classical economics in eighteenth-century Scotland from the economic speculations that preceded Adam Smith was the recognizably modern problems he was dealing with, such as the rise of manufacturing and production rather than just trade, creating a modern conceptual field that included notions like the division of labour,

---

[19] Shearer West, former director of research for the Arts and Humanities Research Council (AHRC), is quoted in the *Times Higher Education* on 3 November 2011 as saying that the arts and humanities disciplines have the potential to benefit more than the sciences from the inclusion of impact in the REF provided methods of measurement are handled intelligently and staff overcome their resistance and embarrassment at demonstrating impact. Writing in the same issue Bill Amos, an evolutionary geneticist (in other words from a science background), disparaged scientists concerned to display impact as Dr Plods, primarily bureaucrats adequate at doing science and more keen to get funding than do pioneering research, whom he contrasted with Dr Sparks, people who live and breathe science, who are passionate and innovative in their research. We might call their respective views 'the impact war', another battle in an ongoing conflict between what Kagan (2009) calls the three cultures.

surplus and economic growth. My point is that the tempo of economic change gave the mid-eighteenth century a suite of problems sufficiently modern to lead to the development of classical economics as a discipline. The same is true for public law, sociology, politics and anthropology; only psychology, with its history based in Germany and the United States, can be said not to have developed in this period. With this notable exception, the social sciences were brought into being as disciplines to emerge out of natural and moral philosophy precisely to diagnose, analyse and solve the problems of modernity.[20] Active engagement with culture, the market and the state is part of their roots. Impact is what they were designed for. And this impulse for engagement continued throughout their growth and development in the nineteenth and early twentieth centuries.

One example of twentieth-century growth will have to suffice. The Fabian tradition of social policy is epitomized by the career of Peter Townsend, who was for a time professor of sociology at Essex but who engaged directly with issues of fundamental social importance to the discipline of social policy (what had earlier been called 'social administration'), such as ageing, health inequalities and, above all, poverty. The arguments between the Fabians – people like Titmuss, Abel Smith and Townsend – were not in the technocratic service of governance but part of a specific social democratic political project that nonetheless helped shape post-war government policy in Britain, as Savage (2010) wonderfully captures. Among other things, Townsend was co-founder of the Child Poverty Action Group in 1965, and its chair for 20 years and Life President from 1989. He also co-founded the Disability Alliance in response to the Thalidomide scandal and chaired it for 25 years.

The impact we are referring to here, however, is quite different in kind from that envisaged in the current impact debate. We need to distinguish, therefore, between two meanings to the notion of impact, its technical and general senses. Its technical meaning is that one which is employed within British higher education policy, where it refers to the value-for-money of the expenditure on higher education as measured by its benefits. Impact is about what society gets from the universities, and in particular from the money given

---

[20] This is far from being an original argument, for it is part of the intellectual history of every social science discipline to see its chief spur coming from the analysis of modernity. One of the earliest to claim that the social sciences emerged out of moral philosophy in eighteenth-century Scotland was Gladys Bryson (1932a, 1932b, 1945).

them for research. This technical meaning is further narrowed by pressures to restrict benefits to economic ones; and the nature of the current impact debate among policy makers, academics and politicians is precisely about the feasibility of employing an economic notion of value-for-money for most disciplines. It is a near universal complaint common across all three cultures, from pure science subjects and the humanities to the social sciences, that the technical meaning of impact is inappropriate for their kind of research. The value-for-money emphasis is widely felt as unsuitable since the research output is only loosely connected to – or not even capable of being directly tied to – the money input, and the narrow attention to economic benefits is inapt. Objections are not based around any inability to produce research outputs, or a wish for unaccountability; it is the nature of their influence that is in dispute.

Impact in its general meaning refers to the influence of research in society (that is, in culture, the market and the state), with influence being unrestricted in its nature and effects, nor by time and the money input. If impact in its technical sense is value-for-money, in its general sense impact is value-for-society. Value-for-money and value-for-society are quite different forms of value. Social scientists are fully aware that they must engage with impact in this general sense, and recently there have been case studies of work collated from the medium past which have addressed it. John Scott (2011), for example, draws together a collection that has Eileen Barker reflecting on the impact of her research on the Moonies for our understanding of cult wars, Susanne MacGregor on drugs and a team from the Plymouth Business School on their work with local government. A web blog run from the LSE, 'The Impact of Social Science' (http://bit.ly/ru/1Uql) is devoted to demonstrating the impactful nature of the social sciences, and has an electronic book associated with it entitled *Handbook for Maximizing Impact* (http://blog.lse. ac.uk/impactofsocialscience/the-handbook), prepared by the School's Public Policy Group.

Current controversies about impact encouraged Crow and Takeda (2011) to look back on the late Ray Pahl's early work on the intersection of human geography, urban sociology and social anthropology, describing him as having had a career of 'fifty years of impact'. Brewer and Hayes (2011) reflected on the impact of social science studies of post-conflict societies, and there have been several surveys of the impact of general fields within contemporary social science undertaken by the Academy of Social Sciences under the rubric *Making the Case for Social Science*. The cases cover topics like well-being (February 2010), ageing (June 2010), sustainability, the environment and climate change (November 2010), crime (June 2011), sport and leisure (November 2011) and management (June 2012), available as pamphlets (see the Academy website at http://www.acss.org.uk/publication. htm). The British Academy's Policy Centre has published booklets on topics as contrasting as electoral systems (2010), stress at work (2010), family policies (two, both 2010), climate change (2011) and heritage (2011) (see http://www.britac.ac.uk/policy/policy-centre-reports. cfm). The ESRC has produced a video it calls *Celebrating the Social Sciences* with eight cases 'where research made a difference', with an accompanying booklet with another 11 cases (see http://www.esrc.ac.uk/publications/multimedia/ index.aspx), ranging, it says 'from military operations in Afghanistan and changing prison practices to reducing firesetting of grasslands and helping young people become more resilient'. The video was launched in November 2011 at a special event attended by the Universities Minister, David Willetts, who spoke in praise of the social sciences and the ESRC (details of his speech will be addressed in the next chapter but it is carried on his personal web blog at http://blogs.bis.gov.uk/blog/2011/11/08/celebrating-the-value-and-relevance-of-the-social-sciences/). Countries which have had impact assessments as part of research grant allocation for a long time, such as The Netherlands, report positive experiences (see Benneworth 2011). Even strident critics of the impact agenda recognize that it is easy for the social sciences to demonstrate their value in this general sense (for example, Collins 2011).

These are issues I will be coming back to, but it is worthwhile noting that in these terms the social sciences can be the most impactful of the three cultures in this general sense, but this is sometimes lost on social scientists themselves when they focus narrowly on combating the technical meaning of impact. However, the two meanings get confused and wrapped up with one another: to the point where I will suggest later that impact as 'value-for-society' is so contaminated by the technical meaning of impact (where it is 'value-for-money'), that we should move the discourse on to more consensual ground and refer to public value more generally.

In order to illustrate the confusion in the meanings of impact, it is useful to return to the ESRC benchmarking reports.[21] To do so will appear ironic since the ESRC is one of the main mediums by which the technical meaning of impact is being imposed. The international assessment panels oscillated between general and technical meanings when commenting on the impact of the social science subjects they were assessing. 'UK psychology research', its report noted, 'has a considerable impact on policy and practice'. The economics report stated that 'economic research in the UK is very influential outside academia and has a large impact on policy. This is a major achievement that results from the high-quality of applied work and the healthy relationship between researchers and policymakers'. Other reports, however, while noting policy impacts, moved well beyond the technical meaning. 'Social Anthropology', its panel wrote, 'has had a signal effect in development policy and practice within the UK and beyond, and Social Anthropologists have become key figures in human rights, asylum and other justice-related work. When viewed from our external perspective, UK Social Anthropology seems considerably more recognized in terms of policy consultations, "cultural" briefings and expert testimony'. The politics and international studies panel 'found considerable evidence of engagement with end-users in the policy community. We found even more evidence of knowledge transfer. If academic research is thought of as a kind of cultural formation, Politics and International Studies contributes greatly to social, cultural and intellectual capital throughout the wider UK community'. Clearly, even the ESRC is incapable of making the technical meaning of impact hegemonic and the broader meaning keeps breaking through to cloud the impact debate. The contest over meaning is part of the current impact war. The key question, therefore, is whose meaning counts? I take up this question in the next chapter.

Conclusion

In its national context, the scale of British social science rivals the natural sciences and humanities; it might be the interloping third culture but, if I could use an analogy from the Holy Trinity, the scale of the social sciences

---

[21] Found at http://www.esrc.ac.uk/funding-and-guidance/tools-and-resources/impact-evaluation/international-benchmarking.aspx, consulted on 31 October 2011. It is noticeable that the sociology panel was the only one that did not comment on impact in its executive summary.

in Britain now makes it equivalent to the other two, more three-in-one than one of three. Internationally, however, it is smaller scale. But what is small in number is large in general impact. The international excellence of British social science makes substantial parts of it truly world class, second only to the United States in international quality (this is the judgement also of the Commission on the Social Sciences 2003: 67). British society had a large effect on the growth and development of this international excellence in the past. What is distinctive about social science in contemporary Britain is the critical mass of its excellence. The great figure syndrome causes many to lament the demise of the goliaths of the past, but this disguises the way in which their reputations were socially constructed by time and scale, and this complaint seriously under-enumerates the critical mass of internationally excellent work done by social scientists in Britain today. However, it is the very *quality* of social science in Britain that is the issue at stake. International excellence puts into particularly high relief the widespread anxiety among social scientists that they are being threatened – that the government is potentially destroying the wisdom of the wise.

3

What is the Threat Faced by the Social Sciences?

Introduction

In this chapter, I will outline current higher education policies and practices on public universities, the audit culture and impact in Britain. These have the potential to drive British universities and the social sciences into the ground and risk destroying the very quality that is their hallmark. Feelings of threat felt by social scientists are high. The high stakes involved in this debate, however, have raised its temperature, preventing us from seeing that the contemporary landscape for social science is very uneven. Policy-related economics in particular is thriving under the impact agenda and large parts of politics – such as security studies and the study of terrorism – prosper under current events. Health studies, sports social science, psychological well-being research, human rights law, medical sociology and educational and birth cohort studies are just a few of the social science fields responding well to current challenges. Public law, international law and environmental law are also flourishing.

It is also necessary to point out that the social sciences are not under direct attack as they were in the 1980s. Social science is affected by the assault on public universities and the onward march of marketization in higher education, but, it is reasonable to claim, no more or less than other subject areas, although there is a largely unsubstantiated feeling among some social scientists that the income they generate is used in their university's internal funding procedures to support science and medicine departments with large deficits (a point made in Commission on the Social Sciences 2003: 108). However, the growth of the audit culture is not directly aimed at social science. There appears equal misery across intellectual arenas, not disproportionate harm for social science.[1]

Indeed, the difficulties Britain has in attracting high-quality university staff because of low salaries and the oppressiveness of the audit culture are more acute in the natural sciences, where the inability to attract high-quality scientists from overseas is matched by the loss of top British scientists to better funded science facilities abroad. Among the social sciences, only economics is badly affected by this process. As we saw in the last chapter, on some measures of regulation and public accountability in the audit culture, the social sciences have been able to demonstrate how very good they are. And general impact – what I call value-for-society – seems especially suited for social science. Social science has, thus, had resounding praise from the Minister for Science and the Universities. David Willetts not only placed social science as central to the future issues facing humankind, he specifically mentions its world class quality (see **Vignette 3**).

The view that social science is *not* under threat, however, warrants close interrogation. Looked at closely, Willetts's endorsement is less ringing than it sounds, for it casts social science's usefulness in a particular utilitarian way. Of course, the tendency to cast the usefulness of social science in utilitarian terms for its contribution to dealing with government policy questions is a fault of all governments. It was also David Blunkett's view, for example, when he was Secretary of State for Education. Speaking at the Annual Conference of the ESRC in 2000, he said: 'social science should be at the heart of policy making. We need a revolution in relations between government and the social research community – we need social scientists to help determine what works and why, and what type of policy initiatives is likely to be the most effective. And we need better ways of ensuring that those who need such information can get it quickly and easily' (quoted in Commission on the Social Sciences 2003: 70). However, such utilitarianism, while distorting government perceptions of social science throughout time, though worrisome, is not particularly threatening. The threat, in fact, lies elsewhere than in social science.

---

[1] STEM subjects (science, technology, engineering and medicine) and languages have not lost all their block grant – money from the public exchequer to fund student places – and while humanities and social sciences have from the 2012–13 academic year, STEM subjects feel greater pressure under the audit culture because of the threat which technical meanings of impact have for basic and curiosity-driven science. This highlights the unevenness of the current landscape.

Vignette 3 David Willetts on social science

Speech at the ESRC Festival of Social Science and the launch of the ESRC video *Celebrating Social Science,* November 2011, carried on his web blog at http://blogs.bis.gov.uk/blog/2011/11/08/celebrating-the-value-and-relevance-of-the-social-sciences/, 8 November 2011.

'Last Thursday I had the honour of speaking at the ESRC's flagship event celebrating the social sciences, held at the British Academy. This forms part of the ESRC's Festival of Social Science, now in its ninth year. The festival is a real celebration of the breadth of social science research, with well over 100 events around the country including major cities like London, Belfast, Edinburgh, Cardiff and Manchester. Social science is a global science, with enormous impact on how we live our lives worldwide. And the UK is a world player – ESRC's international benchmarking exercises have judged the UK to be second only to the US in anthropology, economics, political sciences, psychology and sociology. Social science shapes public policy and services, informs welfare reform and enhances civil liberties. This was effectively demonstrated at last Thursday's event with the launch of ESRC's 'Celebrating the Social Sciences' publication supported by an informative short film. It shows how beneficial our expertise in this area is to policymakers and the public alike. Some examples include: The ESRC-funded Centre for Microeconomic Analysis of Public Policy at the Institute for Fiscal Studies explained the shock to the public finances caused by the recession, informing Government officials, politicians on all sides and the media. A review carried out by the ESRC National Centre for Research Methods/Lancaster-Warwick-Stirling node led to a new policy report and a major revision of the scientific evidence underpinning DNA database policy. Data from the Millennium Cohort Study were used extensively by the Independent Review on Poverty and Life Chances, commissioned by the Government in 2010. The University of Bristol's review report emphasized that the first five years of a child's development life has the strongest impact on their life chances, strengthening the Government focus on 'Foundation Years' services. The £33.5 million investment announced earlier this year in a new Birth Cohort Facility project will take this important work even further. It will support the biggest longitudinal study ever undertaken in the UK – involving 90,000 children – as well as providing computing capacity to ensure we can analyze data from all the previous cohort studies. This will give us a broader and clearer picture than ever before of social mobility over the past 65 years. The studies are a shining example of the UK's support for the social sciences, and our expertise in interpreting research data. However looking ahead, the social science community also faces a series of challenges: The 'fruits' of social science: We need to get better at showing the relevance of our quality research – the ESRC's evidence briefings are an excellent example of this, such as the one on supermarket productivity and planning. Data-mining: We must look for ways to use more data from existing research – the Birth Cohort Facility will provide a great opportunity for this. Transparency: I very much welcome ESRC's continued commitment to work with Research Councils and others to meet the issues around open access facing the wider research community. Evidence-based policy: I want to see us build on social science's already excellent record of informing and shaping Government policy. We should recognize and celebrate the social sciences and the enormous contribution the UK makes to a global body of knowledge. The social sciences vastly improve our understanding of the world around us – our society, our economy, our quality of life and public health – and most importantly they help us improve the outcomes of people from all backgrounds and areas of society. Everything I heard at the Festival of Social Science suggested to me that even in the difficult financial climate we face today, the social sciences are thriving here in the UK.'

As we shall see in this chapter, what differentiates the contemporary period is the drive to marketization and regulation that shapes government relations with HEIs and the threat this poses to the Haldane Principle that protected academic freedom and autonomy in university research.[2] Publicly funded research agendas are under pressure to reflect government policy initiatives – not so much evidence-based policy, as John Holmwood (2011a: 4) puts it, but policy-based evidence. The audit culture impugns ancient practices of academic freedom and research autonomy that helped make British universities distinctive and world class. While this is a universal assault on higher education worldwide (Brown 2010; Burawoy 2011; Christensen and Eyring 2011), its British form, given the special history and quality of public higher education in Britain, makes this moment also one of threat to the very idea of the public university in the United Kingdom. Another feature of the current

---

[2]   There is debate about whether the Haldane Principle ever existed in higher education and, if so, what it really meant. Holmwood (2011c) strongly endorses it, while Edgerton (2009) describes it as an invented tradition. I follow Holmwood.

conjuncture, therefore, is that the principle of public university education has been fatally breached. Decades of hard-won rights and entitlements to public university education have been struck from British history with such vulgar haste that plans for what replaces it are so poorly formed that higher education policies appear to change almost on the hoof. Marketization portends the introduction of private-for-profit-providers to compete for the 'delivery' of higher education, receiving taxpayers' cash (in the form of up-front fee income from the government) without any obligation to provide public benefit.

Again, however, there is need for a caveat to this mood of threat. While public universities are being damaged in Britain beyond repair, it is primarily their status as *public institutions* that is grievously wounded; it is inevitable that they will be threatened as *places of learning* from all these changes, but it is not clear yet in what way or how badly. Social institutions are all capable of adjusting to gradual change. British universities have adapted to rapid change before – notably the building of the Robbins universities in the 1960s and the ending of the binary divide in the 1990s – and prospered as places of learning. It is not my purpose in this chapter, therefore, to speculate on the future of the universities as places of learning and whether or not they are capable anymore of serving their original purpose (this is considered by Christensen and Eyring 2011; Collini 2012; Docherty 2011).

Moreover, I am convinced that whatever threats they are under as public institutions can be turned also into opportunities. I suggest that this moment of degradation for British universities as public institutions simultaneously gives social science a chance to renew its vision for the twenty-first century and to restate its public value. I conclude this chapter by arguing that the new university requires a new form of public social science. The rest of the book will be devoted to elaborating this proposition.

I intend in the following sections to proceed in a jigsaw manner, building up a picture of the current conjuncture piece by piece. I begin with impact before moving on to marketization.

What is the impact of impact?

The vehement criticism social science directs against impact can easily be misconstrued to suggest it is seeking a licence to be unaccountable or worse still that it delights in being irrelevant. Onora O'Neill (2011: vii) spoke for every academic when supporting the case for the public value of the humanities by saying nobody does research except in the hope that it will at some point make a difference, although they are unlikely to think of this simply as a matter of economic benefit. I once wrote that impact is a sheep in wolf's clothing (Brewer 2011a, 2011b). This was a deeply unpopular view among my peers but it is one by which I stand. I mean by it that impact looks more hazardous than it really is, for HEFCE in particular has backtracked to adopt a very friendly form of it which does not require every person to demonstrate impact. I argued, nonetheless, that this sheep in wolf's clothing could well come to be ravaged by the ferocious farm dog (2011b: 256). This is what has happened. The real bite of impact comes from its placement as one part of the more dangerous problem of marketization.

I have argued elsewhere (Brewer 2011b) that impact is a terrain which people traverse from at least three diverse routes. First is the policy evaluation tradition, in which impact is unproblematic. The second is the philosophy and sociology of knowledge, where the social production of knowledge leads to matters around the impact of research, among other things. Mostly, however, people come to impact from the direction of the audit culture in higher education, where it is rejected as part of the audit culture itself. The suggestion that impact is a sheep in wolf's clothing is widely accepted within the policy evaluation tradition, which is bemused by all the fuss, while to critics of the audit culture such a metaphor naïvely underplays the dangers surrounding it.

The first and most basic problem is that there is no consensus over what impact means. Is it the outcomes of research (and are these its outputs?); is it 'user' engagement and dissemination, the benefits of the research, spin-off companies and technology transfers, or changes in behaviour and policy? All these have been suggested at one time or another and they have different connotations and meanings. Of course, paymasters have utilized their position to force impact in its narrow sense upon universities, and inasmuch as paymasters call the tune, one would expect technical meanings to dominate. Impact has been made part of the Research Excellence Framework (REF) on government insistence, endorsed by HEFCE, the chief organizer of the REF, and incorporated as part of the criteria for the award of research monies from the research funding councils, endorsed in the case of social science by both the ESRC and the AHRC, which funds some social science research.[3] Their definitions of impact thus merit exploration.

Research Councils United Kingdom (RCUK), the umbrella body for all the research councils, defines research impact as 'the demonstrable contribution that excellent research makes to society and the economy'.[4] The ESRC's website goes on to say:

> research impact embraces all the diverse ways that research-related skills benefit individuals, organisations and nations. These include: fostering global economic performance, and specifically the economic competitiveness of the United Kingdom; increasing the effectiveness of public services and policy; enhancing quality of life, health and creative output. A key aspect of this definition of research impact is that impact must be demonstrable. It is not enough just to focus on activities and outputs that promote research impact, such as staging a conference or publishing a report. You must be able to provide evidence of research impact, for example, that it has been taken up and used by policy makers, and practitioners, has led to improvements in services or business.

This economic and policy focus is reinforced by the domains in which impact can be experienced. The ESRC's website continues thus:

> This can involve academic impact, economic and societal impact or both: Academic impact is the demonstrable contribution that excellent social and economic research makes to scientific advances, across and within disciplines, including significant advances in understanding, method, theory and application. Economic and societal impact is the demonstrable contribution that excellent social and economic research makes to society and the economy, of benefit to individuals, organisations and nations.

'The impact of social science research can be categorised', it argues, into three types: 'instrumental: influencing the development of policy, practice or service provision, shaping legislation, altering behavior; conceptual: contributing to the understanding of policy issues, reframing debates; capacity building: through technical and personal skill development'. In order to compete for public

---

[3] Research funded by the European Union (EU), a significant source, is required to show impact for Europe and the EU but this is not the same understanding of impact as in RCUK. As I point out below, the European Research Council rejects the impact agenda.

[4] Taken from the ESRC website at http://www.esrc.ac.uk/funding-and-guidance/tools-and-resources/ impact-toolkit/what-how-and-why/what-is-research-impact.aspx, consulted on 11 November 2011.

research monies, therefore, applicants are required to specify their 'pathway to impact'. That is: 'identify your key stakeholders, for example, other researchers; public sector; business/industry; identify how they will benefit from your research – types of impact might include: improving social welfare/public services; influencing public policy; contributing to operational/organisational change; identify how you will ensure they have the opportunity to benefit, for example through organising public events; conferences; interaction with the media'.

The definition pursued in the REF is different in crucial respects. HEFCE's website says the following about impact:[5]

> For the purposes of the REF, impact is defined as an effect on, change or benefit to the economy, society, culture, public policy or services, health, the environment or quality of life, beyond academia. Impact includes, but is not limited to, an effect on, change or benefit to: the activity, attitude, awareness, behaviour, capacity, opportunity, performance, policy, practice, process or understanding of an audience, beneficiary, community, constituency, organisation or individuals, in any geographic location whether locally, regionally, nationally or internationally. Impact includes the reduction or prevention of harm, risk, cost or other negative effects. For the purposes of the impact element of the REF: impacts on research or the advancement of academic knowledge within the higher education sector (whether in the UK or internationally) are excluded. Impacts on students, teaching or other activities within the submitting HEI are excluded.

This is a suitably broad notion of impact, although it notably excludes impact within academia; it is public impact outside their own domain that is treated as the main measure of academics' impact. Nor is there the same lionization of economic and policy impacts as with the research councils. The case study approach utilized by HEFCE in the REF means that not every person returned will need to demonstrate impact. This more liberal approach is in part because HEFCE had a more thorough consultation exercise with the academic community in setting its policies than did the research councils and was more influenced by the voices raised against impact: and rightly so.[6] After all, the

---

[5] See *Assessment Framework and Guidance of Submissions*, Ref 02.2011, July 2011, at HEFCE's website http://www.hefce.ac.uk/research/ref/pubs/2011/02_11/, consulted on 11 November 2011.

[6] Smith et al. (2011) undertook content analysis of the responses in the second consultation and noted people's primary objection was the threat to autonomy implied by the impact agenda.

REF affects everyone, while applications to the research councils have such a low hit rate that applying is now a minority activity leaving most unaffected by RCUK policy (applications will be further constrained by demand policies designed by the research councils to discourage perpetual failures from further attempts). In 2010–11, the ESRC had the lowest hit rate of all research councils at 16 per cent, having dropped further from the year before (although there is no evidence this drop is related to impact assessment). This explains the seemingly unfair paradox that most people's ire is directed towards HEFCE's imposition of impact while the most pernicious policies on impact are pursued by the research councils.

The difference between these definitions of impact is worth reinforcing. Research councils have a very narrow notion of impact. The ESRC, for example, restricts it to value-for-money in the economy and society as measured by its benefits for economic performance, competiveness, policy debates and services, the AHRC to 'economic and social benefits' (see http://www.ahrc.ac.uk/fundedresearch/pages/impactassessment.aspx). RCUK accepts, however, that these impacts can be felt by other academics inside the academy. The REF operates with a broader understanding of the definition of impact, where it is value-for-society, which perforce restricts its display to the public arena outside the academy. In other words, the definitions of impact alive within the audit culture set up an unfortunate choice. Value-for-society, in all other respects a good thing, cuts academics off from domains in which they feel more comfortable – impact on peers, students and to intellectual culture. The impact debate, therefore, makes public value problematic for its effects in minimizing the contribution to knowledge. Knowledge itself is not rendered valuable in its own right, only for what it serves either to value-for-money or value-for-society. Impact, therefore, creates an unfortunate antinomy with public value. While some definitions of impact are, thus, open and inclusive, even these are problematic by setting up resistance to the language of public value. Impact, in short, is counterproductive for debate about public value in higher education. This is a point to which I return in the next chapter when suggesting we need to shift language code away from impact towards public value.

Besides clarifying its meaning, we also need to ask impact from whose perspective? Impact can be approached from the viewpoint of stakeholders, funders, the investigators, the respondents, government policy objectives and on *ad infinitum*. 'Users' are in one sense everyone and thus in another sense no one; they need specification to be meaningful. 'Benefit' is a value judgement and varies according to normative evaluations from a particular standpoint, whereas 'outcomes' are measurable if understood, for example, in terms of outputs like publications. 'Outputs', however, are often the weakest meaning of impact. What matters, paradoxically, is that broad definitions of impact are permissible in order to be inclusive, while narrower meanings should be clarified in specific instances where they are appropriate. Inclusivity of meaning not exclusivity is essential.

The areas in which impact can be displayed are equally broad and diverse, such as policy formation and practice, civil society, the economy, knowledge transfer, heritage and the cultural industry, mass media and so on. Some of these domains are more highly valued than others by those driving the impact agenda, and more relevant to some kinds of social science research than others. Some can be local, others national and transnational. Whatever impact means, however, it is important to accept that it can be displayed in as broad a space as possible, so that no domain is privileged above another. This is crucial in order to avoid the accusation that utilitarian notions of impact are its only prized forms, and that the economy or policy domains the only spaces that matter.

The indicators of impact differ with its meaning and domains. Metrics, such as in the form of citations of published work, objectify the indicators of impact and are favoured in areas of social science which are article-based rather than book-led – since books are often neglected in citation indexes – and where citations of each other's work in small subfields is commonplace. But metrics are no more or less important than local and national press coverage. 'User' engagement and dissemination, policy change, behaviour change and contributions to the local economy are no more significant than, say, contributions to public debate, civil society discourse and NGO and voluntary group thinking. Impact is indexed as much by the take-up of research by other researchers, by teachers, by lay members of the civil sphere and what we might call an 'educated citizenry'. If this makes impact difficult to measure, it is because this complexity is the very nature of the process of impact. It is very important to the sheep-like character of impact that its evaluation is not restricted only to that which can be measured easily. To recycle the phrase with which I have become associated (see Donovan 2011: 176), counting the countable because the countable can be easily counted renders impact illegitimate (first used in Brewer 2011b: 256).

This last point emphasizes that the problems with impact extend well beyond definitional matters. It is not 'owned' by the academy but seen as imposed from outside, thereby challenging ideas of academic autonomy. The fact that it is possible to easily show impact in its general sense does nothing to endear the impact agenda to social scientists who feel no ownership of it. The *language* of impact is a novel imposition even if the *practice* of impact (under different names like 'engagement', 'participation' and 'action research') is routine for social scientists. And impact in its technical sense risks valorizing certain sorts of research where impact is easier to demonstrate, thereby distorting the meaning of impact to things most obvious (like policy, knowledge transfer, contributions to economic enterprise and spin-off companies), shaping the nature of research activity into areas where impact is easier to claim and defend. This has the effect, as Holmwood (2011c: 14–5) noted, of reproducing policy-oriented, technocratic knowledge by large interdisciplinary teams much beloved by politicians, policy makers and civil servants.[7] The contribution of this sort of research is the very benefit David Willetts refers to in his praise of social science, quoted in Vignette 3.

The worst offenders in this respect are the research councils, where applicants are required to speculate on possible impacts sometime in the distant future for a variety of potential users who may find the research beneficial in potential ways. It is not just that this is a new requirement and faces the resistance every fresh procedure provokes, it is meaningless. These impacts may be anticipated now but they can never be predicted; they are even uncertain at the time. The connection between an input (research money) and an output (research findings) is opaque enough to make the assertion that there has been a specific impact (no matter how measured) pretty unreliable, but this is even more untrustworthy when projected forward rather than

---

[7] This is commonly called Mode 2 Knowledge and is associated particularly with analyses from science studies by Nowotny and colleagues (see Nowotny et al. 2001). Mode 2 Knowledge contrasts with Mode 1, created within disciplinary boundaries often under the lone researcher model, which is more conceptual, theoretical and oriented to the disciplinary core. This contrast is much favoured by the sociologist John Holmwood (for example, Holmwood 2011c) and featured greatly in the ESRC benchmarking review of sociology led by Nowotny, which Holmwood co-organized (for details of the Report see the ESRC website at http://www.esrc.ac.uk/_images/Int_benchmarking_ sociology_tcm8-4556.pdf). As President of the European Research Council Nowotny, speaking in March 2012 at the fifth anniversary meeting of the Council's foundation, has said it will not countenance the adoption of an impact agenda.

assessed retrospectively. Impact varies over time and can change, positively or negatively, at the one-point snapshot whenever it is measured. Impact is, thus, conditional, even serendipitous.

We also have the problems of negative and disguised impact which distort this causal chain. Negative impact can be described as research which is rejected, not because it is wrong but for its counter-intuitiveness or its opposition to current policy, government objectives and the like. Social science research is more likely to be sensitive and the politics of social science research increases the prospect of negative impact. Disguised impact arises when research impacts are hidden and unrecognized. This may in part be a failure of researchers to declare or be aware of it, but mostly it is the consequence of policy makers, the press, civil society and the rest being ignorant of it. Benefits have to be recognized as such if research is to have impact, but this does not mean that disguised impact is non-beneficial; its benefits have not yet been valued. The black hole that exists between research and its take up increases the prospect of disguised impact. None of these concerns have yet been resolved.

The heckles of practitioners which are raised at the language of impact used by the research councils, increases many fold when coupled with the research councils' deployment of government research priorities to shape their own research agendas. The furore vented on the AHRC in early 2011 when it was thought that its delivery plan was too close to the Conservative Party's idea of the Big Society makes this point. This blurring of lines augurs the infringement of academic freedom, impinges on academics' autonomy and introduces the prospect of government interference in the independence of research activity. That the research councils should have national priorities for research paid for out of the public exchequer is reasonable, but to frame these priorities using the language of party politics exposes the research councils to criticism on grounds that they are toadying to the paymaster. The ESRC was more astute that the AHRC in the language employed in its delivery plan. Its current 'strategic research priorities' are economic performance and sustainable growth, influencing behaviour and informing interventions, and a vibrant and fair society. These are general enough and encompass large swathes of the social sciences. But they are outworked in particular funding initiatives that can be more narrowly conceived. The 'Big Society' is an ideological project and it is hard to defend the autonomy of the research councils when notions very much like it, such as 'connected communities', become research initiatives within them.[8] As King (2011: 76) reminds us, there has always been publicly funded policy-related social research supported by the ESRC, but the current phase in research council funding, he argues, is distinguished by the adoption of narrower utilitarian notions of research linked to broad research themes that are in tandem with government priorities. This suggests that the long-established Haldane Principle – which, with respect to the universities, means governments should leave individual decisions about fundable projects to academics – while not compromised, since clearly ministers and civil servants do not sit on the committees that award them, risks appearing so (see Holmwood 2011c).

The bigger problem with impact, however, is still measurement. If academics have to live with the impact agenda because they have no choice, we at least ought to be able to measure it. It seems that it is the problem of measurement which has driven policy. Measurement concerns forced HEFCE to apply a wide definition of impact in order to catch as many indices of it as possible; and measurement problems made the research councils take the prospective view of speculating on long-distant impacts in order to avoid having to measure it at all. Measurement problems are not insurmountable. In particular, small subfields where citations of each other's work is common incestuous practice, like the policy evaluation tradition or social studies of science, or larger social science fields that work in an article rather than a book culture, value metrics immensely as a measurement tool, while others to whom it is relevant, favour patents, spin-off companies and other technology transfers or policy impacts. The adoption in the policy evaluation tradition of measurement techniques from health economics, like the Payback Framework, is feasible elsewhere in social science (see Donovan 2011: 176).[9] This explains why economics and

---

[8] It is worth noting that the 'connected communities' initiative was launched by the New Labour Government and predates David Cameron's discovery of the 'Big Society', although this does not excuse the AHRC in seeking to link the two. For further details, see RCUK *Annual Delivery Plan Report 2008–09*, page 4, accessible at http://www.rcuk.ac.uk/documents/publications/anndeliveryplanrep2008-09.pdf.

[9] The Payback Framework is briefly summarized by Donovan and Hanney (2011). It is descriptive rather than analytic, involving breaking the research process into phases, assessing its 'payback' on the way and ending up evaluating its 'health and economic benefits'. It works in health economics because there are clearer indicators of what these benefits are. Its applicability to other areas of social science, currently being championed by its founders at the Health Economics Research Group at Brunel University, is the question which the Donovan (2011) special issue of *Research Evaluation* was partly designed to test. It came to no strong conclusion. The payback framework was used by RAND Europe when, in collaboration with the AHRC and the University of Cambridge, it prepared a report *Assessing the Impact of Arts and Humanities Research at the University of Cambridge* (http://www.rand.org/content/dam/rand/pubs/technical-report/2010/RAND-TR816.pdf), evidence for which was accumulated from peer review interviews, self-reports and interviews with external informants.

the policy-oriented social sciences, familiar with research evaluation methods, have less hostile views on measurement. But even the strongest advocates of the Payback Framework in health economics point to recurring problems around the time lag between input and impact and of attributing ownership to it (Donovan 2011: 178).

SIAMPI (Social Impact Assessment Methods) is another measurement method. It focuses on 'productive relations between researchers and stake-holders', and has been deployed to evaluate some ESRC-funded research (see Molas-Gallart and Tang 2011). But it utilizes a definition of impact far more general than the technical meaning and still has untold concerns in attributing the causal chain of impact. The SIAMPI approach for example, defines impact as 'socially valuable outcomes' (Donovan 2011: 177), and restricts its assessment only to the perspective of stakeholders. 'Productive relations' is also circular in its effects, for unproductive relations presumably rule out impact or restrict it to negative impact. While it is not impossible to employ assessment regimes like this, Martin (2011: 251) makes the astute point that rolling them out to the REF would be so labour intensive and require such expertise that the costs of measuring impact would outweigh the benefits of doing so.

It remains a conundrum, therefore, why something as opaque, diffuse and immeasurable as impact (in its technical sense) should have such prominence in the audit culture. The answer, of course, is its centrality to the imposition of business-led models in social research as part of the marketization of public universities. A value-for-money approach to impact is part and parcel of the market. It is to this element of the current conjuncture that I now turn.

The march of the market

Marketization is captured neatly in four 'C's' – choice, cost, competition and commodification. To understand the link between this powerful alliteration it is necessary to appreciate that marketization is simultaneously both means and end. It is the *means* to effect choice – to compel public bodies to respond to people's demands – but it is simultaneously the *goal*, the preferred way to drive down the costs of the state in meeting them. Markets are presented as mechanisms to respond to people's desire for greater choice, but they involve artificially creating competition as the way to meet them cost effectively. The rhetoric of choice cleverly disguises the introduction of competition. The consequence of competition is commodification: the rendering of all things into objects, products bought and sold on markets, making them subject to the operation of supply and demand. It is one thing to reduce the manufacture of cream crackers to the four 'C's, quite another university education, health care and other public services.[10]

The form of marketization we have in Britain, however, is not based on free market principles, like the opening up of competition, the introduction of deregulation policies, the need to set prices to determine the cost of things and the protection of the rights of consumers. In the context of Britain's neoliberalism, marketization means something significantly different.

Neoliberalism emerged in the 1980s as a radical restatement of classical liberalism and is marked by its strange combination of libertarianism and conservatism, and free market ideology and state regulation. This is a very heady mix. On the one hand it involves rejection of 'Big Government' and a strong central state while advocating state regulation, including regulation of the free market. It advocates the rights of individuals against society and the state while invoking conservative notions about civic engagement, local communities and active citizenship. Neoliberalism, thus, is not simply the free market and the strong state, to use the title of Gamble's analysis of Thatcherite neoliberalism (Gamble 1988), nor is it just about introducing a certain set of economic principles. At one and the same time, neoliberalism is an economic project to promote market capitalism, a political project to roll back the state, a policy project to increase government regulation and a civil project to promote free individuals whose 'self help' mentality turns from self-interestedness into civic engagement (which in Britain is called the 'Big Society' but which means in practice the exact opposite, the 'little society' of small communities

---

[10] Evidence from the British Social Attitude survey (see Curtice and Heath 2009), for example, indicates that the rhetoric of choice is favourably received by the public, who favour consultation and the exercise of their own decision-making in services like education, health and social care, but this declines dramatically when linked to competition and the introduction of private providers. The ethos of public provision is popular and undercuts support for choice. Competition and commodification are unpopular partners in the alliteration.

and tight-knit neighbourhoods of independent people aware of their civic responsibilities).[11]

The Thatcher governments in Britain in the 1980s that first introduced neoliberalism used to refer to their policies as a return to 'Victorian values' (on which see Samuel 1992). This was done in part to reduce the sense of radical discontinuity with the past that neoliberalism provoked to the way Britain had conducted politics, social life and economic policy during the twentieth century. But it was invoked also to suggest theirs was a moral crusade rather than a utilitarian one; that neoliberalism was about the return to virtue and was not crudely economic. 'Victorian values' ennobled a political and economic ideology by turning it cultural. Nothing could be more guaranteed to provoke social scientists.

Social scientists were among the chief analysts of neoliberalism (for critique from within cultural geography see Harvey 2005; economics see Dumenil and Levy 2010; law see Bell 2011; linguistics see Chomsky 1999; race theory see Goldberg 2008; sociology see Crouch 2011). Two factors explain this. First, social science became a chief target of criticism from neoliberalism, for not being a 'science' and for its objectification of society above the individual: who can forget the suggestion of Britain's first neoliberal prime minister, Margaret Thatcher, that there is no such thing as society only individuals and families?[12] This attack led to a stream of social science analysis in response. Secondly, neoliberalism competed with social science for some of the same intellectual ground, and its widely different take on these shared issues – family and marriage, crime, education and educational attainment, the decline of communities, unemployment, women's rights, trade union rights, macroeconomic policy,

[11] In a philosophical outline of the 'Big Society' by the Conservative MP Jesse Norman (2010), former member of the pro-Conservative Party Policy Exchange think tank, an eclectic set of ideas are drawn on from classic liberalism and the philosophy of Michael Oakeshott, among others. In Adam Smith, for example, self-interest is portrayed as necessarily virtuous and encourages social co-operation, while for Bernard Mandeville 'private vices' become 'public benefits' through their encouragement to economic progress. In this classic liberal view, philanthropy and civil society are not incompatible with self-interest. For Oakshott civil society is based on ties like friendship, affection and sentiment which are often distorted by social institutions. For these ties to flourish, therefore, civil society requires minimal regulation and interference from the state. The Big Society is against 'Big Government', portrayed as Labour state centralism, as well as rampant economic liberalism.

[12] Strictly speaking, Thatcher did not actually say there is no such thing as society, although what she did say meant much the same thing. Her actual words were as follows: '[W]ho is society? There is no such thing! There are individual men and women and there are families and no government can do anything except through people and people look to themselves first'. This comment appeared in an interview with the magazine *Women's Own* and can be accessed at http://www.margaretthatcher.org/document/106689.

policing, public order, health provision, social care and the like – promoted vigorous social science engagement with it. This fierce rebuttal only intensified the irritation neoliberal governments felt towards the social sciences.

During the period of the inception of neoliberalism in Britain, therefore, before the Conservative election victory in 1979, social science was in people's sights, and shots were fired (although not all of them by neoliberals). The Social Science Research Council was forced to change its name, right-of-centre think tanks were established purposely to provide the 'proper' sort of social science information and analysis (such as the Institute for Economic Affairs and its off-shoot the Social Affairs Unit, and the Institute for the Study of Conflict), and a select few social scientists wrote highly publicized reports complaining of the takeover of British social science by a variation of lefties and lunatics – the report by the sociologist Julius Gould, *The Attack on Higher Education*, being the best example (for a sociologist reflecting back on this report see Platt 2003: 118–22). The 'Black Papers', so named to contrast with government white papers, attacked progressive education theories and the social science evidence on which they were based.[13] And, as King (2011: 82) notes, there was a general scepticism about social science among government ministers, especially Sir Keith Joseph, for a time minister for education (and it is worth recalling that Mrs Thatcher had been education minister in Heath's Conservative cabinet in the early 1970s). While the university cuts introduced in the 1980s did not single social science out – and the 1982 Rothschild Report recommended the continuance of a research council for the social sciences (on which see King 2011: 83) – it was nonetheless a cold climate for social science.

Thirty years on and marketization proceeds apace.[14] But if social science was once its special target, this is no longer the case. It is universities as public

---

[13] It is important to reiterate that some of these developments predate the 1979 election victory of Mrs Thatcher but assisted in shaping the climate in which social science could later to be attacked. The Institute of Economic Affairs, for example, was founded in 1957, Gould's report dates from 1977, the Black Papers between 1969 and 1977 and the Institute for the Study of Conflict from 1970 (it folded in 1989). Some of the latter's leading figures had connections with the CIA and British and German intelligence services. The fact that it was leading social scientists orchestrating these (and later) attacks – Julius Gould, Leonard Schapiro, Digby Anderson, David Martin, David Marsland, Edward Shils, Caroline Cox, Charles Cox – reinforced the suspicions of the Conservative government about the social sciences. Caroline Cox was given a life peerage under the Thatcher government (Platt 2003: 123 n14).

[14] This volume does not purport to provide a history of higher education policy in the years following the demise of Mrs Thatcher, and it serves the narrative if we leap over the intervening years to connect Mrs Thatcher's policies and those of the Coalition government. Where relevant in the text I distinguish between, or point to continuities with, the higher education policies of the Blair and Cameron governments.

institutions as a whole which bear this burden now. The application of market principles to universities has provoked a torrent. This has two causes. It reflects in part the relative protection of universities in the past from the vagaries of open market competition (making them almost nationalized, the last institution in public ownership, save the National Health Service, which now too is not immune to marketization). There is also extreme doubt among academics that market principles can be reasonably applied to education and that university degrees can be purchased like cream crackers off the supermarket shelf.

A brief digression is necessary at this point. Cuts in university budgets are not the same thing as marketization. The number of university degree courses across the sector is being cut (down by 12 per cent in 2012 alone according to the Universities and Colleges Admissions Service),[15] and staffing levels are being reduced in some subjects and some universities (mostly on an *ad hoc* basis since this is more through voluntary severance schemes than redundancy). However, the concern people properly have with 'cuts' misplaces their attention, for the word does not adequately describe the current problem. Higher education has taken its share of across-the-board reductions in public expenditure, but as Steve Smith, the former Chair of Universities UK (UUK), argues, higher education cuts were not as bad as UUK feared and government funding of higher education continues (2011: 133). He writes: 'The government expects to be spending around £6.5 billion in tuition loans, £3.5 billion in maintenance loans and £2 billion in maintenance grants and scholarships on top of the remaining teaching grant in 2014–15. The balance in funding between teaching grant and loans is currently about two-thirds to one-third. By 2014–15, the balance is expected to be around 80/20 loans to teaching grant' (Smith 2011: 135). Smith estimated that with an average annual fee income of £7,500 per student, the sector will be getting an *extra*

---

[15] A report by the University and College Union (UCA 2012: 3), entitled *Choice Cuts: How Choice has Declined in Higher Education*, published in February 2012, estimated that provision of full-time undergraduate degree courses fell by 27 per cent between 2006 and 2012, but this varied by region and subject matter. England witnessed the largest fall at 31 per cent, Scotland the least at 3 per cent. In subject matter, the report recorded only the patterns for single subject degrees, which in practice is as much an index of the growth of joint degrees as decline in overall provision. There was an overall reduction of 14 per cent in the number of single subject degree courses in the same period. That for social science was the smallest loss at 12.8 per cent, compared with 14.6 per cent for STEM subjects and 14 per cent for arts and humanities (UCA 2012: 5). Courses in human geography and sociology in England were the hardest hit social science single subject degrees, the former likely to be the result of overall decline in provision, the latter simply the growth of joint honours courses with sociology as a partner.

£10 million by 2014–15. This was 'good news' he said (2011: 136). 'Good news' is worth spreading and he further estimated (2011: 137) that subject bands C and D, covering the humanities and social sciences, which from 2012–13 are no longer to receive public money from the government, will have an *increase* of 16 per cent and 41 per cent, respectively, on 2010–11 figures once student fee income replaces block grant (this assumes fees at £9,000 but takes into account monies required to be set aside for bursaries and the like). He makes his point well: this is not the commonly held view. But he also misses the point. Marketization is different from cuts.

The marketization in higher education means two things: the introduction of an artificial market within higher education so that it is run *as if* a free market; and the opening up of higher education to outside market forces to stimulate competition. We might call the one the introduction of an internal market, the other exposure to the external market. The two dimensions are closely related but they manifest themselves in different policies. They combine to cause the commodification of university education and with it the complete degradation of the public university. This involves a loss of public *function* for the universities rather than a loss of money.

The creation of an internal market within higher education is done in order to achieve market differentiation. In true markets, differentiation permits supply and demand to be allocated by market forces and for the true value of the goods to be assessed in order to permit judgements about their value-for-money, both to consumers, now and in the future, and for providers of the goods, in order to assess the efficiency and quality of their provision. This requires that the goods be priced so that suppliers can gauge the costs in producing them and consumers what it costs to acquire them. The marketization of universities, therefore, requires differentiation *within* individual universities, as units compete for resources and have their value-for-money assessed by their university managers in terms of efficiency in their use of resources and the quality of the product. It also requires differentiation *between* universities in the sector as a whole, as they compete with one another in the value of their respective goods and the efficiency and quality of their provision. Competition over price between universities is critical to the operation of a true market. This permits consumers (students, parents, careers teachers and, in this case, employers of students) to make informed judgements about the value to be gained from the goods on offer (which to students are, narrowly, the degrees and certificates earned and more broadly the 'educational experience', and to employers the value of the person with this product) from the various suppliers (the universities).

Market differentiation, therefore, requires dismantling a common – undifferentiated – university sector to introduce differential pricing. This gives the 'educational experience' and the degrees awarded different values in order to trigger supply and demand mechanisms that discriminate between the universities on price. Previous university funding formulae simply did not do this. The block grant for teaching was differentiated only by the costs of the provision across broad subject bands, not between the universities, so all universities received the same money per student within the relevant subject band. The varied academic reputation of universities introduced some differentiation within the sector but there was no market for the high-reputation universities to exploit this in terms of differential prices to their students. The introduction of top-up tuition fees by the Labour government in 1998 did not – nor was it intended – to introduce market differentiation. This has changed.

Distinguishing between Labour and Coalition government policies on marketization is necessary at this point. There were two stages to New Labour's policies. In the first stage, it introduced up-front fees, which were set at a standard level. It then replaced them with variable fees which were supposed to be repaid postgraduation. All institutions charged roughly the same fee, avoiding price competition. While Charles Clarke, the then Labour Education Secretary who introduced top-up fees, supported private investment in universities, he was careful not to privatize the function of universities. The Coalition government, however, has introduced market differentiation by price. The Coalition government's total abolition of the teaching block grant for humanities and social science subjects (bands C and D) with effect from 2012–13 and its replacement by variable fees (up to £9,000 per year) introduces market differentiation. Higher education remains free at the point of entry but the state-guaranteed loan system will require repayment above an income threshold recouped through income tax.[16] The high-reputation universities

---

[16] The income threshold is £21,000. Currently, it is £15,000. It is interesting to compare the cost of education to students in the United Kingdom with other European countries. In terms of the Euro, Britain's £9,000, translates as €10,360, while Germany it is €1,000, France €169, Spain between €9 and €16, Holland €1,627, Italy €850, Slovenia €30 and Denmark zero (quoted in the *Times Higher Education* 2 June 2011).

have favoured this policy because it allows them to charge a higher price for their 'product' in terms of higher fees – which means that they have colluded in the downfall of the public university system they helped to create – and the government has intervened in the market to dissuade universities from forming a cartel by charging the same fee. The so-called 'core and margin' policy has effected market differentiation when at one point it looked like most universities were opting for the £9,000 maximum. Universities were opened up to competition from cheaper providers in the Further Education Colleges and by November 2011, 20,000 student places were created especially for cut-price providers (half of which have been bid for by Further Education Colleges).[17] Economic incentives were also quickly devised to persuade universities to charge less than the maximum (by permitting them to bid for larger numbers of students), and giving elite ones unrestricted access to the best qualified 'A' level students with AAB grades. It has been mooted that this will apply to ABB students from 2013–14, which would mean that roughly one third of student places would fall outside the cap on numbers, increasing the competition between universities for the remaining numbers with the intention to encourage some to lower fees in order to improve their chances. Government interference in the market through its manipulation of a university's ability to bid for student numbers has, thus, created differentiation when variable fees looked as if they might not.

The abolition of the block grant is not about transferring the expense from the public exchequer to the consumer as a cost-cutting device in response to financial constraints, for as we have seen, the burden on the public purse is not eased: academic critics are right when they point out it has actually *increased* costs in the short to medium term. David Willetts (2012: 31) has admitted that higher fees more than compensate for the loss of the block grant. Variable fees are not about reducing government costs but achieving the marketization of higher education – the differentiation of the universities in terms of price, value and costs, so that the learning experience becomes a commodity subject to supply and demand rather than state planning. In short, fees are about neo-liberal ideology.

For market differentiation to work effectively, therefore, universities have to be exposed to performance indicators (such things as teaching quality

---

[17] In February 2012 the government announced that 9,547 of these places had been allocated to FE Colleges, distributed around 143 colleges out of the 167 who applied.

assessments, student satisfaction surveys, research assessment exercises, impact measurement polices, league tables, world rankings, Queen's Anniversary Prizes and the *Times Higher Education* Awards, which includes 'University of the Year') and be made subject to policies of selectivity and concentration (in terms of regulating access to research council funding, and receipt of quality research funding – known as QR – and postgraduate studentships).[18] This gives 'customers' the information to make judgements of the value they get from the different prices charged by the various universities. Quality judgements about universities such as these allocate the value attributed to the 'goods' they supply compared to the price they charge. Value-for-money calculations can, thus, be made, by consumers, suppliers and the government. In all these ways, the government readily offers the universities what education managers eagerly aspire to appropriate – market and product differentiation.

Product differentiation affects the 'goods' universities 'sell' as much as themselves as 'suppliers'. Business speak involves managers identifying the special 'learning attributes' of their degrees – the University of Aberdeen has defined the 'attributes of the Aberdeen graduate' (see http://www.abdn.ac.uk/graduateattributes) – the distinguishing features of their degree structure, their 'innovative courses' and what value-added the particular degree and the university's 'unique' 'learning experience' affords. Universities, thus, emphasize, among other things, their new libraries and the 24-hour library provision, the scale of their IT provision, new sports facilities, luxury accommodation and the attractiveness of the nightlife in the city. The so-called Melbourne Model of 'new generation courses', or as the University of Aberdeen calls them 'sixth-century courses', achieve product differentiation in order to strike a market niche by focusing on 'breadth' not narrow specialism. Product differentiation was once effected solely by quality; it is now sold to us on the market by business-led models of management.

The business-led models of management universities employ within their institution merely reinforce the value-for-money approach to higher education

---

[18] Postgraduate studentships awarded by the ESRC are concentrated in a few recognized Doctoral Training Centres. The Scottish government has announced that it will only provide funding for its studentships at the Scottish Doctoral Training Centre. The Russell Group Universities are expected to be the main beneficiaries of this concentration. This is a radical departure from the situation that pertained at the 2008 RAE when the then Labour government said it would fund QR in whatever pockets of excellence it was found. Concentration policies run against the tendency for research activity to be cross-institutional, even cross-national. Competition at the institutional level for resources permits partnerships only in limited circumstances.

that marketization seeks to enshrine in the sector as a whole. Business-led models of management show themselves in a number of ways. Education managers busy themselves with defining the role attributes of each staff grade, the aims and objectives of our courses and the performance measures by which staff are evaluated for their contribution to value and price. Education managers willingly impose market differentiation within every university structure as its 'units' are evaluated by their quality contributions, assessed in terms of their efficiency and costs, and rendered into value-for-money resource-allocation calculations that can now be closed down or cut for financial unsustainability. Academic criteria are made to seem secondary to financial ones: and so some universities close their bookshops – no longer viable under competition from Amazon – to be replaced in one case by a Kentucky Fried Chicken outlet[19] and others their postgraduate courses 'unless they address skills gaps in the economy'.[20]

Another manifestation of business-led university management is the deployment of the language of business to strike home their market differentiation. They seek 'market and product differentiation' by means of USPs ('unique selling points'), corporate branding, 'brand promises', 'strap lines',[21] mission statements, 'market attuned portfolios', 'value propositions' and logos as much as by scholarship – according to one management consultant who specializes in university corporate branding the purpose is to make universities 'sizzle tangibly' (see **Vignette 4**). Ben Page, chief executive of Ipsos Mori, the polling body, when speaking at a conference on educational services in February 2012, recommended universities adopt the branding strategies of supermarkets (in showing they are listening to students, like customers purchasing cream crackers off the shelves).[22] Jim Northover, from

---

[19] After the sudden closure of the bookshop in Sheffield Hallam University, a poll among students found that humanities and social science students supported the idea of universities having bookshops to assist people's studies, while science, technology and business studies students did not. It is not surprising that those who study within disciplines that work in book cultures should value bookshops; what is regretful is that their needs are secondary to financial concerns.

[20] The latter is a reference to London Metropolitan University, whose 2011 interim report on the review of postgraduate education and research, argued that in order to 'avoid further loss of market share', all postgraduate courses must in future have 'demonstrable demand from students, employers and other stakeholders, address skills gaps in the economy [and] demonstrate good employment and earnings outcomes' (quoted in The *Times Higher Education*, 15 December 2011, p. 11).

[21] Among the 'strap lines' devised by UK universities are 'celebrating 50 years of excellence', 'the achievement of excellence', 'we are exceptional', 'elite without being elitist', 'shaped by the past, creating the future', 'knowledge, innovation and enterprise', 'valuing excellence, sustaining investment', 'distinguish yourself', 'leading the way', 'go beyond original', 'a place of useful learning' and 'a place for possibilities'.

[22] Quoted in *Times Higher Education*, 8 March 2012, p. 12.

Vignette 4 Corporate branding in the university sector

BrandED Consultant Group, Denver Colorado (http://www.brandEDus.net), whose own 'strap line' is 'Branding from the Inside Out', specializes in assisting universities with their corporate branding needs. In a paper accessible on the web by Rex Whisman, Principal and Chief Strategist, entitled 'Internal Branding: A University's Most Valuable Intangible Asset' (http://www.brand channel.com/images/papers/460_Internal_ Branding_final.pdf) the company makes the case for universities to appropriate this market device. The paper begins thus:

'Universities today find themselves competing for students and support in a marketplace made increasingly complex by a convergence of factors. First, their target audience is bombarded by an assortment of marketing messages and consumer information—beginning with the ranking systems that identify the "best" schools and the "top" programs. The audience is also more brand-savvy than its counterparts from previous generations. In fact, students today openly affiliate with various consumer brands, whether Apple, Nokia, Urban Outfitters or Virgin. Any institution seeking to distinguish itself with this group needs to keep in mind that it is sensitive to authenticity and sophisticated about evaluating marketing messages. Making matters even more complex, demographic shifts are changing the marketplace in many regions of the world. In various European countries, for example, the population is aging, and even in the United States, where the children of baby boomers have been applying to colleges in record numbers, the pool of applicants is expected to begin shrinking this year. All this is happening just as many governments across the globe are reducing the resources devoted to higher education. In other words, the competition among universities is getting stiffer and stiffer. As a result, colleges and universities have learned that they must become more accountable to their constituents. They realize that, just like for-profit entities within the corporate world, they must develop sustainability strategies. Many have turned to branding as a solution. In fact, in the last years of the 20th century, branding became part of the higher education lexicon, and today, most colleges and universities around the world have embraced a brand strategy—logo redesigns, catchy taglines and trendy advertising campaigns—with high visibility and some tangible sizzle.'

the branding consultancy group Lloyd Northover, used the publication of the 2012 *Times Higher Education* World Reputation Rankings to self-servingly push for branding in the HE sector 'to separate the wheat from the chaff' (Northover 2012: 26).

The clamour from branding specialists to 'assist universities in product differentiation' is linked to marketization, for, as Northover writes, 'in a market context branding could make all the difference' (2012: 26). Temple (2011), in a recent summary of branding in universities, gave a less sanguine assessment, arguing that reputation was measured by academic excellence rather than branding work. He had no good word for branding consultants, whom he felt wasted universities' time and money. Market differentiation, however, persuades education mangers of the opposite: figures released to the *Times Higher Education* under a freedom of information request showed Lancaster University spent £135,000 on 'brand management' in 2010–11 and Bath Spa £80,256.[23]

The pressure to ensure quality performance across the various indicators has allowed education managers to turn universities into prisons of surveillance, with bursars their jailers. To distinguish this new kind of university, Ginsberg (2011) refers to what he calls the 'administrative university', where administrators turn universities into businesses, and where education managers are suspicious of academics for their resistance, do their utmost to dismantle academic autonomy and run universities to enhance their own pay, prestige and numbers. Those who resist become outmoded 'old style academics'. In my view, this identifies the wrong target. Administrators have grown in number but have become dominant only because they implement marketization rather than breeding ruthlessly for their own aggrandizement. Administrators are merely the warders, the prison system that affords them the authority is marketization.[24]

---

[23] Reported on 5 January 2012, p. 13. The clever sleight of hand in all this comes from the argument of education managers that universities' position in leagues tables is linked to branding and that league tables form rather than reflect reputation.

[24] Figures released by HESA for 2009–10 show that the total number of staff employed in universities fell by 2 per cent over the two previous years, with secretarial staff hardest hit with a 14 per cent drop. Academic staff fell by 1 per cent. In contrast, student welfare and human resources staff grew by 14 per cent and public relations and marketing staff by 5 per cent (*Times Higher Education*, 26 January 2012, p. 13). The longer the time period used in the comparison, the worse the effects. Comparisons between 2004–04 and 2009–10 show that the number of 'managers' rose by 40 per cent compared to 19.2 per cent for academic staff, with one manager for every nine academics compared to one in 11 in 2003–04 (*Times Higher Education*, 8 March 2012, p. 12).

The multilayered nature of performance accountability in modern universities results in a complex number of prison guards, with staff obliged to attend 'training' in writing 'pathways to impact' statements, submit to the regular round of research and teaching reviews, as well as to 'developmental-led' appraisal and end-of-year research development reviews, complete the endless paperwork reporting on their activities, and now inform managers of their whereabouts all year round, if not also to be on campus during specific hours of the day. Work allocation models count the countable in order that staff can be counted for their contribution, forgetting that some things worthy of recognition are just not able to be counted (and which thus go unrecognized).

The adoption of business-led nomenclature in universities has been profound. Registrars are now Chief Operating Officers and senior academics get 'knowledge transfer' and 'internationalization' added to their titles of office. Staff are required to 'push the envelope' and 'think outside the box', be 'outward facing', do 'blue skies thinking' and be 'game changing'. I have yet to hear a senior education manager refer to students as 'customers' or 'consumers' but the business leaders and industrialists nominated to university courts and senates frequently do. A study of the language of university mission statements by Sauntson and Morrish (2010) revealed that they employ a vocabulary of about 25 nouns, modified by 12 different adjectives, in which 'excellence', 'quality', 'impact', 'top', 'leading edge' and 'internationally significant' dominated, although they did note a rare mention of 'academic freedom' and 'intellectual'. But no one seems to defend anymore the idea propounded by Lord Robbins in his 1963 report on higher education that 'reflective enquiry' – 'thinking time' – is crucial to university life.

This language switching, however, is only symptomatic of a much wider cultural shift. Along with marketization has come the decline in manners in universities. I mean by this more than the outbreak of whinging that has emerged as levels of dissatisfaction rise; I suspect academics have always been a crabby crowd. My point is about a change in the discursive practices that mark university culture. The Royal Irish Academy calls its humanities and social science section 'polite literature and letters', which is reminiscent of an academic culture not only in which a subject matter was categorized quaintly but also when it once conducted its business in a particular discursive style.

Now that academic values have given way to those of the market, and business is their business, civility in universities has disappeared with them. Marketization has changed the symbols and culture of universities in many ways: and an ethnographic study of university culture still calls to be written (although Watson 2011 comes near). A minor novelist from the Forest of Dean, John Moore (1907–67), in his little known *The Waters Under the Earth*, published in 1965, that evokes village life in the area, used the decline of the red squirrel as a metaphor of the rapid industrialization of farming that dramatically changed the English countryside after World War II. The disappearance of the senior common room serves a similar purpose in modern universities.

No such room now exists, except in a few universities as a relic, let alone the culture of 'polite' discourse it symbolized. Even those staff for whom the fountain pen is still the only piece of technology needed to pursue their research now eat lunch at their desk, working behind closed doors, disillusioned at spending some of the time filling in the latest census demand from university managers. Technology has partly driven the loss of civil culture in university; so, too unionization, as the job has moved from a craft-like vocation to a trade in the minds of many practitioners – and with it the failure now of both academics-turned-managers and staff to see each other as peers. But marketization has been the main source of value change; manners have given way to the tyranny of the market.[25]

The introduction of an internal market by which universities can differentiate themselves to make supply and demand work is, however, only one part of marketization. Its second feature is exposing universities to the external market. This comes in two forms: private investment in universities and the emergence of for-profit universities. The former shows itself in universities having to become entrepreneurial in order to compete with other public bodies and charitable causes for money from sponsors, public companies and private benefactors, selling the rights to name chairs, research institutes, buildings, libraries and sometime soon perhaps even the name of the university itself

---

[25] There is fear among many academics that the commodification of university education will also lower standards (see Furedi 2012). Wherever customers are king and student evaluations become centrally important, spoon feeding, dumbing down and grade inflation can readily follow unless guarded against. Seymour Martin Lipset once referred to elections as the democratic translation of the class war. In similar fashion, the debate about declining standards is a proxy for anxiety over the negative effects of commodification in education.

in order that benefactors part with money as a supplement to meagre public resources.[26] It is notable always that entrepreneurial Vice Chancellors seek their legacy in new buildings rather than research capacity, libraries rather than people, because they seem more permanent. New buildings – appropriately named after the benefactor rather than an academic – do matter, but so do the researchers and teachers who occupy them.

Permit me a digression about Halifax Town Football Club. It has a wonderfully impressive football stadium indicative of former glory days – the era when they beat Manchester United, the then European Champions two goals to one – but the ability of the players declined and they not only went out of the Football League, they dropped out of the Conference League as well. They went bankrupt and were relegated to three divisions below. And now they play away to teams who change in sheds and use tin baths for post-match washes. There is no point in having excellent buildings if what the people do in them is not first class as well. Treating academics as if what they do is manufacture cream crackers is no way to nurture excellence. The moral of the story is that it is academics in the universities, not the business-led marketeers who manage the universities, who create excellence. Education managers, of course, naturally dispute such a view. Professor Rick Rylance of RCUK, writing in the *Independent* on 19 January 2012, in a pull-out section aimed at postgraduates, thought 'behind every breakthrough lies first-class infrastructure'. Call me naïve, but first-class minds have something to do with it as well.

Exposure to market competition from other providers, however, is perhaps the most dangerous element of the external market. This shows itself in two ways. First, some UK universities have set themselves up as alternative providers on the open market by establishing satellite campuses overseas with local partners in order to benefit from the market in international students.[27] In return, some private but not-for-profit universities from overseas have

---

[26] Some Oxbridge Colleges have changed their names to honour benefactors, such as Robinson College Cambridge and Kellogg and Green Colleges at Oxford, and the old Liverpool Polytechnic was rebranded as Liverpool John Moores University, although this was not as a result of sponsorship.

[27] Among them are Nottingham (in Malaysia and China), Middlesex (Dubai and Mauritius) and Newcastle (Malaysia). The Observatory on Borderless Higher Education has published reports on trends in overseas campuses since 2002. The most recent report found that there were 162 international branch campuses in September 2009, a 43 per cent increase in 3 years. Of these, 78 were American, 14 Australian, 13 British, 11 French and 11 Indian. There were also 14 closures of international branches in recent years. See *Times Higher Education* 3 February 2011 at http://www.timeshighereducation.co.uk/story.asp?storycode=415018.

campuses in the United Kingdom appealing to UK students. Amity Private University from India, for example, has six 'international' campuses, one a Business School in London. US universities have been working in the United Kingdom for a while now but catering to US students wanting years abroad. In 2011, there were 118 affiliates to the Association of American Study Abroad programmes in the United Kingdom. US for-profit providers work in the United Kingdom too, such as the American Institute for Foreign Studies but catering to US students studying in the United Kingdom.

The second, more pernicious, development is that for-profit providers have been allowed to set up in the United Kingdom to compete with British universities for local students; and more are trying to do so. The post-1992 sector of universities is particularly vulnerable to competition from private providers. The centre-right think-tank Policy Exchange, which describes itself as an independent, non-partisan education charity but is heavily endorsed by the Conservative Party (whose leading figures it quotes on its website, with their photographs smiling) wrote a report in 2010 making the case for private funders *Higher Education in an Age of Austerity: The Role of Private Providers* (http://www.policyechange.org.uj/publications/publication.cgi?id=212). There are some fanciful fears raised by this (for example, that there will be a privately funded 'University of the Big Society'). However, McGettigan (2011) is otherwise quite right to draw attention to the way the market for higher education is being distorted by the government trying to drive the price down through its manipulation of the supply side of the market. The Student Loans Company (SLC) has been granted permission to fund student loans at for-profit providers,[28] including at institutions that do not yet have degree-awarding powers. This must be seen in conjunction with proposals from the

---

[28] The *Times Higher Education* on 22 December 2011 reported a parliamentary answer given by David Willetts that indicated 5,900 students had received loans to attend 'alternative providers', which is up 40 per cent from the year before. In June 2012, it was disclosed that the number for 2011–12 had increased to 9,366. BPP borrowed £2 million from the SLC in fee and maintenance loans in 2010–11 and David Willetts announced that students will be allowed to borrow up to £6,000 a year in taxpayer subsidized loans from 2012–13, up from £3,375 in 2011–12 (*Times Higher Education*, 1 March, 2012, p. 9). Students at seven private institutions received more than £1 million in loans from the SLC in 2010–11, even though only five have degree awarding powers. Not all of these are for-profit providers though. Morgan (2012: 39) cites HESA figures which reveal that there were 37,738 students at 65 private providers in 2009–10, the bulk taking business, management and law. Initially only 11 of these private institutions were subject to QAA institutional review. Private providers could, therefore, get degree-awarding powers and attract students with taxpayer subsidized loans, while being exempt from the fair-access policies established and evading the regulatory system public HEIs are constrained by (Morgan 2012: 41). However, the furore over this revelation persuaded the government to subject them to the same regulation and to impose caps on student numbers.

Department of Business, Innovation and Skills to reduce the number of full time equivalent students it takes to legally constitute a university from 4,000 to 1,000, only 750 of whom need be studying for a degree, which potentially opens up competition from many smaller for-profit institutions and companies.

At the moment, there is only one for-profit company with degree awarding powers, BBP, which was given the title 'University College' by David Willetts almost immediately on him assuming office, and it restricts itself to business and law, although Montague Private Equity acquired the College of Law in 2012 for £200 million, which is another of the private providers that have degree awarding powers but is, as yet, not-for-profit (see Thornton 2011 for a study of the impact of privatization from the perspective of the teaching of law). These are primarily teaching institutions that are research-inactive, which contradicts the idea of a university.[29] It is known, however, that the government has been in discussion with other companies that have an interest in following BBP, and in January 2012, the Department of Business, Innovation and Skills, which runs universities, put out a tender for research on supplying it with a 'comprehensive picture of HE provision by private and alternative funders'. It is suspected that the government is worried about the US example, where for-profit providers have a disproportionate number of low income students and a high default rate.

The Apollo Group which owns BPP is a US corporation which also runs the University of Phoenix, the largest for-profit institution in the United States. The *Times Higher Education* reported on 2 June 2011 that its annual accounts in the year up to March 2011 showed it had downgraded the value of BPP by $170.4 million as a result of lower than expected student numbers. For-profit HEIs are more common in the United States, with over three million students, about 10 per cent of the country's university population, most of whom are low-income, non-traditional students who cannot afford the fees of non-profit private or public universities and colleges (cited in Marcus 2011: 40–3). While the British government has been in discussion

---

[29] There is some concern over whether the poor quality research outputs of the major US for-profit institutions qualifies them to the title 'university'. Research by Quentin Hanley, reported in The *Times Higher Education* on 16 February 2012, on the citations in Thomson Reuters's *Web of Knowledge* to research papers produced by staff at the leading for-profit providers there found few examples of well-cited work. Phoenix University mustered fewer than 200 papers with a total citation of 700 since 1993, Kaplan University had 100 papers with just over 500 citations, and Argosy University fared a little better with 200 papers that produced over 1,000 citations. Hanley is quoted as saying that they are 'essentially research inactive institutions' that should not be called universities (p. 7).

with companies like Kaplan Higher Education Group and Apollo with a view to lowering price in the United Kingdom, it is ironic that in the United States these for-profit providers are trying to resist state and federal regulation of their practices. Marcus (2011: 40) reports that 11 states in the United States are investigating the business practices of for-profit institutions, including for misrepresentation of programmes and false promises of outcomes. Kaplan is currently denying allegations that it falsified records to disguise a high drop-out rate. The level of state regulation in the UK university sector may well stem the rush of US for-profit providers moving here (and after public revelation at the absence of QAA oversight, by June 2012 the government was pressured into subjecting private providers to state regulation).

There is something very important to note about these marketization policies: neither the internal nor external market is a true market. For one thing this is not perfect competition since the 'price' is not set by the market itself but by the government. Universities have been told the upper parameters of the fees they can levy; and the government is interfering in the market to lower prices. HEIs intending to charge fees above £6,000 require permission (of the Office of Fair Access, a state-funded body). In some cases, devolved governments in the United Kingdom have created even more imperfect competition by telling universities who it is that they *cannot* charge for the goods. In Scotland, for example, Scottish domicile students pay no fee, and those in Wales and Northern Ireland subsidized fees. Both the price and the buyers are rigged, therefore, set not by supply and demand but by an outside regulator of market conditions. Depending on where they live, UK students will purchase the 'good' for either quite a lot of money or nothing: meaning that there are several markets in higher education not one. Price, in other words, is not a market decision.

Demand is fixed too. The artificiality of the market is emphasized by the fact that demand is regulated by the government. It regulates the number of overseas students allowed to enter the United Kingdom (and has tightened up on access through imposing stricter visa regulation), it manipulates the 'local' market by offering 20,000 cut-price places, some in the further education sector, to stimulate demand at the bottom end to drive down price, and it lifts the cap on student numbers at the top for those with 'A' level grades at AAB or better, fining HEIs if they over-recruit non-AAB students. In 2011–12, 40 universities in England were fined a total of £21 million for over-recruiting in the academic year, representing a total of only 5,750 students, up from £8 million for 14 universities the year before. One was docked £3.4 million in 2009–10 for over-recruiting 913 students (*Times Higher Education*, 7 April 2011).[30] As the *Times Higher* editorial penned that particular week, it is a funny old market in which the state prevents popular institutions from recruiting. The situation grew worse in 2011–12 because universities feared a reduction in applicants from 2012–13 with the introduction of fees and over-recruited to compensate. London Metropolitan alone was fined £5.9 million for over-recruitment in 2011–12. It should be noted that private providers were once excluded from the cap and could recruit taxpayer-backed students unlimited on courses agreed in advance by the government, but this market advantage was withdrawn in 2012.

Value is also not made transparent by the market, contradicting one of the principal features of free markets, which requires that the value of the good be immediately apparent to the purchaser to enable a rational transaction to take place. The benefits accrued through a degree and the wider 'learning experience' that led to it, reveal themselves only over time and decisions about purchasing which goods from which seller on entering university are based on imperfect knowledge. Writing in defence of his government's proposals in the *Times Higher Education* on 26 May 2011, David Willetts saw them as enabling students as prospective buyers to ask before entering the market 'What am I paying for?' They do not know this, nor can they. To assist 'consumers' in obtaining the necessary information to permit 'informed' market decisions, universities will be obliged to provide Key Information Sets (see http://www.hefece.ac.uk/learning/infohe/kis.htm) from 2012–13, which include student satisfaction data; course information; employment and salary data; accommodation costs; financial information, such as fees; and students' union information. HEFCE on its website offers universities a template for presenting this data. Whether this is the information students need to make judgements of value is beside the point; the value is impossible to calculate at the time the information is supplied, for the value of the good is not transparent.[31]

---

[30] This policy particularly affects those universities who recruit through clearing because this makes it harder to plan student numbers, although at least one elite Russell Group university was fined in 2011–12.

[31] What compounds the difficulty in calculating the value is that some of this information is also notoriously difficult to gather and verify in any reliable way, notably student destination surveys, average salaries and graduate-level employment.

All this makes the market in higher education very artificial. Economics tells us that perfectly 'true' markets are rare, for there is always some legal regulation. Mostly, however, this framework of laws is imposed in order to make the competition *fairer*, by eliminating monopoly competition, illegal markets, cartels and the like. The marketization of higher education ends up with *unfair* competition because it is fixed. The absurdity of competition in higher education is no better demonstrated than by the complaints of the Universities Minister, David Willetts, and Vince Cable, Secretary of State for Business, Innovation and Skills which runs universities, about the 'anti-competitive behaviour' of universities in trying to squeeze further education colleges out of the degree awarding 'business' by means of revising their validation arrangements with them, when rigged competition is the very principle on which the whole market in higher education is based. What matters to the Coalition government, of course, is that it is they not the universities who do the rigging. Their creation of a margin of 20,000 places to be auctioned to institutions charging less than £7,500 tuition fees, and inviting further education colleges to bid for them, is rigging the market. In August 2011, Newcastle College and New College Durham were the first further education colleges to be granted foundation degree-awarding powers and in February 2012 the government announced that just under half of these biddable places went to 143 of the 167 Further Education Colleges who applied. Newcastle College, for example, won more of these places (260) than did neighbouring Northumbria University (235).

It is clearly absurd to introduce competitive pricing and then criticize universities for acting competitively – nothing could illustrate better than this complaint how artificial the market is in higher education. James Winter, Head of the Council of Validating Universities, which oversees the arrangements universities develop to validate the degree courses in further education colleges, commented in response to allegations of anti-competitive behaviour that universities were 'being told off for behaving like it's a free market' (*Times Higher Education*, 16 February 2012, p. 17), when the coalition government knows full well it is nothing like a free market – they are rigging it in every way conceivable.

Government manipulation of the market illustrates something else very significant about current marketization policies: marketization involves the withdrawal of public funding through the block grant but not the ending of state regulation. At first sight, regulation seems entirely counterproductive to the purposes of introducing a market. In true markets where there are a lot of suppliers selling essentially the same product, competition is strong and price varies downwards. This is what the government says it wants to achieve in higher education (and, incidentally, in national health). But where the market is tightly regulated by the state, competition ends up being low, since market differentiation is diminished by legislation and regulation. In these cases, competition becomes an illusion, existing as a rhetorical assertion not a real market practice. In economic terms, the higher education market constitutes a monopsony (one powerful consumer that is able to control demand, like a supermarket chain with a local farmer) – the opposite of a monopoly (where there is one supplier) – with the government acting as the single powerful consumer able to manipulate demand. Therefore, for all their business-speak to strike a market niche, what is on offer by British universities is still very much the same.

British higher education remains one of the most highly regulated university systems (Burawoy 2011). In Europe, French and Greek universities are more highly centralized, where academics are civil servants, but traditionally UK universities had autonomy: and they still do in areas like the appointment of staff (including Vice Chancellors and governing boards), and the setting of curriculum, course materials and professorial salaries (and with the move to local bargaining, perhaps also for all staff). The old block grant played a major role in guaranteeing institutional autonomy, since little monitoring came with it. But the marketization of higher education is eroding this autonomy. Indeed, the highly artificial form of marketization we have in Britain *requires* regulation.[32] It is not that the commodification of higher education, turning it into the supply and demand of 'goods', is a different mode of marketization from the regulatory system of university education in highly planned societies. Marketization demands both commodification and regulation. It is the state that

---

[32] Simon Baker (2011: 33) referred to the red tape that once existed in British universities as no more than a sticking plaster, but warned that universities are now facing the situation where almost every aspect of university life will be regulated by funding councils. This arises from the proposal for HEFCE to take over the quality assurance functions of the Quality Assurance Agency, giving it responsibility for teaching quality and protection of student rights and interests, as well as its roles in funding teaching and research, monitoring the finances of universities, from the management of estates to internal auditing of accounts and governance. This would make HEFCE like the watchdogs that regulate competition in the water and energy markets. He raised the prospect that some universities may prefer to go private to evade this level of regulation.

regulates the market and sets its conditions, determining price and buyers. It is the state that regulates the mechanisms for market differentiation by imposing the performance indicators through which value is distributed variably in the market. It is the state that regulates supply by permitting for-profit suppliers to enter the market, and it is the state that has developed the audit culture that facilitates the performance of market behaviour.[33] Since British universities are increasingly persuaded – required – to buy into the Bologna accord, which standardizes higher education practices across Europe, regulation is now as much at the European as the British state level. Regulations, of course, have not everywhere changed behaviour within universities. Universities might now be businesses but sometimes they are still not always business-like. There are still poor practices in teaching, PhD supervision and research, but this is because the regulations are evaded rather than absent.[34]

Conclusion

Good social science requires good universities. While it is not credible to claim the social sciences are under attack by the audit culture, at least not any more, or less, than other subject areas, Britain is witnessing the end of centuries-old traditions with the demise of the public university; traditions which made British universities among the best in the world, gave the country renown and respect, contributed to its civic culture and, it has to be said, also its economic and scientific expansion. Governments, as guardians of traditions, are obliged to hold in trust for future generations what is worthwhile about them and to manage the inevitable process of modernization and change that all traditions have to undergo without destroying what had made them worth keeping in the past. Guardians of traditions render themselves open to unusually fierce contempt when they are careless with what traditionalists believe to be good about customary practice and when they are footloose with valued traditions by imposing rapid and poorly planned change for what appears no reasonable

---

[33] Power (1997), a professor of accounting, shrewdly makes the point that late modern society is an 'audit society' because public accountability and control are necessary features of what is here called 'neoliberal marketization.'

[34] Collini (2012: 134–5) argues that regulation increases inefficiency because it focuses people's attention on what is reportable within the audit system rather than on what needs to be done.

sense at all. As Stefan Collini (2012: 198–9) wrote in the Epilogue to his defence of the idea of a university: 'we are merely custodians for the present generation of a complex intellectual inheritance which we did not create – and which is not ours to destroy'.[35]

Voices raised in opposition to marketization are many and febrile. Some are worth capturing. The Campaign for the Public University (http://publicuniversity.org.uk/) is vociferous; conferences, workshops and public lectures are aplenty defending the principle of university education as a public good. Some musty old learned societies that seemed to be run entirely for the dining benefits of their Fellows have been stirred into life. Learned societies are engaged, so too are trade unions, university staff, students and newspapers, but – and this may sound strange – not many senior university managers are. The connivance of most university leaders in the destruction of the public university in the ambition of stealing market advantage for their own institution is one of the worst features of the destruction of these centuries-old traditions. Craven, commercial, crass: there are so many alliterations to add to our four 'C's'.

I am not going to add to this chorus of utter contempt, nor seek to heap more shame. Among this clamour, there is a need for new voices. I will try to show in the next chapter how this moment of degradation for the public university can be turned into one of opportunity to empower the social sciences by re-envisioning their public value for the twenty-first century.

---

[35] The irony in this remark cannot be passed without comment, for this complaint at what is the destruction of the education legacy for future generations is directed against a government minister noted for a book on intergenerational justice (see Willetts 2010).

4

What is the Public Value of Social Science?

Introduction

Impact is a terrain on which the social sciences can compete with the other academic cultures in Britain, even outperform them, if there were an appropriate understanding of impact and the will among social scientists to do so. While there has been a marked shift in the technical meaning of impact towards a more general approach – although problems of measurement still remain – the attitude towards it among social scientists has not tempered because of its association with the process of marketization. I, therefore, advance four claims in this chapter: (a) British social science is well equipped and easily capable of demonstrating the impact of its research; (b) impact, however, is a deeply flawed way of approaching the public value of social science; (c) it is necessary to shift the terms of the debate away from the public impact of social science to its public value; and (d) value can be deconstructed into several types which show the diverse ways in which the social sciences have value.

I suggest there are four advantages to this change of focus. Public value better constitutes a vocabulary that permits common conversations to develop; it involves rhetoric that is consensual not divisive, thus helping to move social scientists on from the negative tone of the impact debate; it transcends the localized form of the debate about impact, which is perceived to be peculiarly British, to link with an international discourse about public value; and it offers the best prospect of restating for the twenty-first century the principles on which social science can justify itself against the neoliberal push towards using economic impact as their sole measure of effectiveness. I want to begin by showing how feasible the impact agenda is for British social science.

The feasibility of impact in social science research

In the third memorial Gareth Roberts Science Policy Lecture, given at the Royal Society of Medicine on 19 October 2011, David Willetts singled out three subject fields in a domain of over 400 in which he considered Britain 'exceptionally strong' in international quality terms, brain research, health science and social science – and this at a public lecture to honour a molecular electronics scientist. The occasion was used to address the widespread fears and suspicions about the impact agenda among the world class researchers in these – and other – fields. With respect to the REF, Willetts said, 'put simply, academics will be asked to show how, on the basis of excellent research undertaken over a 15-year timeframe, they have made a contribution beyond their institution' (see http://www.bis.gov.uk/news/speeches/david-willetts-gareth-roberts-science-policy-lecture-2011).

'A contribution beyond their institution' can mean anything and thus in a sense everything. HEFCE's definition of impact supports a judgement that at least it has undergone a transition from a value-for-money to value-for-society approach in the REF. As we have already noted in the last chapter, sections 140 and 141 of its July 2011 paper *Assessment Framework and Guidance on Submissions* (http://www.hefce.ac.uk/research/ref/pubs/2011/02_11/02_11.pdf) provide a very broad notion of impact. This has reassured and satisfied some natural scientists. In the view of Stephen Curry (2011: 31), for example, a structural biologist from Imperial College who endorsed this definition – 'it's not' anymore 'just about money'. And it is worth remembering that the case study approach utilized in the REF means that not all people returned will need to demonstrate impact.

It is eminently feasible with this definition for social science to embrace the impact agenda for its technical meaning has merged with its general one (whether it is desirable is another matter and will be discussed shortly). Nor is it particularly puzzling or difficult to do so. Two dimensions of impact require distinguishing in order to demystify it, the *process* of impact and its *assessment*. By process is meant the method of delivering impact, by assessment its measurement. The process of impact can be simplified by reducing it to three questions which all social scientists can ask themselves about their research, even where it is theoretical in its observation and explanation of aspects of culture, markets and the state: Who are the users of our research? How do I engage with them? What has been/could be the effects of this engagement? The assessment of impact revolves around one question. What is the evidence of these effects? This is shown diagrammatically in Figure 4.1, which utilizes culture, the market and the state to represent the broad characterization of society deployed in the generic definition of social science outlined in Chapter 1.

Three points are immediately apparent about these twin dimensions of impact. First, there is a very wide selection of possible answers to the questions that define the process of delivering impact. Secondly, however, many are not directly related to the research itself or its quality but reflect researchers' communication and dissemination skills and their closeness to users. Thirdly, answers to the fourth question, which define its assessment, are more difficult to conjure, especially *evidence* of effects which are independent of the effects themselves rather than duplicates of them. It is particularly tricky to accurately connect the research, its effects and the evidence of these effects. This repeats the observation from Chapter 3 that measurement is the most problematic part of impact and is the issue that has driven REF policy, particularly the development of a very inclusive definition in order to assuage anxieties about the bewildering job of assessing it.

This produces one of the major paradoxes of the current impact debate. HEFCE has abandoned the narrowness of a value-for-money approach to impact while having the hardest task in making impact seem feasible. The process of impact and its assessment operate in opposition to one another, with the inclusiveness of its meaning not resolving the complications of its measurement. The social science community – and I suggest this is common to other academic cultures in Britain – is pulled in different directions therefore, understanding the process of impact but incapable of reliably measuring it. A system that *insists* on its assessment, thus, ends up being heavily criticized and practitioners lose sight of the feasibility of dealing with the *process* of impact.

Some social sciences are better than others in answering these questions and doing so in certain sorts of ways because they are more 'applied' and closer to users of research, but even the high-impact policy-oriented social science disciplines, like areas of economics, business, social policy and public law,

The process of impact
Who are the users of my research?
Culture
NGOs, civil society (national and global), educated citizenry, cultural consumers, librarians, archivists, schools, media, public bodies, private organizations, charities, individuals, families, etc
The state
Governments (local, devolved, national and regional), political parties, politicians, policy makers, civil servants, national and international strategists, etc
The market
business, industry, trade unions, consumers, workers, etc
How do I engage with them?
Culture
mailing lists, newsletters, website, social media, public talks, seminars, publications, popular writings and journalism, radio, television, posters, brochures, conferences and presentations, etc
The state
publications, briefing papers and reports, workshops, talks, popular writing, presentations, etc
The market
same as the above
What have been/could be the effects of this engagement?
Culture
behaviour and pursuits, understanding, civic and humanitarian values, public debate, public benefits, shared beliefs, health and well-being, health promotion, school performance, family relations, etc
The state
evidence-based policy, management and use of public resources, decision-making, strategic thinking, etc
The market
knowledge transfer, spin off companies, product development, evidence-based market behaviour and strategy, decision-making, management of economic and human resources, industrial relations, consumer behaviour and choice, dispute management, etc
The assessment of impact
What is the evidence of these effects?
Culture
take-up of research, influence on behaviours, beliefs, values and civic practice, etc
The state
policy, practice, evaluations, improved public scrutiny and accountability, etc
The market
Knowledge transfer, policy and practice in business and industry, strategic thinking, industrial relations, conflict prevention and dispute management, consumer evaluations, etc

Figure 4.1 The twin dimensions of impact.

do not readily lend themselves to spin off companies as a form of knowledge transfer; and the non-policy-oriented social science disciplines are not devoid of opportunities to display impact in some form. Neither 'applied' nor 'pure' social science fields find it easy. Policy impacts are often the hardest to attribute to specific pieces of research, while other forms of impact, such as behaviour, value or belief change, are difficult to find concrete evidence for. There are some social science-based spin off companies, such as the company part-owned by the University of Leicester Perpetuity Research and Consultancy International, developed from criminological work there by Peter Gill (see http://www.perpetuitygroup.com), which specializes in security management, risk management and crime prevention, doing evaluation research related to business crime, among other things. Risk analysis in economics, business and management and security studies has spurred similar spin off companies elsewhere. These are, however, minority ventures. It is more common to celebrate impact delivered through more obscure effects.

The professional associations, learned societies and funding agencies have been assertive in developing case studies that demonstrate impactful social science, some of them almost transparent in their eagerness to please. The British Academy's two letters to the Queen, the first signed by Tim Besley (economist) and Peter Hennessy (cultural historian) and dated 22 July 2009, responded to her complaint, voiced at the LSE in November 2008 that economists had not anticipated the credit crunch, by drawing to her attention a workshop on just this topic seven months later held at the British Academy. A small selection of less vulgar examples can be highlighted from the last few years.[1]

The 2009 joint report by HEFCE and UUK *Securing World Class Research in UK Universities* (see http://wwe.hefce.ac.uk/research/funding/refund/QR.pdf) reads now slightly ironical given their mutual embrace of tuition fees, for it sought to show what quality impact the old block grant had furnished for British universities. It featured two case studies from social science (most were from natural science and medicine): work at Roehampton University on 'honour killings' that had been widely engaged with by government and civil society

---

[1] The eagerness to demonstrate impact was not just a British phenomenon, for it spread across the Irish Sea. The Higher Education Authority and the Irish Research Council for Humanities and Social Science (IRCHSS) published *Foresight in the Arts, Humanities and Social Sciences* in 2009 to display the public relevance of their work. Cost cutting measures in Ireland, however, have seen the abolition of IRCHSS in 2012 through its merger with its natural science equivalent, giving the Irish state only one research council for all subject areas.

groups, and research at the University of Exeter on Islamic radicalization in British-born youth. The 2010 RCUK publication, *Impacts: People and Skills* (http://www.rcuk.ac.uk/documents/framework/impactspeopleandskills.pdf) profiles a number of researchers from different disciplines whose work had 'impacted on the economy and society' in a variety of ways, arising from 'the application of knowledge, skills and experience developed in their research'. The examples were heavily focused on science and medicine, and it included only three from social science: Professor Tim Jackson, Economics Commissioner to the Sustainable Development Commission, Professor Richard Blundell, director of ESRC Centre for Microeconomic Analysis of Public Policy at the Institute for Fiscal Studies, and Professor Graeme Laurie director of the AHRC Research Centre for Studies in Intellectual Property and Technology Law.

Humanities and social science subjects tend to be neglected in general surveys of this kind because of the ease with which impact can be demonstrated through medical and scientific interventions. The bodies serving the humanities and social sciences, therefore, responded with impact accounts of their own. The British Academy has been particularly active, having established a Policy Centre in 2009 to lead its campaigning. In 2004, it published a report *That Full Complement of Riches* (http://www.britac.ac.uk/policy/full-complement-riches.cfm) devoted to exposing the contribution of the arts, humanities and social sciences to wealth generation, a theme aptly captured by the use of Adam Smith's phrase as its title. In 2008 it made the same point in *Punching our Weight* (http://www.britac.ac.uk/policy/wilson), which looked at the role of these subject areas in policy making. The AHRC's 2009 report *Leading the World: The Economic Impact of UK Arts and Humanities Research* (http://www.ahrc.ac.uk/about/policy/documents/leadingtheworld.pdf) advanced the importance of arts and humanities to UK society, economy and quality of life, suggesting that continued investment was needed to support the many ways in which they contribute to international competitiveness. RAND Europe, in conjunction with AHRC and University of Cambridge, published *Assessing the Impact of Arts and Humanities Research at the University of Cambridge* in 2010 on behalf of the AHRC and the University of Cambridge, using the Payback Framework to make their evaluation (see http://www.rand.org/content/dam/rand/pubs/technical-report/2010/RAND-TR816.pdf). Impact was measured, among other things, by changes in knowledge, understanding, attitudes, beliefs and behaviours and evaluated by peer review interviews, self-reports and interviews with external informants.

Two examples are worth highlighting to reinforce the point that impact is feasible for social science. The British Academy's 2010 report *Past, Present and Future: The Public Value of the Humanities and Social Science* (accessible at http://www.britac.ac.uk/news/news.cfm/newsid/364) draws attention to contributions in strengthening policy making, generating economic impact, tackling social issues, recognition of cultural values, addressing global challenges and advancing international understanding, using ten case studies across these fields. The case studies ranged from social exclusion, humanities in business, intellectual property and technology law, war crimes, multiculturalism, museums, climate change, and bride price, poverty and domestic violence. The impacts claimed in each case are clearly specified. With respect to social exclusion, taking merely the first example, the report stressed improvements in knowledge about how social exclusion works, links to policy through the Sure Start programme of the Labour government and legislation, and working relationships with the Cabinet Office's own Social Exclusion Unit. Moving, randomly, to the last case study, the anthropological research on bride price practices in Uganda, the impacts demonstrated included a constitutional petition on bride price practices seeking to amend the Uganda constitution, round-table workshops in local communities with councils, police, cultural leaders, religious leaders and other stakeholders, changes in legislation making bride prices non-refundable, media engagement and a variety of meetings with civil society groups.

The British Academy's Report runs to over 50 pages of examples of impact indicators. The ESRC produced a handy pocket-sized card brochure, designed more for government and business to read, entitled *Social Science: Excellence with Impact* (see http://www.esrc.ac.uk/_images/Excellence_with_impact_flyer_tcm8-4599.pdf), with case studies organized around three themes, productive economy, healthy society and the sustainable world. The impact indicators are not specified, but under the productive economy theme, it draws attention to the work of the Centre for Market and Public Organisation on the effect of wages on youth unemployment, studies into the effectiveness of training interventions for long-term unemployed, research by the Institute for Fiscal Studies on tax and benefit models that led to the government to abolish the 10 per cent tax band, and work carried out by the Centre for Economic

Performance that persuaded the government that the introduction of the minimum wage would not lead to job losses. Under the healthy society theme it drew attention to the impact of the British Household Panel Surveys on the increased likelihood of unemployed people to be laid off work again within the next 12 months, the Birth Cohort studies on the effect of having obese parents on the obesity of children, the Avon Longitudinal Study of Parents and Children, which proved the link between maternal stress and psychological and medical illnesses later in life, and work on crowd control at football matches which has helped the police to deal with fans in a less confrontational manner.

With respect to sustainability, the flyer highlighted ESRC-funded research on waste management that had helped shape legislation, work on the environment that was being applied by the Environment Agency, work by the Sussex Energy Group that assists in the take-up of low carbon technologies, research by the Centre for Climate Change Economics and Policy which influenced the Treasury's budget policies on the green economy and the Global Uncertainties research programme that focused on global security challenges and cyber crime, among other things. Ian Diamond, then Chief Executive of the ESRC, is quoted thus: 'Social science research is essential to the UK's core needs; economic recovery and skills, security and terrorism, environmental sustainability, helping our children succeed at school and manage our ageing population'.

Before we move on to assessing the desirability of impact, it is worth pointing out how impact has changed practice in another way. Big impact is big business. The attention given to demonstrating impact in these many ways is now matched with research given to demonstrating to practitioners how to do impactful social science. In 2011, RCUK held a conference on user engagement and launched a website (The Research Outcomes System) where recipients of grants have to detail the impact of their funded research (it applies to grants awarded after 1 April 2006), intended as a guide for potential applicants to frame their own impact. I have already referred to the LSE Public Policy Group's handbook on how to be impactful (http://blog.lse.ac.uk/impactofsocialscience/the-handbook), and journals devoted to similar issues abound. There are training courses and research on knowledge transfer, and consultancy groups, often led by former academics, will show us how if we pay a lot for the privilege. As if to emphasize this point, the Centre for Business Research (http://www.cbr.cam.ac.uk/) at the University of Cambridge, to take one example, has undertaken a series of consultancies and published several reports on impact as a research topic (see http://www.cbr.cam.ac.uk/ publications/Special_Reports.htm), some in conjunction with Public and Corporate Economic Consultants, a firm of private economic consultants with offices in Cambridge and London whose core staff have connections with the University of Cambridge (several are its former economics faculty).

Some of this work, for example, has been done for HEFCE, which was eager to understand who it is that engages in knowledge transfer and generates impacts. One such report, *Knowledge Exchange and the Generation of Civic and Community Impacts* (see http://www.pacec.co.uk/publications/Knowledge_ Exchange_and_the_Generation_of_Civic_and_Community_Impacts.pdf), published in 2010, disclosed that female academics are twice more likely than males to work with civil society groups, which the most common form of engagement with is consultancy work for charities. Social scientists were, unsurprisingly, the most likely to work with charities, natural scientists the least. Reports have also been published on establishing connections between the arts and humanities with private and public business, on knowledge transfer in the United States, the possible synergies between knowledge transfer and teaching, and on universities as mediums for business knowledge exchange, among other things. An evaluation was even done for HEFCE on its policies for generating economic impact.

In these many ways, I hope I have shown that impact is feasible, demonstrable, and is one of a number of good ways to show that our research has uses beyond itself. It is easy to imagine that with more attention devoted to equipping social scientists with the skills to understand and demonstrate their impact, the greater will be their facility with it. Many parts of social science, after all, are already comfortable with the language and intent of impact.[2]

It is also the *wrong* way to establish the purposes and principles of social science as a public good. Impact is a deeply flawed way of approaching the public value of the social sciences. I want to proceed in justifying this remark in two stages. In the next section, I explore the reasons why impact is flawed and in the following one begin making the transition from discussing the public impact of social science to its public value.

---

[2] There is an interesting set of impact case studies identified on the Royal Geographical Society's website (see http://www.rgs.org/OurWork/Advocacy+and+Policy/making+the+case+for +geography.htm).

The undesirability of impact in the social sciences

There are many practical difficulties around impact to which I have alluded throughout the discussion so far – its floating meaning, uncertainty about its measurability and its opaqueness – but these are technical matters that one can imagine excellent minds will resolve eventually, especially given the skills training in impact that is looming.[3] There is, however, something wrong with the *principle* of impact. There are four irresolvable problems with impact that impugn its very core: (a) the inherent bias towards economic and policy benefits; (b) its non-linear nature that ensures it does not necessarily involve judgements of quality; (c) it is a circular argument that overlooks negative and disguised impact; and (d) it is inevitably bound up with marketization and the audit culture as an ideological project of neoliberalism. I will address each briefly in turn.

Impact is discriminatory. There is an inevitable – almost inherent – bias towards favouring research whose impact is more readily demonstrable; and this mostly because of its direct policy benefit or user engagement. The examples cited in the previous section illustrate this plainly. These examples are what the learned societies, professional bodies and research councils used to highlight their work – their choosing, not mine. They have spurred a new vocabulary of their own – 'behavioural change policymaking' and 'changes to choice environments' are among the new patois. This language fits that of the Coalition government, whose newly inaugurated Behavioural Insight Team, also known as the 'Nudge Unit', is charged with using behavioural economics to persuade – incentivize – individuals into making better choices in their everyday lives, especially about health, nutrition, wealth and well-being. These examples show the slippage that impact involves, with its unintended but natural tendency to highlight a small range of research with a narrow set of indicators that are incontrovertibly impactful for their policy effects and good links with a limited number of influential users (and a few of the examples keep reappearing and with them, the same named researchers). We know from analysis of research exploitation in the past that this is enhanced whenever

---

[3] Through 2011 and 2012 the ESRC funded a seminar series under the title 'New Frontiers of Impact' designed to explore 'how different types of knowledge creation and application may shape the impact agenda, including examination of how these knowledge processes and outcomes may be appropriated and further shaped and developed by users (and co-producers) of different sorts'.

the findings translate directly into a policy debate, when researchers have close relationships with users, and when status is bestowed by the media on particular researchers as 'experts' (see Bechhofer et al. 2001: 4.3). Sometimes, however, expert status is of the rent-a-quote variety where 'impact' is achieved through insult in order to obtain media notoriety.

Discrimination matters when costs and rewards are attached to impact, for it leaves far too much impactful social science either overlooked or with its impact indicators struggling to command the attention of more obvious markers. The distinction between applied and basic research is not as definite as imagined, for Bechhofer et al. (2001) have shown in their analysis of the exploitation of the findings from 40 ESRC-funded projects at the University of Edinburgh that most research does not fit neatly into these categories. Not all applied research is instrumental, short term and limited; and fundamental research is rarely without some long-term policy implications. One of the negative effects of impact, however, is that it imposes stricter boundaries between these types of research by pushing researchers towards applied projects because of the relative simplicity in demonstrating benefits. In short, it discriminates against fundamental research.

Impact is also non-linear. HEFCE recognizes this but does not accept its consequences. Impact is reducible to activities not directly connected to the quality of the research, for impact is mediated by a large number of processes independent of its findings and their quality, such as the social networks researchers are embedded in for communicating their results and for engaging with users, especially powerful groups, researchers' communication skills and their prior relationships with those who take up the results, like policy makers, the media and other users, the extent to which the field is one where policy debate is settled or still live, and how sensitized users already are to the potential benefit of the research findings. Impact is serendipitous, conditional, involving huge elements of chance and luck. Therefore, impact is not a quality judgement, for high impactful social science depends on these intermediary factors that in themselves are not pointers to quality. It is a poor criterion of quality that the research is impactful merely because it finds favour with powerful groups – or is ignored by them (as MacGregor 2011: 41 argues with respect to UK drugs policy). Good quality research can have little obvious impact and poor quality research high impact. The use of peer review in the REF is supposed to eliminate high impactful but low quality research. It is perhaps feasible to imagine how poor quality work can be identified despite its impact but the measurement problem makes the reverse more problematic – identifying indicators for high quality research that is not obviously impactful. The answer to this conundrum might be that not everyone submitted is required to display impact in the REF, but excluding high-quality low-impact research from the impact cases challenges the relevance of impact in the first place.

This point leads me imperceptibly to another. Impact is circular. Research has impact when it affects policy and brings demonstrable benefits, these policy effects and demonstrable benefits being evidence of its impact. When systems impose the measurement of impact, impact gets reduced to the effects of the research and there is no independent evidence of impact separate from these effects. Impact *is* its measures. This, as I have said many times, is why the problem of measurement has driven the impact agenda. The REF's view on impact permits as evidence that research consolidates current practice, policy and behaviour, but the circularity of the process prevents such indicators being evidenced. If impact is its measures, evidence that things did *not* change because of the research becomes very hard to find.

Circularity leads to other problems. Where the effects of research are disclosed in less obvious ways than demonstrable change, we encounter the problems of negative and disguised impact, referred to already in Chapter 3. Negative impact can be described as research which is rejected by users, policy makers and government for its counter-intuitiveness or its opposition to current policy objectives and the like, rather than its lack of quality or its harmful effects. There is clearly research that is wrong because of its poor quality and harmful effects, despite the impact accorded it by take up in the press, such as medical research that alleged a link between the MMR vaccine and autism. In social science, one thinks of scientific racism that alleged a link between race and intelligence. Negative impact is more than wrongheaded and harmful. With negative impact, researchers are not in a position to encourage take-up by policy makers and other users despite its good quality and beneficial character, since policy makers and others may want to foreclose the debate or restrict it to a more finite range of policy alternatives. Policy makers may be looking for research that legitimates current practice, while researchers are seeking to challenge current ways of thinking. The potential impact of the research in this case is being suppressed. By definition, such research is not said to be impactful because there are no indicators of its effects, but this is because its effects are thought to be negative, harmful, damaging or destructive to current policy preferences and practices, to which no challenge is permitted. One of the most high-profile examples in recent years of negative impact is the sacking of Professor David Nutt from his post as Chair of the Advisory Council on the Misuse of Drugs for suggesting government policy was wrong (see **Vignette 5**).

Disguised impact arises when research impacts are hidden and unrecognized. This may in part be a failure of researchers to declare or be aware of it but mostly it is the consequence of policy makers, the press, civil society and the rest being ignorant of it. The British Academy's 2008 report *Punching our Weight: The Humanities and Social Sciences in Public Policy Making* (http://www.britac.ac.uk/policy/wilson/), which otherwise extolled the potential for impact through policy benefits, was nonetheless realistic about the chasm that can exist between researchers and policy makers, which prevents public policy makers from being better informed about humanities and social science research. The short-term horizons of policy makers, for example, make them blind to the longer-term horizons of researchers, the absence of procedures in government to acquaint it with the latest research, and the few opportunities that exist for dialogue all compound the problems of disguised impact. It might only be some time later, when the policy debate has evolved, that the social relevance of earlier research becomes clearer.

None of these concerns are resolvable (for while it is possible to improve dissemination of social science research, in the many ways *Punching our Weight* recommended, dissemination does not guarantee exploitation of the research, see Bechhofer et al. 2001). The next concern, however, is not inherently irresolvable. In practice, though, it alone justifies moving the debate from public impact to public value.

The final objection to impact is its embedding in the audit culture. It does not have to be part of marketization, for as I made clear in Chapter 2, the general rather than the technical meaning of impact pre-existed the emergence of the audit culture and attention to it seems eminently suitable to social science, since considerations of value-for-society go naturally with disciplines whose subject matter is society. Currently, however, impact is not seen as an opportunity for the empowerment of social scientists – an occasion to celebrate

Vignette 5 Impact, negative impact and UK drugs policy

Drug and addiction studies is a subject area where medical, pharmacological and social sciences meet, including among the latter sociology, social policy, psychology, criminology and economics. It has been noted that psychologists and economists are playing an increasing role, diminishing the earlier dominance of sociology and social policy, by offering answers to questions like 'what works' and 'how much does it cost' (MacGregor 2011: 53 n 1). In a review of the impact of research on UK drugs policy, Susanne MacGregor (2011), drawing on her experience in the discipline of social policy and her own studies in the area, presented a realistic appraisal of the difficulties for researchers to impact government drug policy. On occasions research has legitimized change in policy, while other research which has challenged accepted consensus has been rejected, only to have become influential later in developing alternative policies. Impact varies over time and there can be short 'windows of opportunity' when the exploitation of research is possible, only for them to close as political exigencies change, policy debates become settled, or the public and media interest in drugs policy averts and slows the bandwagon mobilizing for a change in policy. Research that finds favour in one period can be overlooked it another. Findings that do not fit with the dominant paradigm, as she puts it (2011: 41), are routinely filtered out and sidelined, although some may prove more useful in the fullness of time. She argued that research that is 'packaged' purposely for policymakers increases its chances of having impact and gave the following advice (2011: 42): provide accurate information, identify examples of good practice, write with brevity and clarity, attend to the financial and policy implications of the research and to the potential for scaling up initiatives. The advice of the Chief Social Scientific Advisor to government, Paul Wiles, was repeated: offer a one page abstract, a three page summary and a report of no longer than 25 pages for those who are really interested. 'The translation of research findings into a form usable to policymakers and practitioners' (2011: 43) increases the chances of garnering impact. She went on to suggest impact requires a receptive audience which understands the data, communication channels to allow the translation of the evidence, a moment of attention or window of opportunity to focus the issue, and key actors to champion the research (2011: 51). On the other hand, she wisely identified high quality research that had little impact on policy, some of which nonetheless was given public attention in the media. It remains a matter of honest debate as to whether this is impactful or not, given that HEFCE consider dissemination alone not to be an indicator of impact. The *effects* of research on UK drugs policy are what matters, not media attention to the results. On this measure, then, negative impact, a term MacGregor does not employ, is clearly evident in that some research was deliberately rejected on political not quality grounds. The example she cites for research with little impact on policy is David Nutt's work on the relative harm of certain forms of drugs (what follows is taken from MacGregor 2011: 47–9). The Advisory Council on the Misuse of Drugs, set up to advise government on its drugs policy, since 2000 had recommended the reclassification of cannabis to a low-risk category C drug, a move first supported by the Labour government. Political environments change rapidly and when Gordon Brown became prime minister, political pressure mounted to change the reclassification back to the more dangerous categories A and B. In late 2008 Nutt wrote an academic paper and delivered a public lecture pointing to the relative harm of other drugs and activities not banned, which supported the classification of cannabis as a C class drug. He was sacked. The Home Secretary announced in parliament when explaining the sacking that Nutt's role was to advise government not criticize government policy. To have impact in this instance, as measured in effects on policy rather than merely dissemination, Nutt was expected to deliver policy-based evidence not to shape evidence-based policy. Nutt has since formed the Independent Scientific Committee on Drugs.

their contribution to society; it is presented by Martin (2011) as potentially a Frankenstein monster and by Smith et al. (2011) as a constraint and restriction on academic autonomy. Autonomy is a principle proudly protected by practitioners. I have been described in print as 'ambiguous' (Smith et al. 2011), and in the blog sphere much less kindly for encouraging the BSA to engage with the impact debate. To quote the opening to Mrs Beeton's recipe for hare pie, which tells us first to catch the hare, the inhospitable response to impact has to be accepted as the starting point for any discussion of it. Because of this association with marketization, therefore, it is time to move to an intellectual terrain more agreeable to reasoned and polite discourse.

From the public impact to the public value of social science

Impact and public value are different things, despite the British Academy's running together of the two in its otherwise powerful report *Past, Present and Future: The Public Value of the Humanities and Social Science* (British Academy 2010). What is titled a report on their public value reads as an account of their impact. And impact is used narrowly to refer to the benefits deriving from social science and humanities research primarily for policy and in terms of engagement with a limited number of key users, mostly government. Even though the definition of impact is moving in the REF from the narrow technical meaning to extend towards its general one, value-for-society estimations are still measuring social science in terms of what it adds value to. Public value, however, is about the intrinsic worth of social science, what good it is in its own right. What I will be advocating shortly, therefore, is social science as a public good for its own sake.

As I wrote earlier, there are a number of advantages to this transition. Public value better constitutes a vocabulary that permits common conversations to develop; it involves rhetoric that is consensual not divisive, thus helping to move social scientists on from the gangrenous tone into which the impact debate has sunk; it transcends the localized form of the debate about impact, which is perceived to be peculiarly British, to link with an international discourse about public value; and it offers the best prospect of restating for the twenty-first century the principles on which social science can justify itself against the neoliberal push towards using economic impact as their sole measure of effectiveness.

Before I turn to the question of the public value of the social sciences it is worth reinforcing the importance of one of these advantages. Impact is largely a British concern not an international one. Impact provokes incredulity in academics from abroad who snigger at the use of 'REF-returnablity' as a quality control criterion on interview panels; we get pitying sounds of sympathy when they hear of the 'pathways to impact' statements we have to write and the regular surveillance of our REF returns. Marketization, though, is a global phenomenon and even US academics, seemingly working in the least publicly accountable higher education system yet conceived, feel the impulse of the implicit social contract to be publicly engaged. For example, the President of the US Social Science Research Council, Craig Calhoun, in his 'Word from the President' contained in the 2004 President's Report (see http://www.ssrc.org/workspace/images/crm/new_publication_3/%7B0e949a73-f451-de11-afac-001cc477ec70%7D.pdf) stressed the manner in which US social science was publicly responsible. He cited the example of Michael Burawoy, President of the American Sociological Association in 2004, now President of the International

Sociological Association, who has committed both Associations to 'public sociology'. Calhoun noted that the American Anthropological Association had developed a section the same year devoted to 'public anthropology' (in Europe see Eriksen 2006). The American Political Science Association did something parallel in 2004 and there is now even a 'public international relations' (see Lawson 2008). These themes appeared in special issues of several US and British journals given to discussing public engagement, such as *Social Forces, American Sociologist, Critical Sociology* and the *British Journal of Sociology*. Marketization is, thus, not without its effects elsewhere, but the discourse addresses public value not impact. The EU does not impose impact as an assessment criterion and the European Research Council explicitly rejects it.

The impact debate in Britain detaches UK social science from international discussions about public value. Impact is a Jeremiah Pit as described in the Book of Jeremiah in the Old Testament, a well dug deeper and deeper from which it is impossible to be extricated without external assistance.[4] Put another way, impact is a hole leading nowhere. And if for no other reason, the transition from debating the public impact of social science to its public value is necessary to allow British social science to climb out of its isolation and marginalization.

In his 'Word from the President', Calhoun (2004) deconstructed the meaning of 'public' by posing a series of questions about who and what the 'public' means, giving no answers since he was laying out the issues rather than coming to conclusions. These are questions to which I will have to return however, for it is critical to the new public social science that it engages with different sorts of publics and identifies the most appropriate ways to engage each of them. However, I first want to deconstruct the meaning of value. This is a precursor to our prolegomenon towards the new social science for it establishes the different types of value and the various ways in which social science can be shown to have value. In the next section I address the matter of value, after which we are in a clear position to state the public value of social science. The next chapter takes up the challenge of outlining the new public social science that follows on from it.

---

[4] This is not a metaphor to describe endless tasks – like Sisyphean labour or painting the Forth Road Bridge (which, incidentally, in December 2011 just happens to have been completed after 20 years and is not expected to begin again for another 20) – although impact feels a little like that. It is a metaphor about self-destructive behaviour.

What is value?

Neoliberalism puts a price *on* everything and to neoliberals price *is* everything. There is nothing that is not reduced to its price. It puts a price on religious beliefs (called 'spiritual capital'), universities (which I have seen referred to as 'academic capitalism'), the weather, parenthood and the socialization of children, to name just a few: indeed, whatever you name it has a price, since price, after all, makes markets work.

However, price is a poor measure of value. To know what it costs to raise a much loved child (said to be £200,000 up to the age of 18 in the United Kingdom), to get married to a much loved partner (the average wedding is said to cost £18,500 in the United Kingdom) or to experience a much feared extreme weather event (the disruption caused by the Icelandic ash cloud is said to have cost European business £2.15 billion) does not do justice to the meanings surrounding the 'product' to the people involved. Indeed, price can be an offensive and counterproductive form of value: point out the price of the marriage to one's new partner or of raising the child now with the key-of-the-door, and the meaningless of price as a measure of their value is likely to be made very forcibly.

Price, fortunately, does not represent the only way to assess value. If we deconstruct value there are at least three different meanings to the term: value as usefulness and utility; value as quality and worth; value as judgement and evaluation. The first we might call 'use value', the second 'price value', the third 'normative value'. They prompt further deconstruction. Use value can be *direct* or *indirect*, price value *intrinsic* or *added* and normative value *private* or *public*, as represented in Figure 4.2.

Direct use value describes the level of usefulness of an item unmediated by other things, indirect is the utility accorded when used in combination with other things. Use value does not necessarily diminish when it is indirect. A single chair has direct use value (enabling us to sit down) but its indirect use value can be enhanced when set in relation to other chairs and a table (enabling us to dine): sitting down and sitting down to a meal give the chair on which we sit different use values. Intrinsic price value is the worth of the item inherent unto itself which constitutes its cost, such as the price of the raw materials and labour power to make a single chair or set of chairs and table,

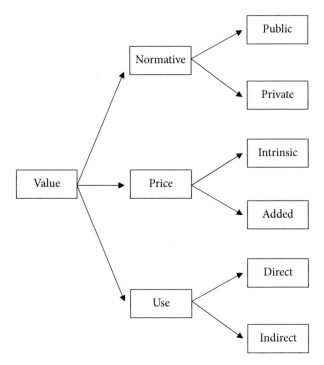

Figure 4.2 Types of value.

added price value describes the worth of things when put to use indirectly, such as the price value of a meal in the restaurant that utilized the chairs and tables, the price of which covers a small proportion of the direct costs involved in the making and partaking of the meal.[5] Private normative value refers to the evaluation attributed to an item by an individual in terms of the pleasure to them derived from possessing it, such as the normative value that comes from eating that particular meal in that specific place. Public normative value refers

---

5   I have resisted using the popular social science term 'exchange value' instead of price value for two reasons. First, strictly speaking, in Marx's original usage the exchange value of a commodity is not identical to its price, but represents what other commodities it will exchange for if traded, and second, because exchange value does not need to be expressed in money prices. I believe retaining the language of price is important because of neoliberalism's thrust to reduce everything to its price and because this price varies dramatically from one exchange to another according to the whole range of factors affecting that particular exchange. This is precisely how the government construes the prices of university degrees as commodities across the different universities in the sector as a whole. Market differentiation is about price differentiation in order to reduce price. The markedly different things that can be exchanged by the different degrees that are 'purchased' across the sector, in terms of life chances, employment opportunities, medical health and the rest, is referred to here as added price value rather than exchange value in order to retain the conceptual link in lay readers' minds with price.

to the esteem attributed to it more widely, such as its social status and cultural significance, represented by dining at the wedding banquet of a high status couple. Personal sentiment can attach immense normative value to an item which is of little meaning and status to other individuals or collectively, and vice versa. Public normative value, however, is about moral sentiment.

Elements of use, price and normative value are run together in current debates so interlocutors mean quite different things when they refer to public value. Impact, for example, is often narrowly reduced to use-value and within that to economic usefulness. Calculations of the economic contributions universities make to society generally or to their regions address price value. Well-meaning arguments about the defining purposes of particular subjects often refer exclusively to their public normative value, such as their contributions to democratic values and civility, an argument advanced recently with respect to the humanities by Martha Nussbaum (2010). Some of these examples are worth instancing in order to show the confusion over what value means and the narrow way in which it is often employed, invoking, as they mostly do, the currency of marketization by concentrating on price and use value.

Price value is what an item costs, either intrinsically or when added to other items. Estimations of price value are at the heart of policies of market differentiation introduced into universities and are, thus, part of the calculations made by governments. They also feature in the defence strategies of those seeking to protect universities. Among the former, price is calculated in order to drive the costs down through competition; among the latter, price is estimated in order to calculate use value, the value-for-money (really better termed, value-for-price) Britain gets from its investment in universities. Costs, of course, are very difficult to calculate for intangible 'goods' like a university education for individual graduates, but are slightly easier when it comes to estimating the costs of universities as institutions.

It is notable that these estimations move well beyond calculations of direct economic use value through such obvious economic benefits as university spin-off companies. This is often the least of the direct economic use value garnered from the price value of universities. Mathews (2011: 36), for example, reports that Manchester University generated 37 spin-off companies between 2004 and 2008, but this represented only 0.1 per cent of the city's start-up companies in this period. Even Oxford, which had the highest proportion of university-based spin-offs, mustered only 1.3 per cent of the city's new companies. Only 890 spin-off companies arising from university research were generated between 2000 and 2012. Calculations of use value now extend very broadly indeed, even beyond direct economic use value, to include social and health benefits to local communities through university voluntary work, service care and cultural activities. Students studying medicine, social work and teaching, for example, often working in deprived communities, bring great benefits to the local community while studying, even though they are unlikely to remain the city where they have been trained once they graduate. Some calculations now try to put figures on just this kind of use value.

Referring to public value in the title of its report, the British Academy's 2010 publication *Past, Present and Future: The Public Value of the Humanities and Social Sciences*, for example, gauged that the British taxpayer pays £12 billion of the estimated £23 billion annual cost of universities, the price of the remainder paid by the private sector. But price and use value were run together in order to show the value-for-money in this price. The Report estimated that the 'economic footprint of universities, in jobs, exports, innovation and added value' was £60 billion (British Academy 2010: 3). This indirect use value, as I would refer to it, was estimated to represent 5 per cent of GDP in 2009. Ironically, these calculations were made on the basis of figures given in a speech by Lord Mandelson at the 2010 Dearing Lecture in Nottingham University, at the point when he was about to lose responsibility for policies towards the universities to the Coalition government.

The eagerness with which similar sorts of calculation of price and use value are made, no matter on what basis and with what reliability, highlights how some who seek to defend public universities have responded to marketization by reducing public value to use and price. In the wake of the new government's enhanced marketization, UUK commissioned the New Economics Foundation (NEF), an independent but left-of-centre think tank founded in 1986 specializing in 'economic well-being', as its website describes it (http://www. neweconomics.org/about), to measure the 'social return' on investment in UK universities. The Report, published in 2011 and entitled *Degrees of Value: How Universities Benefit Society* (see http://www.neweconomics.org/publications/ degrees-of-value), invoked the idea of public value by calculating what is here called the 'indirect use value' of universities over and above their direct economic use value. The Report isolated three indirect use benefits: greater political interest, higher interpersonal trust and better health, alongside a number of community outcomes derived from community outreach activities at two universities, Manchester Metropolitan University and the University of Warwick. The results make interesting reading for the extent to which the HE sector has appropriated price and use values as measures of its worth (for an account of the methodology used in the calculations see **Vignette 6**).

The indirect use value generated from these three social benefits was estimated to be £212 million when set against the cost of the United Kingdom's 1.9 million undergraduates and £1.31 billion for all 11.8 million graduates. For example, Warwick's volunteer programme in primary schools, aimed at improving reading fluency and raising the enjoyment of reading and pupils' reading aspirations brought indirect use value of £290,000. The cultural and community cohesion benefits of the volunteering activities of Warwick's international students realized £48,000. And so it went on. Warwick Art Centre alone was said to contribute £27.7 million through live theatre, music and dance performances. The report concluded on the basis of these two universities: 'it is fair to assume that the university sector as a whole is delivering benefits through facilitating social mobility, community engagement and cultural enrichment to the value of billions of pounds every year'. In the city of Southampton alone, for example, its two universities have been said to generate £500 million in spending power in the city (Mathews 2011), coming from its own workforce as an employer and its students, and £1 million through student volunteering: closure of the two universities would hit the Southampton economy by £610 million per annum.

Another example comes from the National Co-ordinating Centre for Public Engagement, a body established in 2007 by the higher education funding councils, the UK research councils and the Wellcome Trust and supported by the youth volunteering charity called 'V' (see http://www.publicengagement. ac.uk/about/our-vision), which is designed to facilitate the 'higher education sector in making a vital, strategic and valued contribution to twenty-first-century society through its public engagement activity'. It is based in Bristol jointly at the city's two universities (University of Bristol and the University of the West of England). Its 2011 Report, *Through a Glass Darkly: Measuring the Social Value of Universities,* by Kelly and McNicoll (2011), sought to

Vignette 6 Calculating the social return on investment

The NEF study *Degrees of Value* drew on the standardized Social Return on Investment (SROI) methodology. The Report described the method as follows (http://www.neweconomics.org/sites/neweconomics.org/files/Degrees_Of_Value.pdf, page 5):

> SROI is a method for measuring and reporting on the social, environmental and economic value created by an activity or intervention. Although based on traditional financial and economic tools such as cost-benefit analysis, SROI builds on and challenges these. It includes a formal approach to identifying and measuring the things that matter to stakeholders. These are often outcomes for which no market values exist, for example an improvement in quality of life. As such outcomes can be difficult to quantify, they have tended to be excluded from more traditional analyses, preventing a full understanding of value being created or lost for society.

> Carrying out an SROI analysis involves six stages:

> *Establishing scope and identifying key stakeholders.* We spoke to university faculty staff, students and representatives of the local community in both Manchester Metropolitan University and the University of Warwick.

> *Mapping outcomes.* We used information gathered from the interviews and workshops, alongside academic literature to develop an impact map, or theory of change, which shows the relationship between inputs, outputs and outcomes.

> *Evidencing outcomes and giving them a value.* This stage involved finding data to show whether outcomes have happened and then valuing them.

> *Establishing impact.* Having collected evidence on outcomes and monetised them, those aspects of change that would have happened anyway or are a result of other factors are eliminated from consideration.

> *Calculating the SROI.* This stage usually involves deducing a ratio of inputs to value of outcomes. However, as this study was only able to value an isolated number of outcomes for a handful of programmes we focused on the total value of the outcomes alone.

> *Reporting, using and embedding.* Easily forgotten, this vital last step involves sharing findings with stakeholders and responding to them, embedding good outcomes processes and verification of the report.

To illustrate the methodology, we can focus on the example of the Warwick Art Centre (see page 20). The Report described the social return of the Centre as follows:

> Warwick Arts Centre offers a high calibre cultural centre to all attracting over 250,000 visitors a year. It is the largest of its kind outside the Barbican Centre in London with an ensemble of live musical performance, theatre productions as well as comedy shows. While the Centre itself leads on a number of community engagement projects, we focus on the value of the cultural enrichment for those who attend performances. In particular, the variety of shows at the Centre extends the cultural offer available in the area. We valued the benefits of the Centre through three outcomes: more cultured society. To account for the value that society places on the shows that WAC hosts, on top of the individual enjoyment, we used the Arts Council grant given to the Centre for a year as a proxy monetary value. More cultured local community: As a value of the cultural enrichment that all visitors receive at the Centre we take the price of an average ticket. This, alongside the travel costs saved for visitors and the Arts Council grant, brings the total value of the cultural benefits to the local community to £8.98 million. Increased local reputation: Finally, there is an additional value added from more highly skilled individuals attracted to the area. Cultural amenities have repeatedly shown to be one factor when highly skilled individuals chose to relocate to a given area. An increase in the highly skilled in an area has a number of benefits to a local community, such as an increase in incomes circulating in the local economy. When including this economic benefit we estimate the total value to the local community from the Arts Centre to be £27.7 million.

quantify the various ways in which universities are socially responsible, in a similar manner to the way businesses put a price on what they call 'corporate social responsibility'.[6] They utilized the 'socially modified economic valuation' approach (SMEV), which is slightly different from the SROI approach since it quantifies the economic value of all the public services offered by universities, from public lectures to student volunteering, and quality of life to political stability. The authors argue that a price is capable of being attached to all these

---

[6] A charity newly established in the summer of 2011, called UKHE (United Kingdom Higher Education) has urged that universities' corporate social responsibilities in third world countries should be included in league tables in order to encourage competition between them over such matters.

services, although the Report does so only for the more tangible ones. Public lectures, for example, were priced as realizing £356.80 in economic value (based on government calculations of an hour's leisure time being worth £4.46 across an attendance of 80 people at the lecture). It was further suggested that some of these services should have a 'social weight' attached to their price value depending on their use value, referred to as social priority, making a public lecture delivered at university to poorer people realizing between £405 and £442 in economic value.

SMEV owes much to the human capital approach to calculating non-market private and social benefits of higher education when set against total investment costs (see McMahon 2009). This assesses the use of human capital by graduates at home and in the community during leisure-time hours and estimates it use value set against price. As McMahon (2009: 5) explains, time spent at home uses human capital in producing non-market private satisfactions like better health, greater happiness and improved household welfare, while time spent in the community or in helping others uses human capital to generate social benefits for others and future generations, including the benefits accruing to a graduate's children from being raised by someone with a higher education. These include contributions to the operation of civil society, political democracy and even criminal justice. Drawing on long-established formulations in economics, McMahon felt confident enough to assert that the private non-market benefit to the individual graduate in the United States in 2007 was $8,462 for every year at university, $38,080 after graduating with the bachelor's degree (2009: 173). The spill over to others, including future generations, from such an education, referred to as its social benefits was calculated to be $27,726 per year of the post-education life of the graduate (2009: 254). These include the direct benefits to the quality of life from higher education's contributions to democratic values, human rights, political stability, lower crime rates, equality of opportunity, lower inequality and the like.

The purpose of these calculations is to demonstrate that the worth of universities extends much further than contributions to the economy – which is laudable – but the thrust is blunted by the wish to render universities' 'true worth' in financial terms. These calculations honour the variety of ways in which the public value of universities might be established but the price and use values attributed are for all intents and purposes meaningless because of the questionable assumptions made in their calculation.

These sorts of calculations of public value have proliferated with marketization but they focus on use and price value since this is the currency of marketization, and they do so for universities as institutions, since price value is easier to cost at the institutional level. It is more difficult to calculate price and use value for subject areas because of the difficulties of gauging costs. Nonetheless, the logic of the contemporary conjuncture facing public universities in the United Kingdom has led some defenders of public universities to attempt this calculation, including previous governments. For example, the Labour government's science minister, Lord Sainsbury, published a report in 2007 called *The Race to the Top* (see (http://www.rsc.org/images/sainsbury_review051007_tcm18-103116.pdf), reviewing his government's science policies which made estimations of the price value of the cost of investment in science set against their use value. He claimed there was a net gain in economic terms through the contribution of science to economic growth. The humanities and social sciences have sought to make similar calculations of their own price and use value.

Creative industries, for example, are particularly amenable to calculations of this kind. The government Department of Culture, Media and Sports, keen to establish its own monetary value within Whitehall's bun fight over claims to public value, publishes a *Creative Industries Economic Estimates Statistical Bulletin*. Its January 2009 issue reported the following data for industries 'which have their origin in individual creativity, skill and talent and which have a potential for wealth and job creation through the generation and exploitation of intellectual property'. Their contribution to the United Kingdom's gross added value (simply the value of the goods and services produced in a sector of the economy minus intermediate consumption) in 2006 was 6.4 per cent; they exported £16 billion in services, roughly 4.3 per cent of the United Kingdom's total export of goods and services in 2006; and in 2007 they provided employment for over 2 million people (see http://www.culture.gov.uk/images/research/creative_industries_economic_estimates_bulletin_jan_09.pdf). Heritage also sells well and its direct and indirect economic use value is calculable. The number of paying visitors to exhibitions, the number of people employed and the economic return from the spending power of both, among other things, enable the use value of museums, archaeology, history and art to be gauged. The *At Home in Renaissance Italy* exhibition in the Victoria and Albert Museum during 2006–07, for example, was estimated at contributing £2.85 million to the London economy and £1.33 million to the UK economy (quoted in British Academy 2010: 38). The AHRC's 2009 report *Leading the World: The Economic Impact of UK Arts and Humanities Research* (http://www.ahrc.ac.uk/about/policy/documents/leadingtheworld.pdf) was replete with examples like this.

The ESRC does less of this, but on occasions it emphasizes the economic use value of its research, stressing, for example, that work carried out at the Centre for Economic Performance on the minimum wage made a contribution to the British economy of £1.2 billion (http://www.esrc.ac.uk/_images/excellence_with_impact_flyer_tcm8-4599.pdf). This is true also of the Academy of Social Sciences' *Making the Case for Social Science* pamphlets, which do not address these monetary benefits. That the ESRC and Academy of Social Sciences are less impressed by calculations of price and use value may reflect the subject matter of social science, in that there are fewer tangible equivalents to museum visitors, art exhibitions and the productive value of the creative industries, although large parts of the humanities are also unsuited, the availability of more obviously demonstrable impact measures for social science, such as policy effects, as well as the cynicism of social scientists in making these sorts of calculations. The difficulties of estimating use and price value in the humanities and social sciences have led some who seek to debate public value to emphasize instead what I am calling normative value.

Normative value is an evaluation of social worth, involving judgements and evaluations of the esteem involved in possessing something, which can be entirely independent of its price and use value. Normative value can be very high despite the 'good' having little to no use value but a high price value (an original Queen Anne chair that is unsafe to sit on) or low price value (a broken old rocking chair but which just happened to be passed down from a much loved granny on whose knee one sat while on the rocker). Private normative value can attach high value for a range of emotional, sentimental and personal reasons not shared by anyone else. Public normative value differs from private normative value in that the esteem is widely recognized and culturally disseminated and adheres to the collectivity that possesses it. Putting it another way, personal sentiment is replaced by moral sentiment.

Public normative value refers to public acclaim, representing social rather than personal worth (although individuals can attribute great private normative value to possessing something precisely because it has great public normative value, like the pleasure of owning a well-known piece of fine art in one's private collection). Public normative value, in other words, can shape personal norms, increasing the personal motivation to possess a good and thereby extending its public worth. This may appear to suggest it is related to price value, but they are independent.

Public normative value is not about price. Price value can increase the cost of an item to the point where owning it becomes rare and a mark of social status. Price alone can confer esteem. Conspicuous consumption would not work as a social process if this were not so and brand merchandizing as an economic process would not trigger market differentiation without it. Public normative value, however, refers to items that are collectively recognized as worthy regardless of price, even where they have no price, such as the social worth of holding particular sacred beliefs in a religious society, or of participating in public ritual acts of remembrance of the dead. Public normative value, thus, tends to appeal to generalized norms and cultural practices, reproducing grand narratives that are symbolic more than tangible, abstract rather than concrete, evoking themes to which price value cannot be attributed. Many such grand narratives exist to place the normative public value of universities as institutions and whole subject areas. Grand narratives like 'science is civilizing', 'the humanities underwrite democracy', 'knowledge is truth and the truth sets you free', or 'universities educate character and intellect', for example, evoke an entirely different set of moral sentiments than notions like the 'knowledge economy', 'policy based evidence' and 'behavioural change policymaking' (which refer to use value).

Two examples are worth citing, one from the humanities, the other social science, which have addressed public normative value through grand narratives and by invoking broad moral sentiments, eschewing mention of use and price value. The first is Martha Nussbaum's *Not for Profit: Why Democracies Need the Humanities* (2010). The key ideas are twofold: that the humanities create competent democratic citizens, with the sympathies, values, civility and knowledge content to appreciate democracy and practice it; and that this democratic sentiment (as I refer to it) is threatened whenever university education is evaluated against its contribution to national economic growth. In such a situation, 'delivering' rather than 'educating' becomes the process of transmission within universities, and economically productive citizens the output of a university education not democratic citizens. What matters for democratic sentiment is that students learn to think critically, including developing the intellectual skills of deliberation and communication in order to critique authority, garner an openness of spirit to the marginalized, excluded and dispossessed, and an interest in civic engagement and social activism to deal with complex global problems. When university education is reduced to instrumental themes about economic gain and national productivity democratic sentiment is uncultivated and democracy as a political system undermined. Nussbaum sees the humanities in particular as the least instrumental university subjects, the ones most concerned with cultivating education for life rather than for work, and the best at facilitating people in developing arguments, mounting debates and inspiring curiosity. They are also the best at encouraging students to think from the perspective of another person or group, and at cultivating a sympathetic imagination towards others' plight.

This is not an argument about *decline* in humanities provision. The humanities are increasingly popular as subjects and student numbers in the United Kingdom have risen above the national average, as we saw in Chapter 2, and even though Nussbaum's focus is primarily on the United States, she recognizes that liberal arts education there is expanding. Numbers are not her target. What matters to Nussbaum is the kind of educational experience humanities students are getting as a result of the marketization of higher education. Of course, grand narratives can be annoying as discursive styles, irritatingly obtuse and abstract. One blogger was incensed when reviewing the book for The Monkey Cage, a virtual site for philosophy and political theory (see http://themonkeycage.org/blog/2011/06/07/roundtable-on-martha-nussbaums-not-for-profit-why-democray-needs-the-humanities/). 'The book, too often, bores me. I read certain passages, they sound like buzzwordy boilerplate, they sound like declaimed mini-lectures, they sound like cut-and-paste clip-jobs from longer Nussbaum tomes, they sound like academic blah blah blah (with citations), and my eyes gloss over. I want to be moved. I want to be inflamed. I want to be inspired. I want others to be inspired. I don't think this book will do the trick. That saddens me'. Much of the contempt proves her point however.

Marketization makes understanding grand narratives difficult: use and price value are its currency not public normative value.

Nussbaum might be thought of as being unnecessarily disciplinary in associating democratic sentiment and a sympathetic imagination only with the humanities. Medicine, natural science and social science could claim as much. Indeed Charles Wright Mills's *The Sociological Imagination* (1959), now in print for over half a century, referred to an attitude towards social science – which he referred to as 'the promise' – that was similar in its grand narrative and moral sentiments. We know from his letters that the book was to have been entitled 'The Social Studies', and in a revealing second footnote to the first chapter, which he called 'The Promise', Mills explains that it is a social science imagination that he is describing, and was being referred to only by one discipline as a result of being a sociologist himself (1959: 18–19, n 2). The promise, so termed, was to cultivate an imagination in the social sciences that helped ordinary men and women grasp the intricate patterns of their own lives and to see how these connected with wider structural forces and processes about which they had no understanding and over which no control. This was in order to help them cope with 'private troubles'. Among practitioners, the social science imagination should persuade us to make public issues out of these troubles and so undertake social science that improved the lives of ordinary people by addressing urgent social problems and persistent human concerns. This involves what I call a moral sentiment towards social science research on the part of practitioners and students that garners the same sort of sympathetic imagination to marginalized others that Nussbaum referred to 60 years later.

This moral sentiment in social science does not start with Mills, nor end with him, and as counterweight to Martha Nussbaum's grand narrative in the humanities to address public normative value, I want to address as my social science example Michael Burawoy's writings on public sociology.[7]

When first advocating public sociology in 2004 Burawoy acknowledged his debt to Mills (while also distancing himself from him, see Burawoy 2008), as

---

[7]   I could have selected the Commission on the Social Sciences, whose report had a very short section on 'what the social sciences are for', in which they summarized the view of the Commission (2003: 30–1). Social science enhances the quality of life and they mentioned three benefits within this: better understanding; garnering a more civilized, globally aware and tolerant populace; and critical commentary in community debates about values. They mentioned also that social science is an end in itself and should be thought valuable despite some social science research having no utilitarian value. They did not develop these points. Some of these arguments presage my own views about the public value of the social sciences and are elaborated in later parts of this chapter.

well as to several others, and since that time he has expanded on his theme and linked it to a thoroughgoing analysis of marketization, commodification and the degradation of the public university (for the earliest statement see Burawoy 2005; for the fullest statement so far, see Burawoy 2011).[8] Burawoy develops a 'manifesto for the public university', and public sociology's place within it, which in the terminology I have deployed here, constitutes a grand narrative that defines the normative public value of social science. Like Nussbaum, there is an explicit attack on the way university education is being re-envisioned as an instrumental good and in the process destroying the very idea of the public university; and, like Mills, he recognizes that some forms of social science research are technocratic and oriented to meeting national economic and policy goals. He sees a role for this sort of work: it is just not the *whole* purpose of social science.

His manifesto envisages four functions for a public university characterized by types of knowledge and their associated audience. The first is the generation of professional knowledge, which is the knowledge produced in research programmes defined in the academic world evaluated by fellow academics and designed for communication with them. It is knowledge produced for the specialist. This knowledge can be applied in the policy realm, but this is limited by the discursive style and in-jargon used, and its longer-term horizons compared to the short-term demands of policy. Policy knowledge is more meaningful to policy makers and written in a manner suited for them, since it is geared to dialogue with clients and their problems, and involves advocacy. Critical knowledge by contrast is rooted in a community of scholars and maintains the conditions of professional knowledge but it is not incestuously restricted to them and cut off from the outer world. It is not technocratic Type 2 Knowledge geared to policy, but it is world engaging. Public knowledge on the other hand is oriented to conversation between social scientists and wider publics about the broad direction of society and its values.[9] Public knowledge resists policy definitions of the worth of knowledge and elaborates longer-term horizons and broader sets of interests but is also engaged with publics.

---

[8] Burawoy is a prodigious writer on the theme of public sociology and he generously makes available his many contributions to symposia on public sociology on the website dedicated to the idea, See http://burawoy.berkeley.edu/PS.Webpage/ps.mainpage.htm.

[9] He distinguishes between 'traditional' and 'organic' public knowledge, depending upon the kinds of public engaged with (2011: 36ff), and Burawoy has a preference for the latter, since it involves local, community-based, critical publics. This distinction is not relevant to the argument at this point but will be taken up in the next chapter.

Burawoy writes that public knowledge is about building society into the university and placing the university in society (2011: 33), but creating public knowledge is not the sole purpose of the new public university. He envisages that the public university gives weight to each of the four types of knowledge, without privileging one over the other. They are entwined.

> Thus, public knowledge requires the value discussions inspired by critical knowledge and the scientific work of professionals, but also draws on the policy context. Professional knowledge shrivels up if it does not enter into dialogue with the policy world, if its foundations are not subject to interrogation from critical knowledge and if it does not translate itself into public debates about the direction of society. Policy knowledge becomes captive of its clients, and thus more ideology than science, if it loses touch with public debate, with the accumulation of knowledge in research programmes, and with the organized scepticism that comes from critical engagement. Critical knowledge, itself, depends on having the professional and policy worlds to interrogate, but also gains much of its energy from the public debates to which it also contributes (2011: 33)

Burawoy argues that the balance among these types of knowledge varies from discipline to discipline. Hard sciences veer in their emphasis on professional as opposed to policy knowledge, although they also engage in discussion of the implications of their science for the wider society through forms of public science. The humanities proffer public and critical knowledge but also explore policy. However, he claims social sciences form the pivot around which the four types of knowledge revolve since their central task is to negotiate academic and extra-academic knowledge. The social sciences play the mediating role within universities by connecting them to the wider society. In my terminology, this becomes Burawoy's grand narrative for the normative public value of social science: social science reshapes the meaning and practice of the public university.[10]

---

[10] In a private communication with the author, dated 15 January 2011 after we appeared together on a platform at the Royal Irish Academy the week before, Michael Burawoy was kind enough to comment on my contribution and reflected on the symmetry between my deconstruction of the meaning of value and his of types of knowledge. He suggested use value and price value (he preferred the term exchange value) would relate to policy knowledge, whereas public value belongs to public knowledge (he preferred the term social value). He noted this left professional knowledge without a corresponding notion of value, suggesting it might be found in the value of science for science's sake. Shortly I will argue that professional knowledge is a form of public value by helping make social science a public good in its own right. In other words, public value is more than public knowledge.

The foregoing deconstruction of the meaning of value has been necessary to supply us with a new conceptual vocabulary with which to describe value. The lexicon means we have to assess the value of the social sciences across different dimensions of value, and that the assessment of their value varies accordingly. Focusing solely on their normative public value is as one-sided and limited as concentrating on their price or use value. This means for critics of marketization, that use and price value cannot be ignored, and for champions of marketization, that normative public value cannot be dismissed.

With respect to government policy makers and education managers, for example, who are driving the marketization, commodification and degradation of public universities, this conceptual deconstruction allows us to argue that the value of the social sciences is not to be found solely in direct use value (say, economic usefulness), as if this can be assessed in isolation from indirect use value (say, their economic usefulness when assessed in relation to other things, such as the economic usefulness of social science graduates across their working lives). And the indirect use value of social science research should be assessed in combination with other scientific research (in the form of medical-social science research, biological and social science research, and climate change science and the sociology of climate change, and so on).

Furthermore, we can argue that the price value of the social sciences (their cost to the public exchequer set against what they realize by their direct use value) is a very poor measure of value. If price value is to be deployed, as marketeers insist, price value should properly calculate both the indirect use value of the social sciences and their 'value added' price value – the price value of the social sciences when measured by what they add to the use, price and normative value of other things. The price value of the social sciences, for example, should be set in the context of what they add to the price value derived from, say, student exchanges, intellectual tourism and social and cultural events, or the benefits of social science research on transport policy, housing, the welfare state, 'race' relations, better hospital care for the dying, crime rates and so on, and what added price value accrues from having people educated in the social sciences (in terms of, say, socially informed citizenry, workforces, communities and the like). The social sciences as a rule do not have direct links with industry and the market, and knowledge transfer in the social sciences does not tend to reflect in spin-off companies and the like, but social science research on intercultural and interethnic relations, ageing and population demographics, sport, heritage and so on can be stressed as part of their added price value.

For supporters of the principle of public university education who criticize marketization and its malcontents (and all the other alliterations they conjure for it like madness, murder and mayhem), while this new conceptual vocabulary helps us identify the normative public value of social science it also forces us to accept that use and price value are appropriate measures against which to defend the social sciences and by means of which we can make a case for their value.

However, stressing their use and price value is not my purpose here. Some of these calculations have been made and discussed above; and more should be encouraged where they can be reliably estimated. I want instead to address the topic of my interpretative essay – the public value of social science: but first, a plea.

A cautionary note

Shakespeare has Prince Hal commenting on Falstaff's bar bill: 'O monstrous! But one halfpennyworth of bread to this intolerable deal of sack'. Readers may consider I have delivered them a halfpennyworth of bread for all the time and effort it has taken to bring them to this point: but we can now clearly state what the normative public value of social science is and the moral sentiments underlying it. However, this first requires a reminder of what social science is and I want to complete the circle and refer readers back to the arguments in Chapter 1 where I defined generic social science, for the normative public value of social science is predicated on this definition.

I wrote that the subject matter of social science is the social nature of society and that society needed to be understood in its inclusive sense to mean culture, the market and the state, existing across time and space. I elaborated by going on to state that generic social science is the observation, description and identification of the social nature of society by empirical and theoretical investigation in order to explain what culture, the market and the state mean to people, groups and institutions, how they understand, make sense and reproduce culture, markets and the state across time and space, and what people, groups and institutions believe, how they act and interrelate in culture, the market and the state, in local, national and global settings. Put more succinctly, I argued that social science is the scientific study of the processes of societal production and reproduction in culture, the market and the state across time and space. It is to the public value of this generic set of activities that I now turn.

So what is the public value of social science?

The succinct description of the public value of social science is as follows:

> *The normative public value of social science is that it nurtures a moral sentiment in which we produce and reproduce the social nature of society, enabling us to recognize each other as social beings with a shared responsibility for the future of humankind through understanding, explaining, analyzing and ameliorating the fundamental social problems stored up for us. Social science thus becomes a public good for its own sake for cultivating this moral sentiment and sympathetic imagination through its subject matter, teaching, research and civic engagements.*

My own grand narrative is, therefore, simple and clear cut: social science has normative public value by making people aware of themselves as comprising a society, helping in the development and dissemination of key social values that make society possible – social sensibilities like trust, empathy, altruism, tolerance, compromise, compassion, social solidarity and senses of belonging – and assisting in society's ongoing betterment and improvement. The social sciences help us understand the conditions which both promote and undermine these values and identify the sorts of public policies, behaviours and relationships that are needed in culture, the market and the state to ameliorate their absence *and* restore and repair them. In short, social science is a public good in its own right, for nothing else than it is a moral sentiment, a sympathetic imagination, which makes society aware of its social nature.[11]

I find myself in disagreement once again, therefore, with Collini (2012: 98) who differentiates his privileging of the humanities from Nussbaum's (2010) by arguing that humanities scholarship proffers primarily cognitive achievements not direct moral ones. The humanities do not necessarily turn practitioners

---

[11] My Presidential Address to the BSA conference in 2011 held at the University of Leeds was on the public value of sociology and someone was overheard to remark that what I had said could apply to other social sciences. How true that was: it is my whole point here.

into 'better people', he argues, and practitioners' personal morality can be abominable and their political views deplorable (2012: 98–9). Tolerance for other people may not always be the outcome of a social science education and training, but this is a measure of the failure of people's personal morality. I am referring instead to the moral sentiment and sympathetic imagination that makes social sensibility possible within society generally, despite the failure of personal morality, without which society could not function effectively. In addressing, therefore, the question of what makes society possible, the social sciences deal with inherently moral questions that privilege their public value beyond their many cognitive and scholarly accomplishments.

The public normative value of the social sciences lies in their direct engagement with the DNA of society – individuals, groups, social relations, social institutions, civil society, culture, the market and the state. Social science is a mode of thinking for understanding – and helping make ordinary men and women understand through the routinization of social science knowledge – the mechanisms through which we live socially. As such the social sciences are essential for producing and reproducing the social nature of society. The medical analogy with DNA is worth emphasizing, especially since an organic analogy was so important to the public understanding of the social sciences at their inception in the nineteenth and early twentieth centuries. DNA is not only important to helping us understand biological life, knowing how DNA works helps improve the quality of biological life. The mapping of the genome, for example, has revolutionized medical care, both for treatment and prevention, and it is no exaggeration to claim that the discovery of DNA has been as remarkable as the microchip in marking the extent of human progress in late modernity. Similarly, social science dissects the DNA of society (in its inclusive sense) and the information this discloses helps them improve the quality of social life.

As such, the social sciences exist as *sciences* within a normative framework and simultaneously consolidate this framework as the sentiment within which everyone exists as social beings. This is their moral sentiment and sympathetic imagination, sensitizing us to each other as social beings, including the strangers in our midst and the marginalized and dispossessed outsiders across the globe. The anthropologist Marc Augé (1998) captured this wonderfully in his reference to cultivating sensitivities *of* the other and *for* the other (readers wishing to explore the way in which social science analyses these humanitarian sensitivities and is affected by them should see **Vignette 7**).

Vignette 7   Social science and humanitarianism

An interesting issue in this portrayal of the public value of social science is the *social science* evidence to support it. Feelings of responsibility towards others are highly structured by other sets of feelings, particularly about shared belonging and identity. This is why we feel obligated to neighbours, and other close members of our social networks and social groups. It is among these that feelings of reciprocity – of being done to ourselves as we do to others – underwrite and support feelings of shared belonging. The key to this notion of public value, however, is the development of humanitarianism and feelings of responsibility towards strangers and their 'distant suffering' (Boltanski 1999). This might be, as moral philosophers argue, because compassion is the basic social emotion (see Nussbaum 1996), but it is embedded also in social processes explicated by social scientists. Globalization has compressed time and space in a way that brings distant others into the daily experience of late modern life. Television brings distant suffering into people's living rooms and new forms of social networking technology like Twitter and YouTube collapse time and space, giving distant suffering immediacy to the point where images of distant suffering bombard late modernity. Global digital media give visual form to the material conditions of political economy that cause the distant suffering and which provoke the humanitarian response. The link between the moral economy of late modernity and its political economy is a strong theme in Sayer's work (2000). The 'global village' we all live in now reinforces the sensibilities we feel towards distant others. Neighbours, of course, still help neighbours, as was evidenced in the public spiritedness of people during the 2011 English riots, and consanguinity remains a very strong source of social sensibility, but moral awareness has been widened to reflect a much broader humanitarianism. This is in part due to a sense of the shared vulnerability of humankind, which affects our notions of human rights (Turner 2006b) and our understanding of civic responsibilities (Alexander 2006), and is reflected in Misztal's (2011) attempt to chart the sociology of vulnerability, in Delanty's outline of late modernity's 'cosmopolitan imagination' (2009) and in notions of justice that prioritize human dignity over socio-economic redistribution (for example, Margalit 2009; Wolterstorff 2010). It is undergirded by forms of humanitarian law (Hirsh 2003) and the development of an international regulatory system of law and institutions to monitor the conduct of harm. People's ethical commitments to distant others usually transcend the context behind the suffering, which might link it to the policies of pariah states or victims' own culpabilities for their suffering, to represent a decontextualized humanitarian obligation towards them as 'innocents' caught up in material circumstances which evoke empathy. This ethical universalism tends not to extend to 'perpetrators' of the suffering, since theirs is a plight we mostly find it difficult to identify with. Since identification with suffering is the trigger to ethical universalism, the moral boundaries between perpetrator and victim can be flexibly categorized however, to permit identification with some perpetrators, such as combatants fighting in the Arab spring (for a thoroughgoing analysis of humanitarian obligations towards suffering in late modernity see Wilkinson 2005). Anti-foreigner sentiments and aggressive xenophobia are evident and exist alongside ethical cosmopolitanism, and are the result of the same cause, globalization (on globalization and cosmo-politanism see, for example, Beck 2006). As Beck (2012) argues, the world is in a process of cosmopolitanization, of arriving towards rather than yet having achieved cosmopolitanism. Cross-national comparative research by Pichler (2012) on cosmopolitanism at the interpersonal level (rather than the usual macro-level attention to cosmopolitanism) shows it to be uneven across its various dimensions (also see Norris and Inglehart 2009), such as in politics (global governance), identity (notions of global citizenship) and ethics (empathy and trust towards others). Using World Value Survey data from 49 countries between 2005 and 2008, Pichler (2012: 28–31) shows ethical cosmopolitanism to be more prevalent than political cosmopolitanism, especially in the global First World and among urban dwellers, the highly educated and professionals. People with university degrees are the most likely to have cosmopolitan identities, in the sense of recognizing global citizenship, although he noted young people in failing nation states in Africa and Asia had strong senses of global citizenship as an alternative to identification with weak nation states (2012: 38). The upshot is that the very people social scientists educate in universities, at home or overseas students, are the ones most predisposed to ethical cosmopolitanism.

The appreciation we have of globalization as a result of social science helps with the garnering of humanitarian and cosmopolitan sensibilities and how local – or glocal – factors can promote or undercut these sensibilities. The public value of social science research is, therefore, enhanced by the way the social sciences compress time and space and thus make society aware of both the global dimensions to local issues and the catalogue of dangerous issues stacking up for humankind in the future. Use and price values are located in the immediate here-and-now of current time and space; public normative value is attentive to the humanitarian future. Part of the moral sentiment and sympathetic imagination of social science is, thus, its capacity to alert humankind to its potentially threatening future. This is what makes the public value of social science relevant to the twenty-first century.

The normative public value of the social sciences comes in part, therefore, from its engagement with the 'big issues' of future industrial, scientific and economic change in the twenty-first century – economic sustainability, labour migration, climate change, organized violence and peace processes, psychological well-being, pollution, the link between demographic shifts and welfare demands and the like. If the traditional standards by which we judged the purpose of social sciences research have been replaced by economic utility as a result of marketization, then the new public value narrative should not ignore this but stress that scientific, economic, political, industrial, climatic and social changes in the future will be mediated by the capacity of the social sciences to enable culture, the market and the state to make sense of these changes.[12]

This new vocabulary for understanding the public value of the social sciences in the twenty-first century proffers a view of their normative public value that is very broad. Public value is more than the social and cultural relevance of social science research, significant as this is; more than its policy engagements, as profound as these can be; and greater than the many cognitive accomplishments and learning skills derived from a social science education. There are two qualities against which the normative public value of the social sciences should be evaluated: they not only generate information about society, they are a medium for society's reproduction. Put another way, they are the way in which society can find out about itself and in so doing generate the idea of society itself.

This does not render social science into theology or turn it into religious eschatology.[13] It is not 'moralistic' or 'religious', as one friend thought on reading this manuscript, to want to produce socially conscious graduates who seek to

---

[12] In the companion volume to this in Bloomsbury's portfolio, on the public value of the humanities, which is edited by Jonathan Bate (2011a) and which collates various specialists reflecting on the value of their respective disciplines, an entirely different enterprise than to mine here, Bate makes the point in his Introduction that it is only with a humanities education that it is possible to understand the meaning of the question 'what is the value of research in the humanities?' (2011b: 3). My argument at this point reflects similar sophistry: social science research is necessary if society in the future is to make sense of itself. That is to say, both the humanities and social sciences are subject areas sufficiently sensitizing to permit questions about value to the properly answered.

[13] However, see Cloke (2002), among others, who invokes Christian notions of *agape* love as the foundation of ethical practice in human geography. The re-enchantment of social science is a modern trend. See Brewer and Hayes (2011) on the Christianization of social science discourse with respect to studies of the management of emotions in post-conflict societies.

make the world a better place. Nor is it anti-science: social science remains scientific in my view of public value. Let me invoke Adam Smith, the favourite of neoliberals, to explain how.

I am aware that in referring to social science as nurturing moral sentiment and sympathetic imagination by making us aware of ourselves as social beings, I am declaring my debt to the Scottish moralists in the eighteenth century, particularly Smith and Ferguson, who portrayed human nature as inherently sociable, with people being both bound up with and interested in the fortune of others, in which feelings of sympathy and broader social morality hang together.[14] Smith's *The Theory of Moral Sentiments* (written in 1759) and Ferguson's *An Essay on the History of Civil Society* (written in 1767) are key texts for they link the origins of social science in Britain with discourse about moral sentiment which their *science* was intended to disclose. Social science *reveals* moral sentiment when studying culture, the market and the state scientifically. For this reason, there is no incompatibility between the 'two Smiths' (also see Cam 2008; Smith 1998), the Smith of *Moral Sentiments* and *The Wealth of Nations*, since studying economics (Smith) or sociology (Ferguson) scientifically – to take just two examples of social science – itself uncovers the social nature of society and thus exposes our shared future as social beings. That is to say, there is no incompatibility between the status of social science *as science* and its normative public value as a moral sentiment through its disclosure that culture, the market and the state – society in its inclusive sense – are social entities that are premised upon our moral nature as social beings. So important is it for lay readers to understand that social science remains science regardless of its cultivation of moral sentiments that I will be returning to this point in the next chapter.

The marketeers and neoliberals will respond to this depiction of the public value of social science with another objection: that it is incalculable. One answer to such a comment is that this notion of public value is no more incalculable as is the *proper* enumeration of the use and price value of the social sciences. However, my second answer is that such a comment fundamentally misunderstands my argument. I have been at pains to stress in the deconstruction of the meaning of value that public value (as distinct from price and use value) is not reducible to monetary calculations and can only

---

[14] There are many studies on eighteenth-century notions of sympathy and sociability, from a wide number of disciplines. For a selection, see Forget (2003), Frazer (2010) and Mullan (1988).

be construed in terms of grand narratives. I am not saying that social science does not have a use and price value – it clearly does – although distinguishing between price and use value and calculating them fully is more difficult than current calculations suggest and, if done properly, would reveal social science to have even greater price and use value than present calculations enumerate. What I am saying is that normative value is a form that by nature *is* incalculable. This is why SROI, SMEV and the human capital approach, well-meaning as they are, are misguided in believing a monetary calculation can be attached to public value.

It is for this reason that normative public value is problematic as an idea to neoliberalism: it defies price. Hence neoliberalism's currency of price and use value instead. Public value is not, for example, a term in the lexicon of David Willetts when he praises social science; or at least, when he mentions it, it is confused with price value.[15] Normative public value challenges the very principle of marketization that reduces everything to use and price. And it is for this very reason that the transition in debate from the public impact to the public value of social science has been so important. Public value is the language of anti-marketization. Establishing the normative public value of social science has been very important, therefore, for placing the debate back on our terrain, not that of the marketeers, and for using our language not the government's.

Conclusion

Impact is a deeper and deeper hole leading nowhere, a Jeremiah Pit. Public value, on the other hand, leads social science to engagement with our humanitarian future. The multidimensional view of value I have developed here is useful by enabling us to see that the normative value of the social sciences is as important as their use and price value. This is not just meant in the narrow sense of what they add to the quality of life and status of individuals educated in the social sciences or to the lives of people affected by social science research,

---

[15] In *The Times Higher* on 1 March 2012, David Willetts wrote: '[an allegation] is that we lack any understanding of the public value of the university, as shown by the withdrawal of public funding. Public money will continue to get to the universities in a host of ways: the loans for fees; grants for high-cost subjects; more generous maintenance for students; and research excellence funds. All these payments reflect the public value of what universities do' (Willetts 2012: 31). Of course, these 'payments' refer to use and price value not normative public value. He is essentially denying that public funding is being withdrawn and is not addressing what public value might be.

important as these are a measure of *private* normative value; it is that the *public* normative value of the social sciences can be assessed by their contribution to the social sensibilities they help garner and disseminate in culture, the market and the state deriving from people's awareness of themselves as forming a society, whether local, national and global.

Social science contributes to all forms of value, use, price and normative value, and one way of summarizing the normative public value of the social sciences is through itemizing the following range of contributions which social science makes in order to realize its normative public value:

- Social science engages with the social nature of society itself, in culture, the market and the state.
- Social science generates information about society, the market and the state that informs society, the market and the state about themselves.
- Social science promotes moral sentiments and a sympathetic imagination that realizes a body of citizens educated to social awareness and appreciative of the distant, marginalized and strange other.
- Social science teaching and learning has civilizing, humanizing and cultural effects.
- Social science contributes to social amelioration and improvement in society, the market and the state, that extends well beyond short-term policy effects.

However, it is *not* inevitable that social science can or will fulfil all these imperatives to realizing its normative public value. In order to accomplish this, we need a specific kind of public social science. Therefore, simply establishing the normative public value of the social sciences is not the end point of my interpretative essay. Prince Hal's complaint about the halfpennyworth of bread may have been premature, for there is still substantial fare to come. I contend that this portrayal of the public value of social science requires a new kind of social science itself, publicly oriented, conscious of its responsibilities to inculcating moral sentiments and a sympathetic imagination, geared to social amelioration and directed towards addressing the potentially destructive humanitarian future facing us. I outline the new public social science in the next chapter.

5

What is the New Public Social Science?

Introduction

I ended the last chapter by arguing that the normative public value of social science is that it nurtures a moral sentiment in which we produce and reproduce the social nature of society, enabling us to recognize each other as social beings with a shared responsibility for the future of humankind through understanding, explaining, analysing and ameliorating the fundamental social problems stored up for us all. Social science, thus, becomes a public good for its own sake by cultivating this moral sentiment and sympathetic imagination through its subject matter, teaching and research. I pointed out that by studying the social nature of society itself, in culture, the market and the state, social science generates information about society, the market and the state that informs society about itself, promoting moral sentiments and a sympathetic imagination through garnering a body of citizens educated to social awareness and appreciative of the distant, marginalized and strange other, so that social science teaching and learning has civilizing, humanizing and cultural effects.

I also said that there is nothing inevitable about social scientists practising this form of social science, and in this chapter, I will sketch the implications of this view of the normative public value of social science for the conduct and practice of social science by outlining what I call the new public social science. I will reflect on its potential in three areas: research, teaching and civic engagement. I contend that the public value of social science implicates some new practices for social science in these three areas, reinforces the importance of many existing ones and offers a serious challenge to other modes of practice. In the next chapter, I will suggest that by adopting this form of social science, practitioners will make themselves relevant to the big issues of the twenty-first century.

Three caveats should be stated at the beginning, however. There is now a thin chorus of voices raised calling for public social science and some of my arguments have been rattling around for a few years in the separate social science disciplines – sometimes in little known books and journals or out-of-the-way websites – although they have yet to get a stranglehold in any one discipline or be applied to generic social science. Nor have they been brought together in a manifesto for public social science in the twenty-first century. It is the case, though, that the more I read in order to support my arguments with the conventional intellectual apparatus of scholarship, the more I became aware of just how unoriginal they were becoming. However, I also became more and more frustrated that these ideas had not been heard much or made more use of. As I said in my characterization of the genre of interpretative essays in the Introduction, the purpose of this style of writing is to shed new light on existing ideas rather than come up with new ones, which is why I stress in this chapter that my formulation of the public value of social science implies a few new practices but also reinforces some existing ones. Therefore, I see myself tapping into and representing an emerging mood already evident in some colleagues for a new kind of social science, and giving it public prominence by linking it to popular debate about value.

But if change in the way we should conceive social science is already underway my second caveat addresses those with directly opposite concerns. If not universally so, British social science is world class in many areas and in many respects and the popular response to the current conjuncture is to assert that they are in need of no change at all; stasis is a natural tendency when defending against an external attack. However, this excess of self-defence in the social sciences stymies reflexivity. If it is true that bunkers are good places to hole up, they are so only temporarily and they are bad places from which to lead forward charges. I contend that change is inevitable for British social science as a result of making itself relevant to the twenty-first-century problems facing humankind. As I have suggested, we can respond to the opportunities and threats that define the current conjuncture emanating from marketization and regulation by confidently restating our public value, but this conceptualization of our inherent worth and good brings its own demands and challenges. It is necessary, therefore, to complete this depiction of the public value of social science by also depicting the new public social science that has to accompany it, in research, teaching and civic engagement.

Thirdly, I feel I need to explain my motives at this point so that I am not misrepresented. Most social scientists have preferred working either with what Burawoy (2005, 2011) calls 'organic publics', local, community-based and non-market groups, without much access to formal power, or with people in these very systems of formal power, such as governments and policy makers. A lot of technocratic policy-oriented social science is predicated on the latter, most other social science the former. My notion of public involves engagement with both at the same time.[1] The obligation to address 'wicked problems' within late modern political economy implicates engagement upwards as well as downwards, with the formally powerful as well as the formally powerless. The new public social science requires subtle judgements about which publics are the key stakeholders in a 'wicked problem' and no churlishness in engaging with whichever publics are necessary to understand, analyse and ameliorate it. But I am not arguing that social science needs to change in order to make our critics – and government paymasters and education managers – like us more (or give us more money). Neoliberal marketization of public universities may have provoked interest in engaging with value, but it is the essential worth we have as a subject area, which is encapsulated by our normative public value, that is the real driver of change, for this notion of our worth requires us to be relevant to diagnosing, analysing, understanding and ameliorating the conditions of culture, the market and the state in the twenty-first century. Working out the balance between continuity and change in our conduct and practice will mark the challenges social science faces in the future and shape the meaning of the new public social science as it evolves.

There is another reason why I am not ceding the terrain to the government and our wider critics. Arising from this conceptualization of public value, it is clear that they too need to alter their essentially utilitarian view of the worth and value of social science. We are not their handmaidens, valuable only when supplying them with Type 2 Knowledge that allows them to answer policy questions and satisfy policy needs. This is one way social science is relevant

---

[1] Byrne (2011: 38) criticizes Burawoy for suggesting that only useful engagements are found by engaging downwards to civil society, since this demonizes the state, pointing out that civil society and the state are profoundly interpenetrated.

to the future of humankind but there are many more, all equally valuable and deserving of recognition. There is, therefore, a dynamic in the new public social science that obligates our critics and paymasters to widen their understanding of social science and its relevance, improve their relationship with social scientists and utilize some of our rhetoric of public value rather than impact, for they face the same driver of change as social science does – equipping themselves to diagnose, analyse, understand and ameliorate the conditions of culture, the market and the state in the twenty-first century.

In a meeting at the British Academy on impact in November 2009, I heard the issues lying ahead in the twenty-first century described as 'wicked problems', because of the scale of devastation they portend and their complexity, and so enormous in scope and frightening in potential are the complex problems stored up for the twenty-first century that it seems quirky – but highly appropriate – to invoke medieval map makers. They had the practice to write 'here be dragons' when referring to areas of the globe that were unknown and uncharted. The new relationships that need to be fostered to realize the public value of social science and to deal with the problems of culture, market and the state in the twenty-first century, require us all to confront our dragons. This is our imperative as social scientists but also for governments, natural scientists, medics, public universities and their managers, arts and humanities scholars and everyone concerned with the future of humankind.

This imperative is deeply paradoxical for social science: inheriting the future will be difficult for everyone, social science especially. It requires social science to seek to improve its links with people who currently attack public universities and pare their budgets; it forces social scientists to come out of disciplinary bunkers at a time when security seems to be found in hunkering down more solidly in them; the new public social science requires us to be post-disciplinary rather than championing particular social science disciplines as 'ourselves alone', collaborating with our 'strangers' in other social science disciplines and further afield, including natural and medical scientists; and to challenge intellectual orthodoxies that have in the past marked social science as science.

My arguments about public value suggest, for example, that social scientists need to rethink two key scientific orthodoxies in particular, moral relativism and value neutrality. It is this confrontation with what it means to be scientists when answering questions that have a moral dimension that will enable us in our practice as social scientists to live ethically and act politically, as Orlie (1997) terms it. I take this to mean that in our teaching, research and civic engagements as social scientists we are obligated to deal with good and evil, justice and injustice, human dignity and indignity, social enablement and impediment, political and economic empowerment and constraint and the like; not as philosophers, moralists or theologians, but as social scientists. The complex problems we are inheriting now make social science one of the most perspicacious subject areas in the future, yet simultaneously these 'wicked problems' offer the most serious threat to our practice as scientists. Complex problems that are inextricably bound with moral and ethical issues call forth our skills as scientists for analysis and amelioration in a way that risks the very attributes of science that mark our contribution as special. In this paradox lies the essential role of public social science, for the scale of the 'big issues' we have to deal with requires 'big science'.[2] It is to this notion of our enterprise as social scientists that I now turn.

What is traditional social science?

I want to set up a contrast with the new public social science by first mentioning for the sake of symmetry what we might call 'old' or traditional social science.[3] Much of social science as currently practised is disciplinary, conducted from bunkers where practitioners are trained to believe in 'ourselves alone', hence the frequent urge for change towards multidisciplinarity (made in another manifesto, for example, by the Commission on the Social Sciences 2003: 116–18). Thus, it is mostly resistant to working across traditional intellectual boundaries (commented on, for example, by Gulbenkian Commission 1996), and preoccupied with orthodox issues that have long defined the intellectual

---

[2] Of course, 'big science' that deals with 'big issues' also needs 'big resources' but I do not wish to detract from my argument by making it appear that its point is special pleading for more money. However, I feel I must point out that big science, with its big issues, also generates big expectations. The big expectations placed on social science in the context of reduced resources will be difficult to satisfy. This will cause problems for social scientists and their various expectant publics. There is another point worth mentioning. Miller and Sabapathy (2011: 53) argue the short-termism garnered by the RAE/REF puts people off studying 'big issues' because they require a 'big timescale' to be analysed properly, which is inimical to the short census period for outputs adopted in research assessment. I find this point less persuasive than the former one about resources.
[3] This is not a derogatory term.

arena of the separate disciplines as they professionalized rather than with key social problems (as noted, for example, by Lauder et al. 2004; Rubington and Weinberg 2003). It is also limited in its engagement with the public, indeed, often with a very restricted notion of how 'public' can be defined (Calhoun 2007), with preferences for 'organic publics', and mostly written in a style designed for communicating with the specialist rather than non-professionals and in outlets only other professionals read (this is what Burawoy 2005, calls 'professional' social science). It was mostly cautious when engaging with government and hesitant in doing so, with a condescending attitude towards policy research, with so-called Type 2 Knowledge implicitly felt to be inferior to theory-driven knowledge grounded in strong disciplinary enclosures. Max Steuer, one of the ardent science loyalists in economics once wrote (2004: 132) as a 'great defender of the disciplines', that interdisciplinary research is only permissible where there are strong disciplines. Type 2 Knowledge is inherently multidisciplinary and thus at fault because of it. This snobbery often extended towards developing working relations with the media, resulting in what is commonly called 'the dissemination and understanding gap' (see, for example, Commission on the Social Sciences 2003: 87), criticisms of which also featured prominently in the British Academy's 2008 Wilson Report *Punching our Weight* (http://www.britac.ac.uk/policy/wilson).

Governments returned the feeling of suspicion (see **Vignette 8**). They were often critical of social science research, rarely using it to inform policy despite the mantra of 'evidence-led policy', and often disagreeing with its findings or ignoring critical ones. While there was a marked improvement in relations with government in 1997 with the New Labour government, on the part of social science there was still a position of mostly principled distance from and critique of government under the ethos of academic freedom, intellectual autonomy and research independence. Public universities were *sui generis* as largely unregulated ivory towers, with the principles of academic freedom and academic autonomy used to support professional-driven social science. On the part of government, this gave us 'negative impact' (social science research that governments ignored because they disliked its findings or because it showed policy to be wrong and ill-founded). On the part of social science, freedom, autonomy and independence were often disguises for disconnected and disengaged research, removed from community concerns, and people's

Vignette 8 Governments and social science

There have been critical moments in British political and social history when governments have developed good working relations with social scientists. The elimination of poverty, the need for new town planning or housing and slum clearance, shifts in population trends, education reform and schooling, immigration, improvements in 'race' relations, gender inequality and the wages gap, unemployment, industrial restructuring – the list of issues on which governments wanted social science policy input throughout the twentieth century is near endless. The post-1945 period and the 1960s–70s are particular high points in positive engagement. The technical expertise of social scientists was drawn on for advice, to help shape policy, to initiate many longitudinal panel surveys and the like; and there was hardly a government ministry that did not do so. The emergence of government-employed social researchers reflected this demand. Currently there are 1,000 people working on government social research (cited in the BSA's *Network*, Issue 109, Winter 2011, p. 24), and the Government Economic Service is one of the largest employers of economics graduates (Johnson 2004: 27). This growth in demand for social science information occurred even in the Thatcher governments of the 1980s. But government nonetheless remained ambivalent about social science. It wanted a specific kind of policy-relevant social science and was often seeking simplicity in solutions when all social scientists seemed to offer was complexity in their understanding of the problems. Governments wanted answers, social scientists challenged the question. They looked for deep structures, governments for policy fixes. A great deal of the reformist veal and utopian spirit that fed social science, which attracted practitioners with the ambition to change the world, and which for many long years concentrated social science interest in class and inequality in all its various dimensions across culture, the market and the state, came up against governments who thought this made social science too critical and too political. On the one hand, therefore, governments wanted a specific kind of social science, formulated and written in a way that directly served their policy needs, while many social scientists resisted this utilitarian approach to their work and preferred to maintain critical detachment from government. The election of New Labour in 1997 improved the relationship. The number of economists and social researchers in government rose by 50 per cent and 80 per cent respectively between 1997 and 2004 (Johnson 2004: 23). Social scientists with established reputations as excellent researchers were brought in as advisors – Giddens, Stern, Bew (on the Northern Ireland peace process), Plant, Le Grand, Hall, the first four ennobled in the House of

Lords as a result, the latter knighted. However, Le Grand's comment on his experience is telling: 'if you are an academic who works in the policy area, who works in government, or in some sense is enthusiastic about participation in government policy, there is danger you will be labelled either as a sycophant or a naïf' (interviewed in BSA's *Network*, Issue 109, Winter 2011, p. 24). Civil servants still complained of problems in exploiting social science research, of the ways policy makers behaved and social scientists worked (Johnson 2004: 25), resulting in too little social science research being directed at what the government thought the important issues (Johnson 2004: 25). Social scientists who made the transition to work on a seconded basis as advisors, such as Paul Wiles, then the Chief Scientific Advisor and Director of Research to the Home Office and a criminologist by training and background, were no more positive, criticizing the specialist vocabulary used in social science research, and the inability to speak to a broader public (Wiles 2004: 32). The relationship between government and social science, however, has deteriorated further with the Coalition government and the rise of policy-led evidence rather than evidence-led policy, and its imposition of government policy objectives on the research agenda of the funding councils. One way to understand this tension is to appreciate the different interests the parties bring to any relationship as a result of the contrast between we might call the 'contractor' and 'critique' models of social science research. The former sees social science as an instrumental service to government policy needs and tends to emphasize the importance of removing the impediments that exist in social science practice to better serve these needs, such as improving modes of communication, shifting research agendas on to government policy objectives and developing a more short-term focus. The impact debate has encouraged some social scientists to want to improve engagement with government in precisely these sorts of ways since it is a significant 'user' of social science research. Not surprisingly, those social scientists already with good links to powerful elites are the keenest advocates of these forms of impact. The critique model by contrast sees the role of social science to hold governments to account, to sponsor broader-ranging debates about values, so that various policy options are explored for their civic purpose rather than providing evidence for the efficacy of the government's preferred choice, and generally to initiate democratic dialogue. Here, the focus is on the impediments in government that inhibit its receptivity to social science research, such as its quick-fix fixation, its resistance to suggestions of complexity and its short-termism. The idea of impact in this model is either rejected or replaced by discussions about public value, which incorporate broader notions of the publics that need to be engaged.

'private troubles' and public issues, as C. Wright Mills (1959) once put it, and written in a style that the public could not comprehend. The old social science often wrote only to the like-minded and was impenetrable to public and policy makers alike. The old social science was against policy and public engagement on the part of social scientists, and government neglect or misuse of social science on the other. Policy-oriented social science was done aplenty but it was marginalized and ridiculed within mainstream social science, and, deeply ironical, mostly ignored by policy makers. 'Disguised impact' was, therefore, real, being that social science research that had benefits but of which policy makers, governments and the media were wholly ignorant. Disguised impact fills the black hole that often exists between a research input and its eventual outcome.

The fact that there are so many critics of traditional social science among social scientists themselves is significant for the transition to the new public social science. These criticisms are disclosed in many ways: in demands for new kinds of universities that operate outside their ivory towers and are more responsive to the needs of society and the problems of the twenty-first century, such as Miller and Sabapathy's (2011) notion of 'open universities' (2011), Christensen and Eyring's (2011) idea of the 'innovative university' or Burawoy's (2011) new 'public university'; in demands for disciplines to widen their civic and ethical responsibilities, for example, in the form of 'public sociology' (Burawoy 2005), 'public international relations' (Lawson 2008), public social anthropology (Eriksen 2006) and new ethics-led human geography (for example, Proctor and Smith 1999; Sack 1997); in precursory outlines of new forms of 'policy science' appropriate to addressing big issues (Lauder et al. 2004) or in outlines of the political relations of applied social research (Byrne 2011: 195); through calls for social science to establish better links with the natural sciences (Gulbenkian Commission 1996), of the kind practised already particularly by medical social science and the social studies of science tradition;[4] in the various and many encouragements given to social

---

[4] It is worth noting that the 5th ESRC Research Methods Festival in July 2012, held at St Catherine's College Oxford, had as one of its five themes 'the interface between social and natural sciences'. In the early 1970s the then Social Science Research Council funded conversion scholarships for natural scientists and some of the popular social studies of science degrees, like the Masters in Sociology at Bath under Steven Cotgrove, were attractive to such people. Funding was not in the opposite direction and soon stopped altogether. I am grateful to Rick Wilford for this observation. The RCUK PhD studentships that are cross-council are a recent return to this tradition.

science to distinguish the types of 'public' it should increase its engagements with (Calhoun 2007); in demands for social scientists to become more involved with the research needs of civil society by, among other things, involving them in the design and practice of research, widely known as participatory action research, and so on. This brief mention does not do justice to the tide swell of criticism of traditional social science, the urgency of some people's demand for change or the many proposals suggested for its implementation.

However, continuity and change are twins. The current conjuncture threatens to reinforce traditional social science. Seemingly opposite pressures actually pull in the same direction to solidify traditional notions of social science. The marketization of social scientific knowledge (via ideas of 'impact', 'use', 'knowledge transfer' and 'benefit'), combine with the privatization of public university education (through the withdrawal of public funding for social science, and enhanced state regulation of universities through the audit culture), to reinforce mutual suspicion and contempt between government and social science, which has made government approaches to social science ideological. This is the horn of a dilemma that stymies the development of social science. Social science research risks being rendered by the government and advocates of the audit culture as impactful only when carried out on narrow government policy objectives, like the Big Society, while social science researchers that try to engage with impact are negatively stereotyped by social science critics of the impact agenda for conducting narrow, 'professional', policy research. However, as I have stressed all along in this interpretative essay, the present conjuncture can be turned to the advantage of social science and current exigencies used as a form of empowerment. A new public social science can emerge from the current crisis.

So what is the new public social science?

The new public social science can be described in a way that embeds it in the discussions that have preoccupied this entire volume about the nature of generic social science and its public normative value, as follows:

> *The new public social science studies the social nature of society – the way in which society is produced and reproduced in culture, the market and the state,*

generating information about society, the market and the state – which informs society about itself and the big issues that shape the future of humankind. This form of study simultaneously promotes moral sentiments and a sympathetic imagination by garnering a body of citizens educated to social awareness and appreciative of the distant, marginalized and strange other. This means that social science teaching and learning has civilizing, humanizing and cultural effects in addition to whatever use and price value the new public social science might have.

It has teaching, research and practice dimensions, the cumulative effect of which is to realize the normative public value of social science, and below, I flesh out this definition by exploring its implications for the research and teaching agenda of social science, as well as its commitment to civic engagement and its status as science.

The new public social science as a research agenda

As I have stressed throughout, social science is theoretically informed and empirically driven, committed to developing evidence-based observations, descriptions and explanations through theoretical and empirical investigations. This makes social science explanatory rather than just descriptive, combining theoretical insight with empirical rigour. The research agenda of the new public social science is distinguished by applying these scientific skills to the analysis of the fundamental 'wicked problems' of culture, the market and the state in the twenty-first century, to what Calhoun (2007) calls 'pressing public agendas'. This is at once more profound and difficult than it sounds.

It is difficult because it is resisted; and it is resisted for several reasons. For some social scientists, it simply does not sound very new, for others it challenges long-held commitments to generating specific types of knowledge. As Burawoy (2011) makes very clear, many social scientists prefer to develop what he calls 'professional knowledge' from within the bunker of their preferred disciplinary boundaries, pursuing agendas set by the arcane debates within that discipline. On the other hand, 'public knowledge', as he termed it, is reflexive and critical and involves civic engagement and can be disliked as a result. The new public social science may also be resisted because this research agenda challenges existing scientific and normative practices and calls into question the distinction between them, a point to which I shall return below.

It has been argued that traditional social science has long been concerned with fundamental social problems, so what Martyn Hammersley (2004: 439) asks is new? 'Social problems research', though, is unfortunately ghettoized as a subfield and often disciplinary. It is also conventional in the sorts of social problems it addresses and in its manner for doing so. It offers a good example of what Wallerstein (2004) called 'unidisciplinarity', an essentially nineteenth- and early twentieth-century view of social science in which analyses were developed from within autonomous and secure disciplinary boundaries, something Calhoun (2007: 5) dismisses as 'simply accumulating esoteric knowledge inside disciplines'. Since the 'wicked problems' of the twenty-first century are complex and have technical features incapable of analysis by a single discipline, and are not even the responsibility of any one branch of science, the research agenda of the new public social perforce privileges post-disciplinarity in a way that distinguishes it from traditional social problems research.

Byrne (2011: 176) also uses the term post-disciplinarity with respect to his outline of applied social research, seeing it as linked to the importance of complexity theory, of which he is an advocate, realizing that twenty-first-century analyses cannot be based on the outdated practices of disciplinary closure developed in the nineteenth and twentieth centuries. He notes that the term is fuzzy and often elides with the more popular language of multi- and interdisciplinarity, but argues that a good deal of actual research is now already post-disciplinary (2011: 178). He means by it research that draws on a range of methodological tools and which transcends traditional academic boundaries within applied social research. He recommends a 'horses for courses' approach to applied social research (2011: 186). The difference is that I do not see it as characteristic of a small branch of social science; I see it as the hallmark for collaboration across all the branches of knowledge.

Like Byrne, I mean by post-disciplinarity more than the ritualized calls for inter- or multidisciplinarity, although these research modes are transitions towards post-disciplinarity. I use it to refer to two features: it is problem not discipline oriented, and it encourages collaboration across all branches of knowledge, not just across the social sciences.

At the League of European Research Universities' 10th anniversary conference in Barcelona in May 2012, Robert-Jan Smits, director general of research and innovation at the European Commission captured my sentiments about post-disciplinarity well: 'the social sciences and humanities have . . . to get out of these silos and contribute to the enormous challenges that we're facing' (cited in *Times Higher Education* 17 May 2012, p. 20). Helga Nowotny, president of the European Research Council, explained at the same conference how the social sciences should do this. 'We need the social sciences to take part in and work with other disciplines, and the other disciplines need the social sciences to tackle the grand challenges' (cited in *Times Higher Education* 17 May 2012, p. 20). This is what I mean by post-disciplinarity. Post-disciplinary social science is problem oriented rather than discipline oriented, with disciplinary ideas, of theoretical and empirical kinds, used in combination as the problem determines across all the 'three cultures' (Kagan 2009) that mark research pursuits. Problems are no longer defined in terms of the received wisdom of individual disciplines, but by the technical features required to understand, analyse, explain and ameliorate them. I am only too pleased when this advocacy of post-disciplinarity elicits a reaction along the lines of 'that's what I and many others do' – I'm merely suggesting we want more of it.

The Metanexus Institute in the United States has coined the phrase 'big history' for this kind of post-disciplinary enterprise (http://www.metanexus. net/big-history), by which they mean overcoming the separation of science and humanities, and the search for a single account that is integrated across all the disciplinary boundaries. I prefer the notion of post-disciplinarity because of its connection with the 'big issues' that need to be dealt with, but this notion of post-disciplinarity has also been called 'permeability' (Steuer 2002) and the 'hybridization of specialities' (Dogan and Pahre 1990).

This may or may not involve collaboration with others across disciplinary boundaries, as inter- and multidisciplinarity usually mean; it may involve instead single researchers moving outside their intellectual orthodoxies to themselves approach the topic from perspectives outside their own discipline. In terms of economics research, for example, some of the leading US-based economists are pushing out the boundaries of their own field so as to be able to understand grander challenges. This is notable in experimental economics, where laboratory experiments are used to better understand the bounds of rationality and decision-making, and among behavioural economists, who are using biological and psychological models to understand better individual and group behaviour. This can involve revisiting and reworking ideas taken from other branches of knowledge. Behavioural economics is contributing to our understanding of market behaviour by returning to ideas now out of favour in social psychology that explore the cognitive and affective bases of decision-making.

One of the best examples of the limits of disciplinary lenses is provided by Wilkinson's (2000) exploration of the relationship between poverty and health. Usually cast in material terms as a problem of bad diet, Wilkinson suggested instead that psycho-social and medical feelings of well-being mediate the relationship (also see Marmot and Wilkinson 2001). This example illustrates an important feature of post-disciplinarity. It extends the range of collaborations to include natural and medical science. Again this may or may not involve large research teams with disciplinary skills combining to deal with the various technical features of the problem; it could involve single social scientists becoming familiar with the science or medical research necessary to address their topic. Transgendered sexuality, for example, can no longer be understood solely from within social science but requires biological and medical knowledge. Neurological research animates some anthropological studies of culture and sociological studies of child behaviour. The study of organized violence, genocide and post-conflict recovery, for example, now popular in the social sciences in international relations, transitional justice studies, political science, social psychology and what is called 'conflict economics', sees healing as a medical and social process, relevant to the human and social body, and not able to be accomplished properly without also involving trauma studies, cognitive science, medicine and victimology studies, among others.

I am not dismissing social problem research or suggesting that the social problems of the twentieth century have been dealt with and no longer require attention; far from it. Mostly located in the material inequality and injustices that marked aggressive market capitalism in the twentieth century, problems like poverty, unemployment, poor housing, multiple deprivation, under-performance in schools, the various and many dimensions of inequalities of 'race', gender, class and nation and the like, have not disappeared and still need to be addressed. But they have been added to by further 'wicked problems' that are not so easily reducible to disciplinary approaches and ideas, nor are the preserve of any one, as so many of the above are unfortunately approached. Climate change, population growth, sustainable development, pollution, a rapidly expanding elderly and aging population, economic and political instability, terrorism and organized violence and the like require post-disciplinarity because they demand complex treatments that go well beyond redistributive justice. They invoke moral and philosophical ideas about human dignity but also have technical dimensions that are best understood by breaking down barriers between medicine, the natural sciences, like biology, chemistry and environmental science, and the social sciences. Paul Davies (2004: 448), at the time a member of Tony Blair's Strategy Unit in Downing Street, when commenting on proposals by Lauder et al. (2004) for a new form of policy science, captured well this vision of post-disciplinarity in a new public social science that is concerned with fundamental 'wicked problems'. His view of social science practice is worth quoting at length:

> [It] should be able to use the analytical concepts of economic evaluation, understand the concepts and approaches of social psychology, cognitive science and social anthropology, have well developed knowledge-management skills, including effective and efficient searching abilities, critical appraisal skills, and the ability to synthesize and summarize social science research in ways that make it clear and accessible to non-specialists. [It] must be able to go beyond being just technical and be able to offer explanations of why, how, and under what conditions [things] work or not. The ability to challenge what constitutes 'working' or 'not working' and to identify theories of change is also a pre-requisite (Davies 2004: 448).

Being problem rather than discipline focused in this way means that issues demand a multidisciplinary approach that adds to our understanding of them and encourages individuals to step outside their disciplinary comfort zones in order to address them.

There is another distinguishing feature of the research focus on fundamental social problems within the new public social science. This is its collaboration with government, NGOs, civil society and different forms of publics in what is researched, the way it is researched and in the proposed outcomes of the research. Research becomes participative, in which research questions are not defined solely as the preserve of professionals; it is a form of co-produced knowledge. Public social science needs to be co-produced with the publics that name it as such.[5] Fear of the loss of research autonomy (which is not the same as fear over the loss of academic freedom), associated with disciplinary closure to all influences outside professionally driven science, must be secondary to involving publics in the research. Miller and Sabapathy (2011: 50) refer to this as university academics becoming responsible to society as well as themselves by developing 'knowledge that helps us understand and live in our world'. But which public are we to be responsible to?

This is the key question Calhoun (2004, 2007) asks when he wrote position papers trying to move the US Social Science Research Council, of which he was President between 1999 and 2012, towards more publicly engaged social science. He argues there are multiple publics that extend beyond the tyranny of the majority and we require openness to them all. 'The heart of the matter', he writes, is that 'public social science depends on addressing public issues and informing public understanding. Making the sorts of social science we already produce more accessible is not sufficient. We have to produce better social science. This means more work addressing public issues' (2007: 2). This view of our research agenda requires, I suggest, that the new public social science is open to insight from all stakeholders involved in a problem, including the very different publics associated with it, some of whom may be regressive and, using Alexander's (2006) phrase, 'uncivil' (for an analysis of the tension between civil and uncivil tendencies in religious peacebuilding in Northern Ireland see Brewer et al. 2011).

If 'big issues' direct our attention, the multiple interests involved in them require research agendas that successfully tap the impact on all parties and from all their points of view. This means government as well as powerless and marginalized groups, business as well as NGOs, policy makers as well as the underprivileged subjected to policy.[6] Among the several publics which we should be receptive to and engaged with, we need to speak truth

---

[5] Staff at the University of Lincoln have taken this idea a step further by establishing an independent Social Science Centre intended to operate like a free university, with staff giving up their time to work with civil society groups in collaborative research projects and joint publications, although it is primarily a teaching and joint-learning initiative (see http://socialsciencecentre.org.uk/). The University of Lincoln has separately changed its model of teaching, and this will be discussed in the next section.

[6] Using social network analysis, Griffiths (2010) shows that 200 academics sat on 84 different boards of quangos, which is not that many academics or quangos.

to power – whether ministers, officials, civic groups, parties, trade unions or business organizations. Theoretically driven and empirically engaged research on wicked problems transcends disciplinary boundaries *and* political ones, and needs to rise above the 'strangers' whom social scientists kept at arm's length in the past. If big issues demand big science, this also involves a 'big attitude' by improving social science links with government and policy makers (although in a critique model rather than a contractor one), as well as with the local publics social scientists feel represent their more natural constituencies. This is why Lauder et al. (2004) link their new policy science to the study of new social problems and urge improved relations with policy makers through dialogue. 'A policy science that can challenge the assumptions and explanations on which governments make policy', they write, 'remains central' (2004: 20). In Calhoun's terms (2007: 4) addressing public issues does not mean 'merely bringing social science to already formulated problems. It means analyzing why problems are posed in particular ways and what the implications are'.

Post-disciplinarity has significant consequences also for the organizational structure of social science research in universities and governments. With respect to universities, disciplinary bunkers are not the best way to organize social science research. Single-subject departments much beloved as a result of 'golden age' myths, are exemplary only if they facilitate cross-fertilization with units elsewhere in the social sciences and in other branches of science. Multidisciplinary schools and cross-university research themes are more relevant to the needs of the future and some universities are encouraging these initiatives (see **Vignette 9**). With respect to governments, Miller and Sabapathy (2011: 52) force home the relevant point. If research is to become more open to society and to their local communities, and research is to be co-produced with different publics, including governments, 'the quid pro quo must be that society becomes more open to universities and attaches more value to their intellectual and educational work'. 'Wicked problems' are so complex they do not map on to conventional government departments and government research objectives, and governments need to enter into dialogue with public social scientists and others about the best way to conceptualize and approach them; and to remember that dialogue includes listening.

Vignette 9 University College London's four 'grand challenges'

It is worth noting that SAGE, one of the most significant social science publishers, created a web blog in 2011 called 'socialsciencespace', which is devoted to social science engagement with 'the big issues' (see http://www.socialsciencespace. com/). Many universities have reconfigured their research strategies around a set of multidisciplinary challenges. The Oxford Martin School at Oxford University (http:/www.oxfordmartin.ox.ac.uk/about), for example, has set aside £6.4 million to address six 'challenges of the twenty-first century', which include human rights and the resilience of global systems. In this vignette, therefore, I use University College London (UCL) only as an example of many initiatives. UCL has redesigned its research strategy in a new document called 'Delivering a Culture of Wisdom', in ways that promise a fundamental realignment of research practice and infrastructure to enable it to better meet the challenges of the future. The Vice-Provost for Research at the university, Professor David Price, interviewed in *The Times Higher* on 26 January 2012, argues that research intensive universities can justify their high levels of funding only if they amount to more than the sum of their parts by addressing major challenges, and by applying knowledge 'for the good of humanity'. The language of markets has been replaced by a humanitarian discourse, and discipline-based knowledge replaced by 'synthesizing and contrasting of the knowledge perspectives and methodologies of different disciplines'. Accordingly, UCL has introduced four institutional-wide 'grand challenges' to facilitate public issue research within it. These are global health, sustainable cities, intercultural interaction and human well-being. These are very social science-friendly but suggest fruitful relationships with engineering, natural science and medicine. Post-disciplinary research does not happen naturally and university restructuring is necessary to facilitate it. Price is quoted as saying that addressing societal problems in this way chimes with the emphasis put on 'useful knowledge'. This embraces 'impact' but is much broader, and involves engagement with others beyond policy makers and governments, although these are some of the groups with whom it is necessary to dialogue – but 'this isn't saying', Price notes, 'we should do the research the government wants'. Price also envisaged dialogue with civil society and philanthropic foundations with whom these ideas about social problem research might resonate, in part to obtain funding but hopefully also to co-produce the knowledge. This required senior staff to assume research leadership on these themes in order to excite and develop the next generation of researchers and to nurture students.

The research agenda of the new public social science, as I have just described it, requires a further change to conventional research practice. Post-disciplinary research implicates different modes of communication and language. Inter-working across the social sciences and with other branches of science, and in liaison with co-producers of knowledge among publics with a stake in the research, requires a common language. This will mean lessening the use of in-group, professional vocabulary, and where concepts, theories and ideas are necessary to avoid confusion with common sense usage, it involves a stylistic change, in which social scientists write to make themselves understood rather than for professional acclaim. Public criticisms of the poor quality of research were sometimes judgements about the form of writing by which the argument was constructed rather than the methodology or research design. What they were referring to was its inaccessibility through elephantine prose. However, if the ivory tower is to be dismantled by the research agenda of the new public social science, so must the discursive style that helped erect it in the first place.

I want to close this short section on the research agenda of the new public social science by returning to the earlier discussion about public value. Public social science research is capable of showing how these 'wicked problems' interlock, and how the operations of culture, the market and the state, locally, nationally and globally, are impacting on them, for good or bad. Public social science research can, thus, give scientific considerations to the possible futures of humankind and to the progressive development of a society in which the effects of these problems are ameliorated or eliminated, thereby garnering public value through the cultivation of moral sentiment and sympathetic imagination towards peoples affected by them and who are being marginalized and dispossessed, or privileged and advantaged, by the way we organize culture, market and the state. This is a crucial role for the theoretical and empirical insights of the new public social science. It is no coincidence, therefore, that the US Social Science Research Council has recently inaugurated a 'Possible Futures' programme. Craig Calhoun makes the connection between his reformulation of public social science for the twenty-first century and reflection on our possible humanitarian future, for as President of the US Social Science Research Council he inaugurated a book series entitled Possible Futures, in which leading social scientists write short accessible accounts of global issues (see http://www.possible-futures.org/book-series/).

The new public social science as a teaching agenda

It should be plain by now that there are a number of programmatic statements about the research agenda of public social science and some far-sighted people have already called for research agendas devoted to pressing public issues. It is fair to say, though, that no equivalent attention has been put to the teaching agenda of the new public social science. I am not claiming that new forms of public social science teaching are not practised, only that it is less well known and more localized.

Ask any social science graduate what have been the benefits of their degree – and they are asked such things in twice-annual module evaluations and in annual national satisfaction surveys to the point where there is feedback fatigue – and they can adumbrate a long ream of private normative values. These evaluations of what a degree is worth to the individual are part of normative value and will be as variable as the individuals accounting them, ranging from job prospects to marriage prospects. They may invoke notions of use and price value as key reasons for studying social science, such as employment and salary. They may also include references to collective and communal benefits that are forms of public normative value, like encouragements deriving from their social science education to active citizenship, public engagement, social empathy and intercultural awareness and the like. Research undertaken on students' civic awareness is worth discussing briefly to illustrate the mix of motivations and experiences between individual and public benefits.

For example, research undertaken by a team from the universities of Nottingham, Lancaster and Teesside and funded by the ESRC, interviewed students at four universities about their experience and assessment of social science teaching (see McLean et al. 2012) and found students in sociology-based social sciences (including criminology and social policy) felt the three main benefits of their social science education were enhanced academic and employability skills, understanding of and empathy for a wider range of people and change in personal identity towards changing society for the better. The authors drew the obvious conclusion that at least sociology-based social sciences were assisting in personal and social transformation and that students' ambitions were not solely about individual enhancement.

One of the keys to achieving this effect is teaching that allows students to practise and perform social science (McLean et al. 2012: 8).[7] Transformative social science teaching does not simply hand-down acquired knowledge to students but enables them to perform the life-changing and life-enhancing knowledge they are learning, such as through assisting them to see how this knowledge helps them understand and make sense of their own lives and the lives of others, locally as well as globally. This is in part facilitated by a particular subject matter but also, crucially, by encouraging critical analytical skills, an open-minded and challenging attitude, and capacities to see beneath the surface. Nor is this just about providing students with opportunities for discussion through small groups. Discursive practices are only one performative strategy – and small groups have long disappeared in many mass universities – since what matters is the nurturing of students' sensibilities, what here I have called their moral sentiment and sympathetic imagination, which can be done in a multitude of ways outside the tired format of the largely quiet seminar. (Examples of what I mean by performative pedagogic practice follow shortly.)

The broader issues arising from this study are the relevance of its findings to the non-sociology-based social sciences, by far the largest number, and whether professional identities among economists, lawyers and psychologists are inimical to the cultivation of moral sentiments. Research from Finland (Ylijoki 2000), for example, which compared students from computer science, library science and informatics, public administration, sociology and social psychology found profound differences in students' 'moral orders',[8] suggesting that sociology-based social sciences are predisposed to such views and that a real task lies ahead for the harder, profession-oriented social sciences. These findings run counter to the suggestion today that students are very instrumental in their approach to study, although this perception can largely be explained by the failure of teaching and assessment methods to facilitate the performative strategies that demonstrate the level of personal and public transformation students have accomplished. It may well be that students are picking up their social awareness largely outside the classroom, through engagement in student

---

[7] Also see the research team's website at http://www.pedagogicequality.ac.uk/.

[8] I am grateful to Vicky Gunn, Director of the Learning and Teaching Centre at Glasgow University, for drawing the Finnish research to my attention.

extra-curricular activities, from their peers or student union involvement. The findings might also be highly gendered and class based, in that moral sentiment through personal and social transformation is more likely for non-traditional students, women students with caring responsibilities and those from underprivileged backgrounds, although McLean et al. found these trends across all types of university, including those they described anonymously as 'prestige' and 'selective', with traditional middle class intakes.

It is also the case that these sorts of comments in routine feedback evaluation forms are rare. That is, unless explicitly asked, students do not formulate accounts that routinely reference moral sentiment and personal and social transformation. This is primarily because these qualities are implicit rather than explicit in traditional social science education and students are not pointed to the way in which social science garners public normative value. Nor is there enough stress in social science teaching on big issues and how social science is relevant to them as a route into garnering moral sentiment and sympathetic imagination. Accreditation in the discipline through acquiring its 'unique', 'special' discipline-specific knowledge content is as much a practice of the non-vocational social sciences as those with professional accreditation bodies overseeing curriculum.

There is a fear that the current audit culture stymies innovation by making teachers risk averse and little more than spoon-feeders, concerned more with 'delivering' what students want rather than challenging them by addressing what they need (Furedi 2012: 40).

However, there is an imperative in the public value of social science that affects social science teaching that could well make innovation in curriculum and pedagogy itself attractive to students. Alongside the core areas of traditional social science disciplines the new public social science needs also to teach courses that deal with some of the public issues that affect the future of humankind. Teaching courses on suffering, sustainability, the environment, oceans, East–West, peace processes and climate, for example, makes social science inherently post-disciplinary and helps focus attention of possible humanitarian futures and in the process garner sympathetic imagination towards others. INGOs and civil society groups can be brought into the classroom so that, in our teaching, students see what it means to think globally and act locally. Public social science is a practice for the classroom, in which the real world is brought in through innovative teaching methods in order to try to narrow the gulf between the two. This also means taking students outside the classroom into the real world, through fieldtrips, placements, even walkabouts in the neighbourhood (done, for example by sociologists at Goldsmiths College); and it means providing open, inclusive classrooms, as well as fulsome pedagogic opportunities for students to *experience* the life-changing and life-enhancing effects of public social science, in their own lives and others. The teaching agenda of the new public social science is, thus, not just about changes in curriculum, it also involves change in teaching and assessment practices to facilitate transformative performances by students. This way, the culture of tolerance, empathy, open-mindedness and global cultural citizenship associated with social science teaching becomes a lived experience in the classroom (readers interested in an example to illustrate this type of teaching can see **Vignette 10,** which is merely one example of many and, since I know it best, it comes from my own teaching).

While some of this kind of teaching is already being done,[9] especially with respect to curriculum redesign, there is also a great deal of resistance to change. A major concern is the threat to academic standards. Will Hutton, for example, Principal of Hertford College Oxford, was quoted in the *Times Higher Education* on 26 January 2012 as criticizing those at his institution who said that it was a university's obligation 'to be an academic institution above anything else'. They feared the University of Oxford would 'get into trouble' if they did not maintain a predominantly academic focus. However, there is no inherent incompatibility between academic excellence and public social science; academically excellent *and* publicly engaged, morally aware students should be what every teacher aims to develop. Professor Mike Neary, Dean of Teaching and Learning at the University of

---

[9]　George Mason University in the United States introduced in 2008 a new PhD in sociology that emphasizes public sociology, with two areas of specialization: institutions and inequalities, and the sociology of globalization (see http://www.asanet.org/footnotes/mayjun08/mason.html). The design of the programme is to prepare students to pursue careers in academic sociology, policy research or civic advocacy. Their publicity states that the *Institutions and Inequality* concentration equips students to conduct research on salient disparities that characterize the functioning of various social institutions, such as schools, health care, the workplace and family life. The *Sociology of Globalization* track trains students to apply sociological knowledge to the study of social structures operating at the global or transnational level, addressing questions of development, human rights and the dynamics of transnational social movements.

Vignette 10 The sociology of peace processes, University of Aberdeen, taught by John Brewer

This is a fourth year, 12-week elective course open to all students in the School of Social Science (sociology, politics and international relations, and social anthropology) but is also popular among European Studies students. It is capped at 25 as an elective but is very popular, and normally has a reserve list. I have been teaching it since 2004–05. Its subject matter and curriculum reflect post-disciplinary public social science, drawing on all the above disciplines, as well as economics and social psychology, in order to better understand the process of societal healing after communal conflict, dealing with issues like civil society, memory, truth recovery, victimhood, religion, gender, emotions and citizenship education. It covers cases like Northern Ireland, South Africa, the Balkans, Rwanda, Sudan, Israel-Palestine, Bougainville and Poland. It is designed to educate students into global citizenship with an awareness of the impact of new forms of organized violence on societies emerging out of conflict. I tell students at the beginning that the course will make more demands of them than the standard lecture-seminar format, because they will be co-participants in the course, leading small groups, setting their own assignments, undertaking role plays and having to confront the real world of other people's suffering. One or two normally leave at this point and are replaced by reserves. I conduct the course as a two-hour seminar. Full lecture notes are placed on the web for the whole course in advance, as are Power Point slides. I do this to emphasize the lack of importance of the lectures and note taking and, as a corollary, the importance of reading. Each session starts with a short reminder of the lecture theme, after which we break into seminar mode. This is not a format students are used to and it takes some weeks before the class gels. I do not want here to put stress on the curriculum content as a form of public issue social science but rather to stress the performative strategies I adopt as teaching methods in order to reduce the gulf between the classroom and the real world outside. Seminars take different forms, and I rotate frequently so students have variety in the learning experience and outcomes. One format is a role play in which volunteers take the role of victim/survivor or ex-combatant in order to play out in class the conflicting demands each has in a peace process. Other seminars involve peace activists coming into the classroom to recount their first-hand experiences. In some we play DVDs or videos in which participants in a conflict share their experiences, which can occasionally be harrowing and emotionally demanding. On some occasions I invite local representatives of INGOs to talk to the class about what it is like in Aberdeen to think globally but act locally. Student presentations are organized in a particular way to encourage co-production. A seminar topic is set – perhaps on retributive versus restorative justice, the righteousness or not of victims displaying anger, or sport as a peace strategy – on which opposed positions can be taken. The class is split up into smaller break-out groups within the seminar room and students who have done the reading lead the discussion; sometimes I get them to report back, sometimes not. It is responsibility for leading and managing the group discussion that is the learning outcome, not the communication skills in reporting back. In this way students are taking some responsibility for their own learning. They also get to choose their assignment topic in order to pursue their individual interests. The course is assessed each occasion through comments sent to the class representative and through an anonymous web-based questionnaire that permits more indepth comments. Following is a selection of comments from the 2011–12 class on the effectiveness of the format in realizing what here I have called the public value of social science. 'It was so much better than it looked on the course list. It appealed to me because I've always been interested in the idea of being a global citizen'. 'As a sociologist I cannot help but be concerned about people, and harm to them from conflict. Peace processes was a magnet to me'. 'Interesting and relevant to today'. 'Peace processes is a subject of importance today'. 'Peace processes, conflict, are a personal area of interest and I have been looking forward to taking this course for two years'. What follows now are comments from the same cohort on whether the teaching format helped in the performance of personal and social transformation. 'He effectively integrated the entire class to the extent that at the end of the semester the majority were on speaking terms. He changed the dynamics of a lecture. Every week he changed how the class was taught, different, effective teaching methods that involved you'. 'The course was very innovative in the range of assignments, for example the role play, this turned out to be very interesting, very clear and easy to understand while also showing the complexities'. 'Its form[at] allows for more informal, more personal study atmosphere, moreover, the relation of course content with examples from around the world made for a good mix of theory and practice often lacking in other courses'. 'It gave me new friends and a confidence in my own abilities'. 'It has inspired me to explore future options as a citizenship educator'. 'Going global, being up-to-date, that's what I liked about it'. 'The course opens your eyes to what is happening in the world'. 'It was very nice to be able to engage with the material by myself and gauge my own responses. I enjoyed the flexibility of the course and the different teaching methods'. 'The seminar style of teaching was a refreshing change and made the class more interactive'.

Lincoln and Director of the University's Centre for Educational Research and Development, is one of a number at Lincoln behind a new approach to teaching which it calls the Student as Producer initiative, where students are co-producers of knowledge with staff (see http://www/lincoln.ac.uk/home/studyatlincoln/discoverlincoln/teachingandlearning/studentasproducer/), which is supported by a Higher Education Academy grant (also see Neary and Winn 2009, and see **Vignette 11**). He argues that involving students

---

Vignette 11   University of Lincoln 'Students as Producers'

The University of Lincoln describes the initiative as follows:

> We are the leading partner in a Government project which enables students to learn through hands-on experience. Through practise and primary engagement with research, students build and improve their critical skills which in turn increases their employment opportunities. Students engage directly in all aspects of teaching and learning at the University of Lincoln. This research-engaged teaching is grounded in the intellectual history and tradition of the modern university, and the Student as Producer scheme is the organising principle for all teaching and learning across the University. Students are involved in working with lecturers in the design and delivery of teaching and learning programmes at Lincoln. Academics provide the main substance for courses but we also like to ask what students are interested in learning and how programmes can be designed to fit with their particular interests and passions. 'Undergraduates are no longer here simply to consume information passively: they are here to learn by generating knowledge through real research or projects which replicate the process of research within their chosen discipline' (Professor Mike Neary, Dean of Teaching and Learning). Student as Producer has surfaced at a time when students are demanding greater value for money in terms of quality of teaching and graduate employability. By offering students responsibility and practical engagement, they benefit from a more holistic learning experience which leads to enhanced employment prospects, personal development and satisfaction with their course.

Taken from the University of Lincoln website at http://www.lincoln.ac.uk/home/studyatlincoln/discoverlincoln/teachingandlearning/studentasproducer/

as co-producers, more properly perhaps co-participants in teaching, is the route to excellence. It is also much more appropriate to the 'wicked problems' that exist outside Oxford's dreaming spires: its Fellows may continue to dream while the rest of the world accelerates into potential nightmares.

The new public social science as an agenda for civic engagement

Social scientists can sometimes be their own worst enemies for permitting impact and public engagement to become confused, so that in resisting the former they develop reservations about the latter. The impact industry has made public engagement one of its principal components. A series of initiatives to promote public engagement have, thus, been viewed negatively because they are seen through the prism of impact. The examples I have in mind are the 'Beacons for Public Engagement' scheme (see **Vignette 12**), RCUK's 'Concordat for Engaging the Public with Research', and the many conferences and workshops of the National Co-ordinating Centre for Public Engagement (see http://www.publicengagement.ac.uk) promoting its ambition to make researchers 'more sensitive to the emerging social and civic demands of the twenty-first century', as its Director, Paul Manners puts it.[10] The impact prism can blind us, however. Stripped of these connotations, the purposes of these schemes ought to be widely debated for their contribution to a much broader notion of public social science.

Through initiatives such as these, one of the most familiar features of the impact agenda is the obligation to improve dissemination; dissemination is presented as a form of public engagement and a method of garnering impact, making dissemination another central component of the impact industry. The problem with many of these initiatives is that public engagement is reduced to dissemination as its only form. It, therefore, needs to be forcefully noted that civic engagement is more than dissemination. This is what perhaps distinguishes the various initiatives for civic engagement introduced as part of the impact agenda in Britain from the more thoroughly public form of social science envisaged here.

[10] Quoted in the *Times Higher Education*, 24 November 2011, p. 24.

Vignette 12 Beacons for Public Engagement

The Beacons for Public Engagement initiative (see http://www.public
engagement.ac.uk/about/beacons/) was launched in 2008 with funding worth
£9.2 million from RUCK, the Wellcome Trust and the higher education funding
councils, coming to an end in 2012 when the 4 years' funding ran out. It was
administered by the National Co-ordinating Centre for Public Engagement
(see http://www.publicengagement.ac.uk/), set up as part of the Beacons
project. The intention was to introduce a cultural change within universities
towards more public engagement by funding a series of projects that opened
up higher education to the public. Six regional centres were established in
London, Cardiff, Edinburgh, Norwich, Manchester and Newcastle intended as
collaborative centres to bring in clusters of universities and further education
colleges, and other partner organizations, like museums, charities, the media
and businesses. Projects were designed to assist staff and students in their
engagement with the public, and training courses were designed by the
National Co-ordinating Centre for this purpose. Each regional centre had its
own projects. The Wales Centre, for example, worked with the universities in
Wales to help them show how the work they do was 'relevant to modern Wales'.
It did this through: encouraging university staff and students to listen to the
public to find out what they want from universities and how they want to be
involved; encouraging universities to reward high quality public engagement
by its staff and students; encouraging university staff and students to undertake
more engagement and to learn how to do it better; helping members of the
public and university staff and students to meet with each other to learn more
about the needs of each (see http://www.publicengagement.ac.uk/about/
beacons/wales). The initiative has been replaced by Catalyst, with funding of
£2.4 million over 3 years from RCUK alone. Catalyst projects run from eight
individual universities, including Nottingham, the Institute of Education in
London and UCL, and are designed for them to embed public engagement
in their internal practices and culture, such as by encouraging universities to
recognize public engagement in their promotion criteria and to communicate
to young researchers that public engagement is an opportunity for career
enhancement. Quoted in the *Times Higher Education* on 10 May 2012, the
principal Catalyst investigator at the University of Nottingham expressed
the view that no research done at the university should be without impact on
the community and that 10 per cent of the activities of each project should
involve some form of public engagement.

Civic engagement, as we have seen in the research strategy of the new public social science, begins with the formulation of the research problem when different publics can be involved as co-producers of research, and it also enters into the teaching strategy of the new public social science, when civil society groups, INGOs and other publics can be brought into the classroom – and provide placements and fieldtrips outside the classroom – to lessen the gap between it and the real world of 'wicked problems'. Civic engagement in the new public social science is, thus, not left as the final outcome, to be done at the end. Dissemination and civic engagement are different processes. Dissemination involves communicating the results to broader audiences, which may involve public forms of dissemination. This is as important to the new public social science as it is to traditional social science. There are inventive ways in which dissemination can be done in order to widen the publics informed by means of it, such as web blogs, websites and online networks, popular publications and writings, briefing reports and the like. Civic engagement, however, also involves holding conversations with relevant publics and stakeholders in a problem at all stages of research, as well as in teaching.

Civic engagement within the new public social science requires writing plainly, clearly and well, but civic engagement is not meant to be a communication strategy – that comes with dissemination. Civic engagement involves identifying the network of publics involved in, affected by or engaged with specific research problems, and holding conversations with them in the formulation of the problem, the research design developed to explore it, the conduct and practice of data collection and the writing up. It involves conversations also about the best way to communicate the results to the different publics and the use to which the results are put as far as they are concerned. This will involve different forms of dissemination and communication, depending on whether it is policy makers, politicians or publics in the local community (see **Vignette 13** for an example from criminology). It is a feature of the strategy for civic engagement within the new public social science that no publics are ruled out when they have a stakeholder interest in the 'wicked problem'. The new social science is public not partisan.

Education managers in universities might usefully start to develop these sorts of links for their research staff and teachers; it might be more effective than thinking up strap lines, mission statements and 'tangibly sizzling'

Vignette 13 StopWatch*

Stopwatch was founded in 2011 because of concerns that several academics, civil society groups and community activists shared about the way in which provisions to monitor and regulate police stop and search powers were being pared back. The group is a broad coalition which includes several academics – Dr Mike Shiner (LSE), and Professors Ben Bowling (King's College London) and Lee Bridges (University of Warwick), as well as Dr Rebekah Delsol (Programme Officer for the Open Society Justice Initiative) – who very much see StopWatch as an example of social science in action. Academics in the group have undertaken research independently on police powers, police-community relations and related criminological issues, as well as providing expert witness statements on legal cases. There is a policy group, a legal group and a youth group, plus a co-ordinating committee, each of which meet between once a month and once every 6 weeks. Its website (http://www.stop-watch.org/about.html) explains that stop and search tactics continue to create a wedge between communities and the police. The StopWatch action group seeks to work with communities, ministers, policy makers and senior police officers to ensure that the reforms to the police service are fair and inclusive, and lead to better policing for all. StopWatch aims to ensure that the stop and search agenda progresses on fair grounds. Formed of leading figures from civil society, the legal professions and academia, the action group's goals are to: cut ethnic disproportionality in stop and search by half over the next 5 years and give forces guidance and support on how to achieve this; review the use and regulation of stop and search powers that do not require reasonable suspicion such as section 60, schedule 7 and the Road Traffic Act; ensure that procedures are in place for effective monitoring and external accountability of stop and search; create a parliamentary champion/independent reviewer for fair stop and search use, and equality in policing; promote research on stop and search and alternatives to the use of the power. Along with the work that is featured on the website, the group is currently supporting two legal cases. One calling for a judicial review of section 60 searches under the Criminal Justice and Public Order Act 1994 (http://www.bbc.co.uk/news/uk-england-london-17942299; http://www.voice-online.co.uk/article/racist-stop-and-search-powers- be-challenged) and the other challenging the way police forces have dropped the requirement to record stop and account incidents. Examples of its media work can be found at:

http://www.leftfootforward.org/2012/04/stopping-the-searches-the-need-to-confront-police-racism/
http://www.guardian.co.uk/law/2012/jan/14/stop-search-racial-profiling-police

http://www.guardian.co.uk/law/2012/jan/07/abuse-stop-search-crime-police
http://www.guardian.co.uk/uk/2011/sep/22/police-record-race-stop
http://www.guardian.co.uk/commentisfree/2011/feb/01/police-stop-search-data-equality?INTCMP = SRCH
http://www.guardian.co.uk/commentisfree/libertycentral/2010/may/26/stop-and-search-reform-theresa-may?INTCMP = SRCH

The group is also looking at using creative media to get its message across. The youth group have made a film charting the impact of stop and search (http://vimeo.com/33752075) and organized a flashmob to raise awareness (http://www.youtube.com/watch?v=Xcx-92IB8C0). Finally, the group has recently commissioned and produced a play about stop and search, the idea being to raise awareness and influence decision makers – it held a couple of panel discussions after the show which included Heidi Alexander, the local MP, and Simon Woolley, a commissioner for the Equality and Human Right Commission. The group also produced an education pack for schools designed around the Citizenship Programme Key Stages 3 and 4. This is an excellent example of engagement upwards to government, politicians and policy makers, and downwards to civil society and organic communities.

* I am grateful to Dr Mike Shiner for details that have helped inform this vignette.

corporate branding statements. If British universities were to develop a public mission of civic engagement, education managers might learn where, and in what, it is better for universities to sizzle tangibly.

The new public social science as science

I argued earlier that one of the reasons why public social science is at once difficult and profound is because it challenges the boundaries between normative and scientific practice. Traditional normative social scientists may well dislike the idea of public social science because it challenges their preference for the naysayer role of critic, since they know that in order to make a difference to people's lives they will have to engage upwards to powerful publics. Traditional science affirmers in social science, conversely, may well dislike it because the focus on 'wicked problems' risks their detachment and threatens to get them engaged with issues that have clear moral dimensions.

However, I do not see the new public social science as involving a simple bifurcation between science and normative practice – it is science with a normative dimension and moral commitment scientifically undergirded.

The public value of social science is explicitly normative. The way I have constructed this public value – cultivation of moral sentiments and a sympathetic imagination towards each other as social beings and ethical concern about the humanitarian future of humankind – makes it a particularly normative pursuit. The new public social science which is predicated on this notion of public value, therefore, cannot avoid being normative. Indeed, it is designed in order for social scientists in their practice as social scientists to live ethically and act politically. In traditional social science, normative social scientists tended to be science-rejectionists, as it was termed in Chapter 1. Scientific practice was seen as directly opposite to value-led and normative practice; and they rejected science, thinking it inimical to value. The anxiety among science-loyalists over their scientific status, given the particular subject matter of social science, often made them hostile to any suggestion of normative practice, such that normative social scientists were their *bête noir*. Science and value appeared as opposites. The history of social science shows this to be an entirely false antinomy. I argue in this section, therefore, that public social science is still science, and its normative and scientific dimensions can be easily reconciled. This requires me to return to some of the claims in Chapter 1 about the *idea of science* and the way it is independent of, and does not privilege, any specific set of research methods.

Science is itself a value to which one can be committed as much as is religious belief. I defined the idea of science as a value involving the following commitments:

- The commitment to developing evidence-based observations, descriptions and explanations;
- The commitment to professional and ethical practice, including accuracy, honesty and integrity, in all stages of the investigation;
- The commitment to objectivity;
- The separation of value and evidence.

The importance of the latter commitment is that evidence should not be distorted for the sake of the values scientists hold. When Weber gave us the principle of value neutrality, it was this commitment he had in mind not the absurd suggestion that scientists should hold no values. Scientists can have shared values and ethical inclinations, or differ remarkably in them, but they will never be devoid of them as social beings; what matters is that these values do not impugn their practice as scientists. Partisanship is a problem only if the values it carries distort practice; it is not inevitable that it does so if values and evidence remain separated. What Lather (1986) calls 'openly ideological research' is partisan only if values and evidence elide, and now that we work in a post post-modern research culture (see Brewer 2000) there is no reason to argue that their separation is impossible. It might well be the case, as postmodernists argue, that 'facts' are value laden and need to be critically examined; what matters for the practice of science is that the examination is not distorted by the values the examiner holds.

The ethical commitments of the new public social science make it normative and partisan. These ethical values are explicit. They are its point. Its focus on the big issues facing the twenty-first century is motivated by concern over the humanitarian future we are bequeathing our grandchildren; its public value is to garner moral sentiment and sympathetic imagination towards other social beings with whom we share dwindling resources and space, which makes us aware of our responsibilities to the marginalized and dispossessed worse off than ourselves; its research and teaching agendas are designed to engage with publics, locally organic ones as well as powerful ones, privileged and poor ones, in order to involve all stakeholders affected by the 'wicked problems' we are experiencing; and the scientific commitments to analysis, explanation and understanding are matched with the desire, at best, for solutions and at least amelioration.[11]

This means that public social science is concerned with impact. But this is impact on our humanitarian future. It is impact, through its research and teaching, on people's personal and social transformation, impacting on the sense they make of their lives and of the impact the organization of culture,

---

[11] I emphasize the importance of openness in the publics we should engage, in order to reinforce the scientific status of public social science, since to engage only with publics we liked for reasons of our personal values, would be to elide value and evidence, as well as cutting public social science off from all the stakeholders with a vested interest in the wicked problem under investigation. Public social science needs to go upwards to powerful elites, not only downwards to the marginal outsiders social scientists feel more comfortable with.

markets and the state, locally, nationally and globally, has on their lives and the lives of others. Through its research, teaching and civic engagements, public social science is about creating publics, persuading publics, moving publics, to become committed to civic action in order to impact on our humanitarian future.

This is its purpose in the twenty-first century – as was its purpose in the eighteenth and nineteenth centuries. I realize I am proposing nothing new. Social science emerged out of moral philosophy in the eighteenth century for the same purpose that the new public social science is needed in the twenty-first – the analysis, diagnosis and amelioration of the social condition, in culture, the market and the state, with the hope of social improvement and human betterment. The return of explicitly normative public social science might appear shocking only because the professionalization of the separate social sciences in the twentieth century made us forget that science and value are compatible. They were not thought of as incompatible by Hobbes, Locke, Smith, Ferguson and the Victorian improvers who appropriated the status of science enthusiastically when founding organizations like the National Association for the Promotion of Social Science (NAPSS), which John Stuart Mill supported as a 'means to understand and tackle the problems of their society' (Huch 1985: 280). A range of statistical societies – a fad of the period, established in the belief that statistical science aided understanding and that understanding led to social improvement – were affiliated to it. The science was a route to public engagement and motivated by normative concerns (Goldman 2002). Earl Shaftesbury, a former government official and President of the NAPSS, used his 1859 presidential address, to make this point. 'We are called to consider the greatest amount of interest and improvement for the greatest number' (quoted in Huch 1985: 281).

The Victorian scientific reformers did not see it as complicity to try to work with the people who had the power best to alleviate and solve these problems; they were pragmatic in believing it necessary to mediate between the people suffering and those with the power to do something about it. Of course, nineteenth-century public social science was limited by the narrowness of the upper class paternalism that motivated it (Abrams 1968). In a sense, these Victorian improvers were both hope makers and myth makers. They generated hope through their almost utopian belief that social science could benefit society, and myths in the mistaken belief that their notion of public social science would make all the difference. There is nothing wrong with hope[12] and it may well be that twenty-first century public social science will be defeated in the same way the nineteenth-century social scientists were – by the scale and complexity of the 'wicked problems' faced. However, this merely means we need better science; and that we need to keep on trying to improve our science.

The new public social science, therefore, is scientific through its commitment to the idea of science and by its separation of values and evidence, such that the new public social science needs to continue to reflect on methodological issues and research practice in order to improve its science. Nonetheless, the normative enterprise that is the new public social science does challenge some of the orthodox commitments of traditional social science. The new public social science is value-committed, undertaking ethical-based research and teaching, done for the purpose of promoting the public good broadly conceived, in which values matter and notions like 'good', 'sustainability', 'equality of opportunity', 'fairness', 'justice', 'wrong-doing', 'evil', 'human betterment', 'human dignity' and the like are objective rather than moral categories. Some things need to be named for what they are – wrong. Inequality of opportunity is wrong, crime is wrong, wickedness is wrong, injustice is wrong, poverty is wrong, human indignity is wrong, malnutrition is wrong, pollution is wrong, organized violence is wrong, cruelty is wrong and so on; these are not moral relatives, only partly wrong depending on cultural perspectives.

It follows also that the reverse of these conditions need to be named for what they are – good. The elimination of poverty is good, the ending of war is good, the stopping of pollution is good, equality of opportunity is good, fairness is good and so on. These evaluations are made against universal humanitarian claims embedded in the public value of social science. This ethical and normative framework allows us to make categorical judgements between what is good and bad and in the future the new public social science will be about realizing the potential of what is good and eliminating what is bad through its research, teaching and civic engagements, making universal its ethical and normative public value through the research it conducts, the students it teaches and the publics it engages with. Again this is not new. Modern philosophers like Arendt, Margalit, Sen and Nussbaum have debated evil (on Arendt see Cloke 2002), and it has crept into social science

---

[12] Christenson and Eyring (2011) also invoke the language of hope, seeing grounds to anticipate that universities in the United States can become innovative by changes from within.

discussions of suffering (Pickering and Rosati 2008); it just happens to be new to traditional social science. Moral relativism is seriously challenged by the new public social science.

Conclusion

Social science has necessarily always been transgressive and its critical edge is what makes social science distinctive. The new public social science retains its identity as a form of critique by continuing it transgressiveness. There are at least three borders it transgresses – disciplinary, national and political – and it transcends at least one divide – that between teaching and research. It is post-disciplinary and global. Disciplines offer perspectives better in combination than separately, in which the nature of the problem should determine the disciplinary perspectives not the other way round. Nothing less can be done in face of the 'wicked problems' stored up for us in the twenty-first century. This post-disciplinarity is finding expression in hived-off new subject areas, like transitional justice studies, behavioural economics, sexuality studies, security studies and memory studies. However, its home might better be found in the idea of public social science itself. But, it is the political boundaries that make public social science most challenging.

In order to act politically, the new public social science has to engage with those considered by us up to now as 'strangers' – natural scientists, governments, international agencies, like the EU and UN and INGOs. Using climate change as the instance, there has to be useful engagement between sociologists, environmentalists, transport policy makers, oceanographers and the like. Governments are the strangest of all our dragons, but the new social science needs to engage with them as much as civil society and NGOs. Devising strategies for improving government reception to social science is part of the new social science as much as improving social science's attitude towards political and public engagement and the pursuit of publicly relevant research – mostly done in participatory forms in conjunction with communities, NGOs, civil society and the people directly involved in or affected by it. Public social science has porous borders and requires enhanced collaboration between the disciplines; it transcends national borders to engage with global society; and it moves from traditional disciplinary agendas, many rooted in narrow twentieth-century notions of professionalism within the separate social science disciplines, to engage with public issues and 'wicked problems' affecting the future of humankind. This is what it means to be ethical as social scientists in the twenty-first century and to work towards making social science a public good.

Conclusion: A Social Science for the Twenty-First Century?

There are, I believe, social science cohorts. These are very specific generations of social scientists affected by the distinctive and marked conditions, debates, ideas and experiences around at the time of their entry into the profession that remain as enduring legacies throughout their career. Not all generations face remarkable times that leave a permanent imprint but I have evoked two of these cohorts in my interpretative essay, the eighteenth-century Scots and the nineteenth-century Victorian scientific reformers, and have suggested we might learn something from them. In the first case, the example is the necessity to understand culture, the market and the state through humankind's tendency towards moral sentiment and sociability, the second is attaching this normative commitment to the practice of science, thereby linking the value of human and social betterment with the value of science. Both cohorts, of course, were hope makers and myth makers at the same time, full of vision for what social science could do but unable to deliver on it. In that sense they might make poor models.

Two recent cohorts of social science also come to mind. The first is the 1960s, the 'golden age' of optimism in social science, when social scientists believed they could change the world; the second is the 1980s, when fear, contraction and threat abounded, in which the social sciences were explicitly under attack. The 1960s left a legacy of openly normative commitment that largely went unfulfilled, resulting in a cynical, naysayer mentality of critique of systems of formal power that ended up in most practitioners in withdrawal under a preference for identifying the complexities and difficulties of trying to make a difference to ordinary people's lives. The 1980s by contrast gave us doubt, in which social scientists hunkered down within disciplinary bunkers, distancing themselves from the disappointments of the 1960s by generating professional knowledge designed primarily for each other. Hope making and myth making gave way to solid – depressed – realism about the limits of social science and very little wish to try to make a difference. The legacy of both cohorts, therefore, is social science for 'ourselves alone' – either because public engagement is rejected or too complex to achieve.

The intellectual adventure I have been on to define the public value of social science and the new public social science that implements it, encounters the cultural remnants of these cohorts, and will be unpopular (and irritating) as a result. These cultural legacies are found in the contemporary fashion for 'science rejectionism', as I have called it, in the preference for the naysayer role of critique that has given up trying to make a difference, in the withdrawal of professional social science from public engagement in favour of narrow scientific abstraction, and in the partisanship that engages only with certain sorts of organic and community publics, portraying social science as complicit with the powerful if it engages upwards. A social science for the twenty-first century, however, needs to be scientifically skilled in its analysis as well as court moral experience, to be publicly enlightening but not partisan in the publics it engages, to be hope making with a better notion of science so that it does not disappoint and end up again as myth making. This is, of course, a return to earlier notions of public social science, found in eighteenth-century Scots and the nineteenth-century Victorian reformers, but grounded on better science and different moral sentiments more suited to the twenty-first century.

I am suggesting, therefore, that social science is on the cusp of a new age, deeply rooted in the past, but facing different conditions, debates, ideas and experiences. I want to close this interpretative essay, therefore, by asking two closely related questions about twenty-first-century social science. What is it about the twenty-first century that poses problems for social science? What are the challenges of these problems for the practice of social scientists?

In the course of this essay, I have identified the following problems that will shape public social science in the twenty-first century and to which it has to respond.

- A set of interconnected and complex 'wicked problems' that constitute themselves as dramatic public issues affecting the future of humankind and which call for 'big science'.
- Neoliberal marketization of higher education and the degradation of the public university that reflects in contraction and cuts in public expenditure and which limit the potential for 'big science'.

- A humanitarian revolution that motivates ethical universalism, signalled by the awareness of distant suffering and the material plight of 'strange' others, reflected in a cosmopolitan imagination that requires social science to make a difference through its practice.
- The fragmentation of power that has led to the empowerment of a variety of different publics, divided by religion, gender, nation, lifestyle and consumption (such as 'green' and 'ethical consumers') and the like, which requires we adopt a pluralist and non-partisan notion of the publics we need to engage through our social science.

These problems pose serious challenges to social science and I have rehearsed on several occasions throughout the text the ways in which social science practice needs to adapt to them. I believe they constrain as well as empower social science, existing as threats and opportunities. It is no exaggeration to say that social science is under threat, nor fantasy to suggest that the future of humankind is under threat. Public social science is a necessary response to both. It defends social science by making it relevant to the twenty-first century, with a post-disciplinary teaching, research and civic engagement agenda directed to analysing, explaining and solving the major public issues of our time. It fits the political economy of late modernity that has bequeathed humankind with complex stubborn problems that can no longer be addressed from within disciplinary bunkers. This notion of post-disciplinary public social science inevitably makes social science significant also to the humanitarian future that lies ahead, with a public value that renders social science into a public good in its own right independent of whatever use or price value it may have. It fits the humanitarian revolution that is occurring in late modernity as humankind is becoming aware of the need to live ethically and act politically in ways that make moral sentiment and sympathetic imagination towards distant others an ethical universalism. It is, if you like, a public social science for its time (readers who wish to see an example from my own work should read **Vignette 14**).

What, thus, is left for a particularly social science perspective? Have I not argued, in fact, for the elimination of social science in a polyglot post-disciplinary mash, with no distinctiveness left for social science?

I do not see that I have. Iain Wilkinson, associated closely with pioneering work on the sociology of suffering (2005), is worth quoting at length on what

Vignette 14 Public social science in practice – Compromise after Conflict Research Programme

This project is funded by The Leverhulme Trust and is a £1.26 million, five year programme (2009–14) at the University of Aberdeen that is addressed to the problem of what compromise means for victims of communal violence and how it might be encouraged and developed as both a social practice by erstwhile enemies themselves and a policy option by government and civil society. It is led by John Brewer (sociology) with Bernie Hayes (sociology) and Francis Teeney (psychology) as co-investigators, and has Post Doctoral Fellows (PDFs) with backgrounds in social anthropology and Latin American studies (Caumartin), sociology (Mueller-Hirth) and psychology (Dudgeon). It is designed to capture the lived experience of victims in three societies emerging out of conflict, Northern Ireland, South Africa and Sri Lanka, by means of qualitative interviews with victims and nationally representative quantitative surveys (Northern Ireland and South Africa) or, where nationally representative samples are impossible, to generate, non-random victim surveys (Sri Lanka). Linked PhDs explore specific case studies: the deconstruction of violent masculinities among former members of Loyalist paramilitary organizations in Northern Ireland (Magee), the role of victim group leaders in the development of social capital in Northern Ireland (Fowler-Graham), the role of the Catholic Church in managing memory after an atrocity in part of Colombia (Rios), the reintegration of girl child soldiers back into their families in Sierra Leone (Anderson), the recovery of memory policies in contemporary Spain and their impact on the school curriculum (Magill) and change in Catholic young people's identity in Belfast and Derry (Smith). The PhD students have backgrounds in social anthropology, theology, peace studies, sociology and politics. Capturing victims' lived experiences in a multi-method approach, however, is combined with abstract and theoretical analysis on the meaning of compromise at the interpersonal level – the nature of which is under-theorized in social science – in order to be able to define it as a social practice independent of attitude or value change. Victim issues feature in the teaching of Brewer's course on the sociology of peace processes at the University of Aberdeen, the content of which is complemented with videos, DVDs and other witness testimonies to bring this lived experience into the classroom. Some of the activists invited to speak to the class over the years have been from victim groups, including from Sri Lanka and Northern Ireland. There is also a programme of civic engagement focused around victim issues. For example, one of our consultants on the Northern Ireland projects, Jennifer McNern, herself badly injured in a bombing, is a member of the pilot Victim and

Survivor Forum in Northern Ireland set up by the Stormont government and is also Secretary to the 'Injured Group' within Wave, a major counselling NGO. One of the PDFs, Mueller-Hirth, is advisor to the Institute for the Healing of Memories in Cape Town in its work with political prisoners. Teeney works with victims for Restoration Ministries in Belfast and has a special interest in those suffering agoraphobia as a result of 'the Troubles' in Northern Ireland. Brewer has delivered peacebuilding workshops for Mediation Network Northern Ireland, with cross-community groups, and on four occasions in Sri Lanka, the last in Jaffna in February 2012, a Tamil area, with a joint group of Tamils and Sinhalese. In conjunction with the Asian Institute of Missiology, which conducts the Sri Lankan fieldwork, Brewer has initiated a project to bring together Sinhalese and Tamil widows and their children on a holiday break together, for which he also fundraises in Ireland and the United Kingdom. Brewer and Teeney work with Republican ex-combatants in Northern Ireland; Magee does likewise with Loyalists, where he teaches conflict reduction courses in hardline Loyalist areas. In the past, Brewer has arranged for Sinn Féin personnel to visit Sri Lanka for dialogue with the Tamil Tigers. Drawing on his personal experience of involvement with and social science study of religious peacebuilding in Northern Ireland, Brewer is working with Catholic Church groups in Sri Lanka encouraging them to greater involvement in the Sri Lankan peace process. This involves work with both grassroots church personnel and bishops (who in the past have disengaged from involvement with the peace process). It should be clear by now that this project brings together various disciplines and touches on research, teaching and civic engagement. It is motivated by humanitarian concern for victims but uses skills of scientific analysis to try to make a difference to their lives and those of the wider society. It is empirical and theoretical, normative and scientific, addressing lived experience while incorporating abstract analysis. It is both detached and publicly engaged, befitting the model developed here of public social science for the twenty-first century.

he takes as the contribution of public social science in the future, for his words speak eloquently and with a passion for future public social science that is inspiring.

I'm not sure that many will grasp the weight of [the] suggestion that social science should be involved with the promotion of social sympathy. It is important to make clear that in this tradition an appreciation for the human social condition is a moral encounter – it engages us in understanding social life as an enactment of substantive human values and that as social scientists we cannot operate above the fray. It is often difficult and can be distressing (as I think both Weber and Mills recognised). Moral demands are made of the social scientist and his/her readers – both to work at understanding the moral condition/experience of people and to question the terms and quality of their moral commitments to others. It cannot be a dry academic exercise – it is a call to know oneself as a moral-social being and as a being morally embedded in relationship with others. Value conflict is inevitable and life conduct must be examined – if not, we may never gather an appreciation for the most important fact about social life, which is that it *matters for people*. In this issue the very condition of our humanity is at stake.[1]

The wicked problems stored up for our grandchildren require the special insights provided by the new public social science, just as much as they do that provided by medics, scientists and arts and humanities scholars. The wicked problems have technical features relevant to perspectives from all branches of scholarship. Not all equally, not all the same for every problem, but there remain opportunities for the social sciences to bring their skills as analysts of culture, the market and the state to bear on a multitude of public issues. Public social science has much to contribute in representing and capturing the 'lived experience' of those distant others with whom we feel empathy and identification, as well as in understanding the material conditions underlying various wrongs. Particular social sciences may well capture different aspects of these lived experiences and sets of material conditions better than others, as part of their contribution to analysing the technical features of important public issues. There will still be need for economic analysis, social anthropology, human geography, psychology, politics, criminology, sociology and all the rest, singularly or in small or large combinations across broad subject areas to add their distinctive knowledge as the problem requires.

There is one final question, and I want to phrase it in the way that deliberately invokes the aggrandizement of Gould's depiction of the 1960s when he observed we were all sociologists then (Gould 1965: 9): should all social scientists be public social scientists now?

Triumphalism is as inappropriate today as it was then and I am not arguing that social scientists all need be the same. The new public social science will exist – and thrive – at the point of tension between four axes that mark its

---

[1]   In a personal communication with the author, dated 8 March 2012. Emphasis in the original.

special perspective as social science. These axes are continuums, along which individual social scientists and the many social science disciplines will place themselves differently. Below are the respective poles of each continuum:

- the representation of people's lived experience-abstract analysis;
- ethical involvement-detachment;
- normative practice-science;
- public engagement-contemplative reflection and 'thinking time'.

These are not antinomies representing once-and-for-all, mutually exclusive choices, and the position individual social scientists locate themselves at on each axis will vary according to different times of their career and particular teaching, research and public engagement projects. The disciplines that constitute public social science, however, must live them all as a constant tension if they are to make a difference to global issues in the twenty-first century and return hope to humankind. Our grandchildren will condemn us if we do not make ourselves relevant by practising them.

Further Reading and Select Bibliography

Further reading

The reader interested enough to follow-up these arguments and who is desirous first of a more limited and directed set of readings, will find benefit in consulting the following. I have kept this list short, in order not to defeat its purpose; specific readings cited in the text follow further below.

Bate, J. (ed.) (2011) *The Public Value of the Humanities*. London: Bloomsbury.
British Academy (2010) *Past, Present and Future: The Public Value of the Humanities and Social Science*. London: The British Academy.
Brown, R. (ed.) (2010) *Higher Education and the Market*. London: Routledge.
Collini, S. (2012) *What Are Universities For?* London: Allen Lane.
Commission on the Social Sciences (2003) *Great Expectations*. London: Commission on the Social Sciences.
Docherty, T. (2011) *For the University*. London: Bloomsbury.
Gulbenkian Commission (1996) *Open the Social Sciences*. Stanford, CA: Stanford University Press.
Holmwood, J. (ed.) (2011) *A Manifesto for the Public University*. London: Bloomsbury.
McMahon, W. (2009) *Higher Learning, Greater Good*. Baltimore, MD: Johns Hopkins University Press.
Orlie, M. (1997) *Living Ethically, Acting Politically*. Ithaca, NY: Cornell University Press.
UNESCO (2010) *World Social Science Report 2010*. Paris: UNESCO Publishing.

Bibliography

Abbott, A. (2001) *The Chaos of Disciplines*. Chicago, IL: University of Chicago Press.
Abrams, P. (1968) *The Origins of British Sociology 1834–1914*. Chicago, IL: University of Chicago Press.
Alexander, J. (2006) *The Civil Sphere*. Oxford: Oxford University Press.
Augé, M. (1998) *A Sense For the Other*. Stanford, CA: Stanford University Press.
Bailey, M. and Freedman, D. (eds) (2011) *The Assault on Universities*. London: Pluto Press.
Baker, S. (2011) 'One Quango to Rule them All?', *Times Higher Education* 22 December: 33–7.
Bate, J. (ed.) (2011a) *The Public Value of the Humanities*. London: Bloomsbury.
— (2011b) 'Introduction', *The Public Value of the Humanities*. London: Bloomsbury.

Bayer, R. and Drache, D. (eds) *States Against Markets*. London: Routledge.

Bechhofer, F., Rayman-Bacchus, L. and Williams, R. (2001) 'The Dynamics of Social Science Research Exploitation', *Scottish Affairs* 36: 124–55.

Beck, U. (2006) *Cosmopolitan Vision*. Cambridge: Polity Press.

— (2012) 'Redefining the Sociological Project: The Cosmopolitan Challenge', *Sociology* 46: 7–12.

Becker, H. (1967) 'Whose Side Are We On?', *Social Problems* 14: 239–47.

Bell, C. and Newby, H. (1971) *Community Studies*. London: Allen and Unwin.

Bell, E. (2011) *Criminal Justice and Neoliberalism*. Basingstoke: Palgrave.

Bendix, R. and Lipset, S. M. (1957) 'Political Sociology: An Essay and Bibliography', *Current Sociology* 6: 85–93.

Bennett, T. (1979) 'The Social Distribution of Criminal Labels', *British Journal of Criminology* 19: 134–45.

Benneworth, P. (2011) 'Dutch Lessons for an Impact Agenda that Satisfied all Parties', *Time Higher Education* 17 November: 28–9.

Berger, P. (1963) *Sociology: A Humanistic Perspective*. Harmondsworth: Penguin.

Blau, P. (1956) *Bureaucracy in Modern Society*. New York: Random House.

Boltanski, L. (1999) *Distant Suffering*. Cambridge: Cambridge University Press.

Bone, J. (2010) 'Irrational Capitalism: The Social Map, Neoliberalism and the Demodernization of the West', *Critical Sociology* 36: 717–40.

Brewer, J. D. (1986) 'Adam Ferguson and the Theme of Exploitation', *British Journal of Sociology* 37: 461–78.

— (1989) 'Conjectural History, Sociology and Social Change in Eighteenth Century Scotland: Adam Ferguson and the Division of Labour', in D. McCrone et al. (eds), *The Making of Scotland: Nation, Culture and Social Change*. Edinburgh: Edinburgh University Press.

— (2000) *Ethnography*. Buckingham: Open University Press.

— (2003) *C. Wright Mills and the Ending of Violence*. London: Palgrave.

— (2007a) ' "We Must Protest that Our Inheritance is Within Us": Robert Morrison MacIver as Sociologist and Scotsman', *Journal of Scottish Thought* 1(1): 1–23.

— (2007b) 'Sociology and Theology Reconsidered: Religious Sociology and the Sociology of Religion in Britain', *History of the Human Sciences* 20: 7–28.

— (2011a) 'Viewpoint – From Public Impact to Public Value', *Methodological Innovations Online* 6(1): 9–12.

— (2011b) 'Commentary: The Impact of Impact', *Research Evaluation* 20: 255–6.

Brewer, J. D. and Hayes, B. C. (2011) 'Post-Conflict Societies and the Social Sciences: A Review', *Contemporary Social Science* 6(1): 5–18.

Brewer, J. D., Higgins, G. I., and Teeney, F. (2011) *Religion, Civil Society and Peace in Northern Ireland*. Oxford: Oxford University Press.

Brinkmann, S. (2011) *Psychology as a Moral Science*. New York: Springer.

British Academy (2010) *Past, Present and Future: The Public Value of the Humanities and Social Science*. London: The British Academy.

Brown, R. (ed.) (2010) *Higher Education and the Market*. London: Routledge.

Bryson, G. (1932a) 'The Emergence of the Social Sciences from Moral Philosophy', *International Journal of Ethics* 42: 304–23.

— (1932b) 'Sociology Considered as Moral Philosophy', *Sociological Review* 24: 26–36.

— (1945) *Man and Society*. Princeton, NJ: Princeton University Press.

Burawoy, M. (2005) 'For Public Sociology', *American Sociological Review* 70: 4–28.

— (2008) 'Open Letter to C. Wright Mills', *Antipode* 40: 365–75.

— (2011) 'Redefining the Public University: Global and National Contexts' in J. Holmwood (ed.), *A Manifesto for the Public University*. London: Bloomsbury.

Burr, V. (1995) *An Introduction to Social Constructionism*. London: Routledge.

Byrne, D. (2011) *Applying Social Science*. Bristol: The Policy Press.

Calhoun. C. (2004) 'Word from the President', *4th Annual Report*. New York: Social Science Research Council. Accessible at http://www.ssrc.org/workspace/images/crm/new_publication_3/%7B0e949a73-f451-de11-afac-001cc477ec70%7D.pdf.

— (2007) *Social Science for Public Knowledge*. New York: Social Science Research Council. Accessible at http://www.ssrc.org/publications/view/49173559–675F-DE11-BD80-001CC477EC70/.

Cam, P. (2008) 'The Two Adam Smiths', *Think* 7: 107–12.

Chomsky, N. (1999) *Profit over People*. New York: Seven Stories Press.

Christensen, C. M. and Eyring, H. J. (2011) *The Innovative University*. San Francisco, CA: Jossey Bass.

Cloke, P. (2002) 'Deliver Us From Evil? Prospects for Living Ethically and Acting Politically in Human Geography', *Progress in Human Geography* 26: 587–604.

Collini, S. (2012) *What Are Universities For?* London: Allen Lane.

Collins, H. (2011) 'Viewpoint – Measures, Markets and Information', *Methodological Innovations Online* 6(1): 3–6.

Commission on the Social Sciences (2003) *Great Expectations*. London: Commission on the Social Sciences.

Crouch, C. (2011) *The Strange Non-Death of Neoliberalism*. Cambridge: Polity Press.

Crow, G. and Takeda, N. (2011) 'Ray Pahl's Sociological Career: Fifty Years of Impact', *Sociological Research Online* 16(3), http://www.socresonline.org.uk/16/3/11.html.

Curry, S. (2011) 'Our Audience Awaits', *Times Higher Education* 24 November.

Curtice, J. and Heath, O. (2009) 'Do People Want Choice and Diversity of Provision in Public Service?', in A. Park, J. Curtice, K. Thomson, M. Philipps and E. Clery (eds), *British Social Attitudes 25th Report*. London: Sage.

Davies, P. (2004) 'Sociology and Policy Science: Just in Time?' *British Journal of Sociology* 55: 447–50.

Delanty, G. (2009) *The Cosmopolitan Imagination*. Cambridge: Cambridge University Press.

Docherty, T. (2011) *For the University*. London: Bloomsbury.

Dogan, M. and Pahre, R. (1990) *Creative Marginality at the Intersections of the Social Sciences*. Boulder, CO: Westview Press.

Donovan, C. (2011) 'State of the Art in Assessing Research Impact: Introduction to a Special Issue', *Research Evaluation* 20: 175–80.

Donovan, C. and Hanney, S. (2011) 'The "Payback Framework" Explained', *Research Evaluation* 20: 181–4.

Dumenil, G. and Levy, D. (2010) *The Crisis of Neoliberalism*. Cambridge, MA: Harvard University Press.

Edgerton, D. (2009) 'The "Haldane Principle" and Other Invented Traditions in Science Policy', *History and Policy* 88. Accessible at http://www.historyandpolicy.org/papers/policy-paper-88.html.

Edwards, M. (2004) *Civil Society*. Cambridge: Polity Press.

Erikson, R. (2005) 'A View from Sweden', in A. H. Halsey and W. G. Runciman (eds), *British Sociology: Seen From Without and Within*. London: British Academy.

Eriksen, T. H. (2006) *Engaging Anthropology: The Case for a Public Presence*. Oxford: Berg.

Fontaine, P. (2006) 'The Intellectuals and Capitalism', *British Journal of Sociology* 57: 189–94.

Forget, E. L. (2003) 'Evocations of Sympathy: Sympathetic Imagery in Eighteenth-Century Social Theory and Physiology', *History of Political Economy* 35: 282–308.

Fox, R. (1965) 'Prolegomenon to the Study of British Kinship', in J. Gould (ed.), *Penguin Survey of the Social Sciences*. Harmondsworth: Penguin.

Frazer, M. L. (2010) *The Enlightenment of Sympathy*. Oxford: Oxford University Press.

Furedi, F. (2012) 'Satisfaction and its Discontents', *Times Higher Education*, 8 March: 36–41.

Gamble, A. (1988) *The Free Economy and the Strong State: The Politics of Thatcherism*. Basingstoke: Macmillan.

Gellner, E. (1975) 'Ethnomethodology: The Re-Enchantment Industry or the Californian Way to Subjectivity?', *Philosophy of the Social Sciences* 5: 431–50.

Giddens, A. (1974) *Positivism and Sociology*. London: Heinemann.

— (1996) *In Defence of Sociology*. Cambridge: Polity Press.

Ginsberg, B. (2011) *The Fall of the Faculty*. Oxford: Oxford University Press.

Ginsberg, M. (1934) *Sociology*. London: Thornton Butterworth.

Goldberg, D. T. (2008) *The Threat of Race: Reflections on Racial Neoliberalism*. Oxford: Wiley-Blackwell.

Goldman, L. (2002) *Science, Reform and Politics in Victorian Britain*. Cambridge: Cambridge University Press.

Goldthorpe, J. (2000) *On Sociology*. Oxford: Oxford University Press.

Gould, J. (ed.) (1965) *Penguin Survey of the Social Sciences*. Harmondsworth: Penguin.

Griffiths, D. (2010) 'Academic Influence Amongst UK Power Elites', *Sociology* 44: 734–50.

Gulbenkian Commission (1996) *Open the Social Sciences*. Stanford, CA: Stanford University Press.

Hammersley, M. (2004) 'A New Political Arithmetic to Make Sociology Useful?', *British Journal of Sociology* 55: 439–46.

Harvey, D. (2005) *A Brief History of Neoliberalism*. Oxford: Oxford University Press.

Higher Education Funding Council for England (2002) *Academic Staff: Trends and Projections*. Issue Paper 43. Bristol: Higher Education Funding Council for England.

Hird, M. (2004) *Sex, Gender and Science*. Basingstoke: Palgrave.

Hirsh, D. (2003) *Law Against Genocide*. London: Glasshouse Press.

Holmwood, J. (2010) 'Sociology's Misfortune: Disciplines, Interdisciplinarity and the Impact of Audit Culture', *British Journal of Sociology* 61: 639–58.

— (ed.) (2011a) 'Introduction', *A Manifesto for the Public University*. London: Bloomsbury.

— (ed.) (2011b) *A Manifesto for the Public University*. London: Bloomsbury.

— (2011c) 'Viewpoint – The Impact of "Impact" on UK Social Science', *Methodological Innovations Online* 6(1): 13–17.

Horowitz, I. (1995) 'Are the Social Sciences Scientific?', *Academic Quarterly* 9: 53–9.

Huch, R. K. (1985) 'The National Association for the Promotion of Social Science', *Albion* 17: 279–99.

Johnson, P. (2004) 'Making Social Science Useful', *British Journal of Sociology* 55: 23–30.

Kagan, J. (2009) *The Three Cultures*. Cambridge: Cambridge University Press.

Kelly, U. and McNicoll, I. (2011) *Through a Glass Darkly: Measuring the Social Value of Universities*. Bristol: National Coordinating Centre for Public Engagement. Available at https://www.publicengagement.ac.uk/sites/default/files/80096%20NCCPE%20 Social%20Value%20Report.pdf.

King, D. (2011) 'The Politics of Publicly-Funded Social Research', in J. Holmwood (ed.), *A Manifesto for the Public University*. London: Bloomsbury.

Kuhn, T. (1962) *The Structure of Scientific Revolutions*. Chicago, IL: University of Chicago Press.

Lather, P. (1986) 'Issues of Validity in Openly Ideological Research', *Interchange* 17: 63–84.

Lauder, H., Brown, P. and Halsey, A. H. (2004) 'Sociology and Political Arithmetic: Some Principles of a New Policy Science', *British Journal of Sociology* 55: 3–22.

Lawson, G. (2008) 'For a Public International Relations', *International Political Sociology* 2: 17–35.

Livingstone, D. (2012) 'Science Wars', in N. C. Johnson, R. H. Schein and J. Winders (eds), *A New Companion to Cultural Geography*. Oxford: Blackwell.

Macdonald, S. (2001) 'British Social Anthropology', in P. Atkinson et al. (eds), *Handbook of Ethnography*. London: Sage.

MacGregor, S. (2011) 'The Impact of Research on Policy in the Drugs Field', *Methodological Innovations Online* 6: 41–57.

MacIver, R. (1921) *The Elements of Social Science*. London: Methuen.

MacIver, R. and Page, C. (1967) *Society*. London: Macmillan.

MacRea, D. (1961) *Ideology and Society*. London: Heinemann.

Madge, J. (1953) *The Tools of Social Science*. London: Longmans.

Marcus, J. (2011) 'Offence is The Best Defence', *Times Higher Education* 16 June.

Margalit, A. (2009) *On Compromise and Rotten Compromises*. Princeton, NJ: Princeton University Press.

Marmot, M. and Wilkinson, R. (2001) 'Psychosocial and Material Pathways in the Relations Between Income and Health', *British Medical Journal* 322: 1233–6.

Martin, B. (2011) 'The Research Excellence Framework and the "Impact Agenda": Are We Creating a Frankenstein Monster?', *Research Evaluation* 20: 247–54.

Mathews, D. (2011) 'What Have They Ever Done for Us?', *Times Higher Education* 24 November.

McGettigan, A. (2011), 'New Providers: The Creation of a Market in Higher Education', *Radical Philosophy*, 167: 1–8.

McLean, M., Abbas, A. and Ashwin, P. (2012) 'Pedagogic Quality and Inequality in Undergraduate Social Science', Paper given to the Research Symposium at the University of Nottingham, 27 January.

McMahon, W. (2009) *Higher Learning, Greater Good*. Baltimore, MD: Johns Hopkins University Press.

Miller, N. and Sabapathy, J. (2011) 'Open Universities: A Vision for the Public University in the Twenty-First Century', in J. Holmwood (ed.), *A Manifesto for the Public University*. London: Bloomsbury.

Mills, C. W. (1959) *The Sociological Imagination*. Oxford: Oxford University Press.

Misztal, B. (2011) *The Challenges of Vulnerability*. Basingstoke: Palgrave.

Molas-Gallart, J. and Tang, P. (2011) 'Tracing "Productive Interactions" to Identify Social Impact', *Research Evaluation* 20: 219–26.

Molesworth, M., Scullion, R. and Nixon, E. (eds) (2010) *The Marketisation of Higher Education*. London: Routledge.

Morgan, J. (2012) 'Enigma Variations', *The Times Higher Education*, 1 March: 36–41.

Morrell, G., Scott, S., McNeish, D. and Webster, S. (2011) *The August Riots in England*. London: National Centre for Social Research.

Mullan, J. (1988) *Sentiment and Sociability*. Oxford: The Clarendon Press.

Neary, M. and Winn, J. (2009) 'Student as Producer: Reinventing the Undergraduate Curriculum', in L. Bell, H. Stevenson and M. Neary (eds), *The Future of Higher Education: Policy, Pedagogy and the Student Experience*. Continuum: London.

Nisbet, R. (1976) *Sociology as an Art Form*. Oxford: Oxford University Press.

Norman, J. (2010) *The Big Society*. Buckingham: University of Buckingham Press.

Norris, P. and Inglehart, R. (2009) *Cosmopolitan Communications*. Cambridge: Cambridge University Press.

Northover, J. (2012) 'UK's Squeezed Middle Needs Brand Openings', *Times Higher Education World Reputation Rankings 2012*, 15 March: 26.

Nowotny, H., Scott, P. and Gibbons, M. (2001) *Re-Thinking Science: Knowledge and the Public in an Age of Uncertainty*. Cambridge: Polity Press.

Nussbaum, M. (1996) 'Compassion: The Basic Social Emotion', *Social Philosophy and Policy* 13: 27–58.

— (2010) *Not for Profit: Why Democracy Needs the Humanities*. Princeton, NJ: Princeton University Press.

O'Neill, O. (2011) 'Foreward' in *The Public Value of the Humanities*. London: Bloomsbury.

Orlie, M. (1997) *Living Ethically, Acting Politically*. Ithaca, NY: Cornell University Press.

Ormerod, P. (1994) *The Death of Economics*. London: Faber.

— (2010) 'The Current Crisis and the Culpability of Macroeconomic Theory', *21st Century Society* 5: 5–18.

Oswald, A. (2011) 'You Want Fame? Here's Where You Start Paying', *Times Higher World University Rankings 2011–12*. 6 October: 15–7.

Parkinson, H. (1920[1913]) *A Primer of Social Science*. London: P. S. King.

Phillips, D. (1973) *Abandoning Method*. San Francisco: Jossey Boss.

Pichler, F. (2012) 'Cosmopolitanism in a Global Perspective', *International Sociology* 27: 21–50.

Pickering, W. S. F. and Rosati, M. (2008) *Suffering and Evil*. Oxford: Berghan Press.

Platt, J. (2003) *The British Sociological Association: A Sociological History*. Durham: Sociology Press.

Porter, D. (ed.) (1981) *Society and the Social Sciences*. London: Routledge.

Power, M. (1997) *The Audit Society*. Oxford: Oxford University Press.

Proctor, J. and Smith, D. (eds) (1999) *Geography and Ethics*. London: Routledge.

Ritzer, G. (2006) 'Who's a Public Intellectual?', *British Journal of Sociology* 57: 209–14.

Robertson, R. (1995) 'Glocalization: Time-Space and Homogeneity-Heterogeneity', in M. Featherstone, S. Lash and R. Robertson (eds), *Global Modernities*. London: Sage.

Rojek, C. and Turner, B. (2000) 'Decorative Sociology: Toward a Critique of the Cultural Turn', *Sociological Review* 48: 629–48.

Rubington, E. and Weinberg, M. (2003) *The Study of Social Problems*. New York: Allyn and Bacon.

Runciman, W. G. (1965) *Social Science and Political Theory*. Cambridge: Cambridge University Press.

— (1999) *The Social Animal*. London: Fontana Press.

Ryan, A. (1970) *The Philosophy of the Social Sciences*. Basingstoke: Macmillan.

— (1981) 'Is the Study of Society a Science?', in D. Porter (ed.), *Society and the Social Sciences*. London: Routledge.

Sack, R. (1997) *Homo Geographicus*. Baltimore, MD: Johns Hopkins University Press.

Samuel, R. (1992) 'Mrs Thatcher's Return to Victorian Values', *Proceedings of the British Academy* 78: 9–29

Sandel, M. (2012) *What Money Can't Buy: The Moral Limits of the Market*. London: Allen Lane.

Satz, D. (2010) *Why Some Things Should Not be Sold*. Oxford: Oxford University Press.

Sauntson, H. and Morrish, L. (2010) 'Vision, Values and International Excellence: The "Products" that University Mission Statements Sell to Students', in M. Molesworth, L. Nixon and R. Scullion (eds), *The Student as Consumer and the Marketisation of Higher Education*. London: Routledge, pp. 73–85.

Savage, M. (2010) *Identities and Social Change in Britain Since 1940*. Oxford: Clarendon Press.

Savage, M. and Burrows, R. (2007) 'The Coming Crisis of Empirical Sociology', *Sociology* 41: 885–97.

Sayer, A. (2000) 'Moral Economy and Political Economy', *Studies in Political Economy* 61: 79–104.

Scott, J. (ed.) (2011) *Methodological Innovations Online* 6(1). Special Issue on Impact at http://www.pbs.plym.ac.uk/mi/.

Smith, S. (2011) 'Afterword: A Positive Future for Higher Education in England', in J. Holmwood (ed.), *A Manifesto for the Public University*. London: Bloomsbury.

Smith, S. O., Ward, V. and House, A. (2011) ' "Impact" in the Proposals for the UK's Research Excellence Framework', *Research Policy* 40: 1369–79.

Smith, V. (1998) 'The Two Faces of Adam Smith', *Southern Economic Journal* 65: 1–19.

Stanley, L. (2001) 'Mass Observation's Fieldwork Methods', in P. Atkinson et al. (eds), *Handbook of Ethnography*. London: Sage.

— (2005) 'A Child of its Time: Hybridic Perspectives on Othering in Sociology', *Sociological Research Online* 10(3) at http://www.socresonline.org.uk/10/3/stanley.html.

Steuer, M. (2002) *The Scientific Study of Society*. Boston, MA: Kluwer.

— (2004) 'Reply by Max Steuer', *British Journal of Sociology* 55: 132–5.

Taagepera, R. (2008) *Making Social Science More Scientific*. Oxford: Oxford University Press.

Temple, P. (2011) 'University Branding', *Perspective: Policy and Practice in Higher Education* 15(4): 113–16.

Thornton, M. (2011) *Privatising the Public University: The Case of Law*. London: Routledge.

Times Higher Education (2011) *World University Rankings 2011–12*. 6 October.

Turner, B. (2006a) 'British Sociology and Public Intellectuals: Consumer Society and Imperial Decline', *British Journal of Sociology* 57: 169–88.

— (2006b) *Vulnerability and Human Rights*. Philadelphia, PA: Pennsylvania State University Press.

UNESCO (2010) *World Social Science Report 2010*. Paris: UNESCO Publishing.

University and College Union (UCA) (2012) *Choice Cuts: How Choice Has Declined in Higher Education*. London: UCA. Accessible at http://www.ucu.org.uk/media/pdf/c/h/Choice_cuts_report_Feb12.pdf.

Urry, J. (1981) 'Sociology as a Parasite: Some Vices and Virtues', in P. Abrams, R. Deem, J. Finch and P. Rock (eds), *Practice and Progress in British Sociology 1950–1980*. London: Allen and Unwin.

— (2011) *Climate Change and Society*. Cambridge: Polity Press.

Wallerstein, I. (2004) *World Systems Theory*. Durham, NC: Duke University Press.

Watson, C. (2011) 'Accountability, Transparency, Redundancy: Academic Identities in an Era of "Excellence" ', *British Educational Research Journal* 37: 955–72.

Webb, B. (1926) *My Apprenticeship*. London: Longmans.

Wiles, P. (2004) 'Policy and Sociology', *British Journal of Sociology* 55: 31–4.

Wilkinson, I. (2005) *Suffering*. Cambridge: Polity Press.

Wilkinson, R. (2000) *Mind the Gap*. London: Weidenfeld and Nicolson.

Williams, J. M. (1920) *The Foundations of Social Science*. New York: Alfred Knopf.

Willetts, D. (2010) *The Pinch: How the Baby Boomers Took Their Children's Future – And How They Should Give it Back*. London: Atlantic Books.

— (2012) 'A Mistaken Conception that the University System is Under Attack', *Times Higher Education*, 1 March: 30–1.

Winch, P. (1958) *The Idea of a Social Science*. London: Routledge.

Wolterstorff, N. (2010) *Justice: Rights and Wrongs*. Princeton, NJ: Princeton University Press.

Ylijoki, O.-H. (2000) 'Disciplinary Cultures and the Moral Order of Studying: A Case-Study of Four Finnish University Departments', *Higher Education* 39: 339–62.

Index